CLOSED LINGUISTIC SPACE

CLOSED LINGUISTIC SPACE

Censorship by the Occupation Forces and Postwar Japan

Etō Jun

Japan Publishing Industry Foundation for Culture

PUBLISHER'S NOTE

- Japanese names are given in Japanese order, family name first.
- There are a number of lengthy quotations that the author provided in Japanese translation in the Japanese book. While every effort has been made to locate and use the original English, this has not always been possible. In such cases, we have translated the author's Japanese back into English. As a result, there is no guarantee that the English here matches the original English—meaning that they are gist paraphrases and not quotations in the strict sense. Although laid out to look like the quotations as the author intended, such passages are prefaced by "paraphrase" in parentheses.
- Readers will notice some inconsistency in the use of macrons for renderings of extended vowels in Japanese. In many cases, this is because macrons are absent from primary documents from American sources; for the sake of faithfulness to the source, we have presented the quotations as they were written (often without macrons). Paraphrased translations (for unlocatable source texts) generally employ macrons.

Closed Linguistic Space: Censorship by the Occupation Forces and Postwar Japan
Etō Jun. Translated by The Japan Institute of International Affairs (JIIA).

Published by Japan Publishing Industry Foundation for Culture (JPIC)
2-2-30 Kanda-Jinbocho, Chiyoda-ku, Tokyo 101-0051, Japan
First English edition: March 2020

Originally published in Japan by Bungeishunju Ltd. under the title of *Tozasareta gengokūkan: Senryōgun no ken'etsu to sengo Nihon* in 1989, then released in paperback in 1994 by the same publisher.
English publishing rights arranged with Bungeishunju Ltd.

This book is the result of a collaborative effort between The Japan Institute of International Affairs (JIIA) and Japan Publishing Industry Foundation for Culture (JPIC).

Book design: Miki Kazuhiko, Ampersand Works
Jacket and cover photograph: aflo
Printed in Japan
ISBN 978-4-86658-114-9
https://www.jpic.or.jp/

CONTENTS

PART I

How the United States Prepared for Censorship in Japan

CHAPTER 1

Introduction

Between the fall of 1979 and the spring of 1980, I spent six months visiting three institutions in the United States every few days on a rotating basis. They were the Woodrow Wilson International Center for Scholars (Wilson Center) in the heart of Washington, DC ("Washington," for convenience's sake), the McKeldin Library at the University of Maryland, and the Washington National Records Center (WNRC) in Suitland, Maryland.

At the time, I was hoping to uncover the realities of the censorship of newspapers, magazines, and other print media that the occupation forces instituted during the Allied occupation of Japan between 1945 and 1952. I wanted to accomplish as much as I could toward that end during my stay in Washington, which was limited to nine months. I first encountered the issue while I was contributing the serial essay "Wasureta koto to wasuresaserareta koto" (What We Have Forgotten and What We Were Made to Forget) in Bungei Shunjūsha's monthly *Shokun!* (literally "Gentlemen!") every month for three years.

The common belief is that Japan was granted freedom of speech by the Allied forces when the country was occupied after World War II. A closer scrutiny of the situation in those days, however, reveals that, in actuality, the occupation authorities ordered Dōmei News Agency to suspend business for twenty-four hours at 5:29 p.m. on September 14, less than two weeks after the signing of the surrender document. The agency was permitted to resume business at noon the next day under instructions that the its communication "be limited to within Japan, and all communication. . . be subject to full inspection by representatives of the United States Army stationed in the agency."[1]

The daily *Asahi Shimbun* was also ordered to suspend publication for forty-eight hours between 4:00 p.m. on September 18, 1945, and 4:00 p.m. on September 20. The *Nippon Times*, an English-language daily, was ordered to suspend publication for twenty-four hours between 3:30 p.m. on September 19 and 3:30 p.m. on September 20. It was later discovered that the occu-

1 Etō Jun, *Wasureta koto to wasuresaserareta koto* [What We Have Forgotten and What We Were Made to Forget], Tokyo: Bungei Shunjūsha, 1979, p. 62.

pation authorities ordered a recall of the September 29 issue of the quarterly *Tōyō Keizai Shimpō* on October 1 and had the recalled magazines destroyed in cutting machines.[2]

These incidents give the impression that an immeasurably great power was imposing itself on organs of public opinion in Japan in the early days of the occupation. From actual publications of the time, it is also obvious that the period marked a drastic conversion in the tone of newspapers and magazines in Japan.[3]

While it was self-evident that the shift in journalistic tone was a product of the censorship under the occupation authorities, I still wanted to know as accurately as possible what was going on in the minds of the Japanese and what the outside circumstances were. Mine was not mere curiosity about the past. Although some may find my attitude rather peculiar, I just could not shake the rather mysterious notion that what had happened in those days was still happening in Japan.

If my hypothesis were correct, attempting to disclose the reality of the occupation authorities' censorship would be tantamount to questioning the very fundamentals of Japan's postwar era. Do we, in other words, really believe what we think we believe? If we really do, then how have we come to believe it? If we don't, then what should we believe instead—and how should we live our lives?

When I asked myself these questions, it dawned on me that, in fact, I had been repeating this same questions over and over long before I wrote the serial essay "Wasureta koto to wasuresaserareta koto." From late 1969 through the late autumn of 1978, I contributed a monthly literary review to the daily *Mainichi Shimbun*. Those nine years began with the Mishima Incident (the failed coup attempt in which novelist Mishima Yukio committed ritual suicide) and witnessed the fall and decay of literature in Japan. Reading literary works month after month, I was struck by a sense of frustration at how our linguistic space—in which we were presumed to be breathing freely—was being strangely closed and constrained.

Figuratively speaking, Japanese novelists in those days devoted themselves to weaving a fiction within a linguistic space that was itself a fiction. And every time I followed that train of thought, I felt the urge to explore the true nature of this fiction that had confined and constrained U.S. Article 21 of the 1946 Constitution of Japan which guarantees freedom of speech and expression—yet even that very constitution must have been a component of this fiction.

---

2 SCAPIN-79, dated October 1, 1945.

3 Etō (1979), p. 209–48.

"Wasureta koto to wasuresaserareta koto," my monthly essay, grew out of the debate I had had in the fall of 1978 with literary critic Honda Shūgo on Japan's unconditional surrender. In fact, the debate itself was just one of the consequences of the questions that I had been asking myself. In order to work out the true nature of the "fiction" situation, I had to measure the reality of the censorship under the occupation. By the time I finished contributing my monthly essay, I was convinced that the censorship by the occupation authorities held clues to my questions' answer.

But how could I investigate? Once I set to the task, I soon discovered how scarce documents on censorship during Japan's occupation were. I was able to dig up only three relevant documents: the books *Senryōka no genron dan'atsu* (Suppression of Freedom of Speech in Occupied Japan) by Matsuura Sōzō,[4] the book *Okinawa genron tōseishi* (History of the Regulation of Speech in Okinawa) by Monna Naoki,[5] and a treatise by Fukushima Jurō under the title "Senryō shoki ni okeru shinbun ken'etsu" (Newspaper Censorship during the Early Occupation Period).[6]

That scarcity may explain why Tanii Seinosuke's "Kindai shuppan sokumen-shi: Chosakuken no hensen to hatsubai kinshi" (Side History of Publications in Modern Japan: Transition of Copyrights and Book Banning),[7] a detailed account of the 108-year-long history of book banning between 1868 and 1975, hardly touched on censorship by the occupation forces and mentioned no cases of suspension of publication during the occupation period. While these documents offered me several hints, they were not particularly useful for what I wanted to know.

It seemed my only option was to attempt to unravel on my own the truth about censorship—and to do so by relying on primary historical documents. I decided that my research theme at the Wilson Center, which had already invited me as a visiting research fellow, would be the "censorship by the U.S. occupation forces and its impact on postwar literature in Japan." I notified the center's president, Dr. James Billington, accordingly. Just around

4 Matsuura Sōzō, *Senryōka no genron dan'atsu* [Suppression of Freedom of Speech in the Occupied Japan], Gendai Jānarizumu Shuppansha, 1964.

5 Monna Naoki, *Okinawa genron tōseishi* [History of Regulation of Speech in Okinawa], Gendai Jānarizumu Kenkyūkai, 1960.

6 Fukushima Jurō, "Senryō shoki ni okeru shinbun ken'etsu" [Newspaper Censorship during the Early Occupation Period] in *Kyōdō kenkyū Nippon senryōgun no hikari to kage* [Joint Research on Positive and Negative Aspects of the Japan Occupation Forces], edited by Shisō no Kagaku Kenkyūkai, Tokuma Shoten, 1968, p. 339–381.

7 Tanii Seinosuke, "Kindai shuppan sokumen-shi: Chosakuken no hensen to hatsubai kinshi" [Side History of Publications in Modern Japan: Transition of Copyrights and Book Banning] in *Nippon kindai bungaku dai-jiten dai 6-kan* [Encyclopedia of Modern Japanese Literature, Vol. 6], Kōdansha, 1968, p. 133–210.

that time, I received a letter from Mr. Okuizumi Eizaburō at the University of Maryland's McKeldin Library. He had apparently been transferred from the Keio University Library to the Asian collection at McKeldin. His letter read, roughly, that he had learned from my "Wasureta koto to wasuresase-rareta koto" essays that I was interested in Japan's occupation period and invited me to visit his library when I came to the United States. Considering that the documents there would most surely be of use to me. The letter included a couple of reference materials as well.

As a matter of fact, I had known that the McKeldin Library housed a tremendous number of Japanese documents—including books, newspapers, and magazines—that had been censored by the U.S. military during the occupation. Not until I had a look at the attachments to Mr. Okuizumi's letter, however, did I learn that this collection had been named the Gordon W. Prange Collection, that it had been designated as an official collection of the McKeldin Library's Asian collection, and that its opening presentation ceremony had just been held on May 6, 1979.

According to the materials Mr. Okuizumi kindly sent me, the Prange Collection consisted of 45,000 books and booklets, 13,000 magazine titles, and 11,000 newspaper titles that the Civil Censorship Detachment (CCD) of the Supreme Commander for the Allied Powers (better known in Japan as "GHQ") had censored during the occupation period. The huge collection had come into the possession of the University of Maryland because Dr. Prange, a professor of history at the University of Maryland since the prewar days, had served in the office of war history of GHQ's General Staff Section 2 (G-2) for six years during the occupation period and as GHQ's chief historian when he returned home in 1951. Before he left his post, he decided to bring back censored documents to be disposed in the United States. He packed the documents in 500 wooden crates, which the U.S. Army used as containers in those days, and sent them to the University of Maryland, where he resumed his post as professor of history.

The collection had been in dead storage in the McKeldin Library basement for 26 long years until 1977, when Dr. Frank Shulman, a renowned bibliographer, and Mr. Okuizumi began sorting the collection. The sorting effort got off the ground thanks to a grant from the National Endowment for the Humanities in the amount of $117,000. The process, however, ended up extending only to books and magazines; children's literature books went completely untouched, as did newspapers.

That background knowledge came from Mr. Okuizumi's letter and the attached documents. It appeared to me at that time that, along with the WNRC in Suitland, Maryland, the Prange Collection would be a good place to frequent while I was in Washington.

Mr. Hata Ikuhiko, a Japanese historian, made a brief introduction about the WNRC in Suitland in the annotated bibliography of *Showa zaiseishi 3: Shūsen kara kōwa made: Amerika no tainichi senryō seisaku* (Financial History of Showa 3: From the End of the War through the Peace Treaty; U.S. Occupation Policy toward Japan), edited by Ōkurashō Zaiseishi-shitsu.[8] From that profile, I knew that the Center stored more than 10,000 cardboard boxes full of documents related to the U.S. occupation forces. Since it was easy to assume the 10,000 cartons contained documents related to G-2, including those of the CCD, which was under G-2 jurisdiction, it was clear that what I had to do in Washington was to look for documents from the censorship authorities' side in Suitland and documents from the censored side in the Prange Collection. Still, at that point, I did not know what it all meant, exactly.

It was the morning of October 8, 1979, exactly one week after my arrival at the Wilson Center, when I first visited the Prange Collection. It took me about forty minutes to drive from the Wilson Center to College Park, the small town where the main campus of the University of Maryland is located. College Park is about ten miles northeast of Washington, via U.S. Route 1. Seeing as I have written elsewhere about that bright campus town situated over a gentle hill from Washington, I will refrain from describing it here. The East Asian Library, where the Prange Collection is located, is on the third floor of the University's McKeldin Library. At the time, it was managed by Dr. Schulman, Mr. Okuizumi, and several other staff members.

On that first visit, I had the good fortune of encountering the galley proof of Yoshida Mitsuru's "Senkan Yamato no saigo" (The Sinking of the Battleship Yamato), which had been scheduled for publication in the inaugural volume of the quarterly *Sōgen* in December 1946 but was banned by the occupation forces' censorship. See my book *Ochiba no hakiyose* (Sweeping

8 Appendix to Ōkurashō Zaiseishi-shitsu (Ministry of Finance Financial History Dept), ed., *Shōwa zaiseishi 3: Shūsen kara kōwa made: Amerika no tainichi senryō seisaku* [Financial History of Shōwa 3: From End of War through Peace Treaty: U.S. Occupation Policy toward Japan], Tōyō Keizai Shimpōsha, 1966, p. 69–70.

up Fallen Leaves)[9] for the details of that encounter, which I will not recount here. In any event, my first day at the Prange Collection was a rather promising start.

I paid my first visit to the WNRC in Suitland on October 15, 1979, one week after my first trip to the Prange Collection.

Even though it was only October, it was a cold, snowy day. When I arrived at the National Archives to register myself and my research assistant, David, in the morning, it was still snowing, though lighter than before.

To visit the WNRC, it was procedure to first register at the National Archives in Washington. There, one needed to receive a researcher registration card, report the purpose of one's visit to the file clerk, and request an introduction to the file clerk at the WNRC. It was past noon when I completed all the requirements and David and I went to a small canteen in the basement. When I unwrapped the sandwiches we had bought for lunch, I found the bread quite soggy.

But I went ahead and ate my soggy sandwich and washed it down with tasteless, lukewarm coffee. There was no time for me to bother about the bad food. I was eaten up by an obsession with the limited time I had to tackle the vast amounts of reference materials and documents at hand.

After I returned to the Wilson Center that afternoon, I telephoned the WNRC in Suitland to ask for directions. The voice, which sounded like it belonged to a mature, good-natured woman, instructed me to take Pennsylvania Avenue south, cross the Anacostia River, turn right at Branch Avenue, and turn when I came to the intersection with Suitland Road. She informed me that the entrance to the Federal Center, where the WNRC was located, faced Suitland Road.

Although the directions sounded easy enough, I missed the turn from Branch Avenue onto Suitland Road and ended up circling around and around. It did not help that the car that I had borrowed from a friend had a broken speedometer, either. It had already stopped snowing. I saw patches of blue sky. But the street remained deserted, perhaps because of the low temperatures.

What with one thing and another, we finally arrived at the WNRC after

---

9 Etō Jun, *Ochiba no hakiyose* [Sweeping up Fallen Leaves], now available as *Ochiba no hakiyose*: *1946-nen kenpō; Sono kōsoku* [Sweeping up Fallen Leaves: The 1946 Constitution; Its Restrictions], Bungei Shunjū, 1981. Enclosed in this volume are "Shisha tono kizuna: Senryōgun no ken'etsu to 'Senkan Yamato no saigo'" [Bondage with the Dead: Censorship by the Occupation Forces and "Sinking of Battleship Yamato"], which first appeared in monthly *Shinchō* (January 1980, p. 233–248) and "'Senkan Yamato no saigo' shoshutsu no mondai" [The Issue of First Publication of "Sinking of Battleship Yamato"], which first appeared in monthly *Bungakukai* (September 1981, p. 142–173).

2:30 p.m. I had driven around for more than 40 minutes to cover a distance that would have taken only 20 minutes under normal conditions.

The WNRC was situated at the farthest corner of the Suitland Federal Center, which consisted of several buildings. The neighborhood was full of cemeteries, and the Suitland Federal Center compound shared a border with one, while there was another vast cemetery across the street. For a split second, I was struck by the irony of a graveyard of documents lying right next to a cemetery for humans. But, then again, I decided that, unlike dead people, documents could be revived from their burial sites.

While the National Archives building in Washington was a grand piece of architecture that resembled a Greek temple—like many other government buildings in the heart of the city—the WNRC in Suitland was a low, single-story building. Looking more like a barracks, it did not appear to be a repository of historically important documents, at least not from the outside.

Turning right after entering the building, I found a small reading room on the right side of the corridor. The room was divided into two sections, and the one closer to the entrance was the office-cum-lounge equipped with a receptionist's desk and a sofa. Smoking was permitted there. The reading room section, separated from the lounge by a glass partition, was a barren space with about ten carrels for two people each. Seven or eight people were already there, indulging in documents they must have taken out of the cardboard boxes piled up beside the carrels. There was also a woman typing at a furious pace.

When I told the receptionist the purpose of my visit, I was told that, for whatever reason, the file clerk whom I had been referred to at the National Archives had not shown up that day. The receptionist offered to call another clerk who could help me. In about ten minutes, a smallish African-American gentleman with a mustache and dressed in what looked like a laboratory coat showed up. He introduced himself as Mr. Pernell, and he was the file clerk who ended up assisting me throughout all my visits to Suitland.

Mr. Pernell explained to me that documents at Suitland were known for being difficult to search through for information. There was no index, nor any index cards. All the facility had was a cargo manifest that had been filled out when the documents were shipped to the United States after GHQ's dissolution in 1952. Therefore, Mr. Pernell said, all I could do was to make a wild guess from the cargo manifest and ask for the file clerks' help.

At the entrance to the reading room was a notebook in which visitors were supposed to fill in their names, research registration numbers, and times of entry to the reading room. After entering the required information in the notebook according to Mr. Pernell's instruction, I took a seat at one of the vacant carrels. Having nothing to do until Mr. Pernell brought me the cargo manifest, I just looked around. On top of all the other carrels were piles of cardboard boxes. It was a moment of excited anticipation, knowing that those were the "boxes" that I had heard of and that I, too, was on a hunt for my own boxes.

At the far corner of the reading room was a pair of visitors, apparently Japanese, who were typing as if possessed. I later found out that they were staff members from Japan's National Diet Library on dispatch to Suitland to find documents related to GHQ's Government Section, convert them to microfilm, and bring them home.

When I saw the cargo manifest that Mr. Pernell brought me in the crook of his arm, I realized that there were easily more than 200 boxes of G-2-related documents alone. Those 200 boxes were sure to include boxes of documents pertaining to the Civil Censorship Detachment that had conducted the censorship, but there seemed to be many more than ten or twenty boxes that I had to look into. As I started to jot down the numbers assigned to the boxes that seemed relevant, I was momentarily haunted by the thought that it could take me months or even years to read through all the documents.

I was so engrossed in this note-taking work that nearly one hour had passed before I knew it. My watch told me it was close to 4:00 in the afternoon. I left my carrel and asked the receptionist to page Mr. Pernell.

When he arrived at the reading room, Mr. Pernell took a look at my cards with box numbers. Picking one up, he put a check mark on it and said, "You might as well start with this one."

I looked at the card: "Record Group #231, Box #8568." I had no idea why it would be better to start with this box rather than another. Resigned that I had no choice but to trust Mr. Pernell, I asked him if he could bring me the box. I was somewhat taken aback when he unexpectedly shook his head and pointed at his wristwatch, saying, "It's already 4:00, Mr. Etō. Here in Suitland, we retrieve all the documents in the reading room at 4:00 p.m. and close the reading room at 4:45. When are you coming back? When are you returning to Japan?"

When I replied, saying, "I'm coming back on October 18. I won't go back to Japan until next summer," Mr. Pernell answered, "So you have plenty of time. Box #8568 will be ready when you come back on October 18."

"Thank you, Mr. Pernell."

"It's Fred. Fred Pernell."

"Well, then, thank you, and good day, Fred."

That was how my first day at Suitland went.

According to my research notes, I subsequently returned to Suitland on October 18, 22, 23, and 24, making almost back-to-back visits. The box, which was filled to the brim with files, proved to be a mixture of wheat and chaff, so to speak, and I found it much more time-consuming than expected to select pertinent files and have them Xeroxed.

In order to make Xerox copies, I had to fill out a request form identifying all the documents to be copied and pay the fee in advance. It took, on average, two to three weeks, but sometimes longer than a month, to get the copies. The fee was 15 cents per page, payable to the receptionist at the entrance to the reading room.

The receptionists at Suitland worked in shifts, and I saw a different face every time I went. Some receptionists were friendly, and some were not. One day, when I approached the day's receptionist, a sulky-looking young man, to submit a copy-request form, he looked alternately at me and my request form before asking, "What are you investigating?" When I answered, "I'm looking into the censorship conducted by the CCD," he gave me a questioning look and remarked, "Censorship? But the point of the censorship was to democratize Japan, wasn't it?" As I wrote a check for the amount to be paid, I replied, "Well, I'm investigating why the censorship was conducted."

It would have been so much easier if I could have reached the state of clean decisiveness that this young man had. But it seemed to me that it could not be so simple and easy to answer the very fundamental questions of who had conducted censorship in occupied Japan and what purpose it had served.

As for "who did it," it seemed too self-evident from the documents at the WNRC in Suitland, and in the Prange Collection, that it was GHQ's CCD that actually conducted the censorship. Nevertheless, I had no clue at that point as to whether the censorship took place as an independent GHQ policy or under orders from the U.S. government in Washington. As long as the "who" was an unknown, it would be impossible to obtain an accurate answer to the "why." As I continued to read the unsorted documents in the box, one by one, I came to secretly wish for a clue about the "who" question.

The clue arrived on the morning of October 24. I was still struggling with documents in Box #8568 when I came across a rather voluminous file. Skimming through the document inside, I realized it was a draft of a long memorandum by Major General Charles Willoughby, General Douglas MacArthur's chief of intelligence (G-2), addressed to Major General

Edward M. Almond, GHQ's chief of staff.[10] It was dated March 1949, but it had no specific date. The memorandum mainly pertained to the relocation of censorship personnel, but when I read (A) of "Basic Facts Pertaining to This Issue," which came after the body of the memorandum, I could not believe my eyes. The memorandum stated:

> (Paraphrase) JCS 873/3 of November 12, 1944, (Appendix Table A) stipulates that the responsibility for censorship of civil communication within the area under U.S. jurisdiction falls on the theater military commander and that such censorship should be conducted by the military authorities throughout the period of occupation of an adversary's territory. The same directive also states that the range and severity of censorship can be relaxed at the theater military commander's discretion. <u>Nevertheless, censorship cannot be terminated in any area without the prior approval of the Joint Chiefs of Staff.</u>[11] (emphasis added)

It appeared that I had to conclude that the censorship had taken place on orders from Washington—the Joint Chiefs of Staff, in this case. Obviously, after my encounter with this draft memorandum, my search for relevant documents expanded to include the National Archives in Washington. The document JCS 873/3, or Joint Chiefs of Staff Directive 873/3, had to be at the National Archives, not the WNRC in Suitland, and I knew that a close scrutiny of the document would reveal the planning and decision-making processes for the censorship policy.

Before long, I was able to obtain not only JCS 873/3 but also a series of related documents at the National Archives. Close inspection of those documents pointed me to a government organization called the United States Office of Censorship, which I had not previously been aware of. As I investigated the history of this federal organization, I had to stretch my search further to cover the Library of Congress in Washington and the MacArthur Memorial in Norfolk, Virginia. Needless to say, in the meantime, I continued to frequent the Prange Collection at the University of Maryland to collect documents from the censored side.

In retrospect, I cannot help but think that October 24, 1979, marked a major turning point in my investigation and research. Not only did I discover the

---

10 Memorandum for the Chief of Staff (draft), March 1949, Signed Charles A. Willoughby, Major General, GSC Ass't Chief of Staff, G-2, The National Records Center, Suitland, Maryland. GR #331, Box #8568, File #211.

11 Ibid., p. 1.

Willoughby memorandum, but I also found—in the same box—the censorship guidelines of the Civil Censorship Detachment, comprising thirty prohibited matters, including documents on criticism of SCAP's drafting of the constitution and references to the censorship system.[12]

At that time, of course, my goal was not to know everything about the censorship that the U.S. occupation forces conducted in Japan. Nor is it today. After nine months of meticulous investigation, I was only able to look into ten boxes in Suitland. There were also countless documents in the Prange Collection that time limitations hampered me from investigating. What follows, then, is nothing more than what I was able to discover given the limits of time and my own ability.

This book is divided into two parts. Part 1 reviews the process of the formulation of the censorship policy. Part 2 attempts to explain how the censorship was conducted, with a few personal comments of mine. The question of how the censorship affected the Japanese mind is one I hope to touch on in the future.

To begin, we turn back the clock to early June of 1943, when World War II was at its peak.

12 Etō Jun, *1946-nen kenpō: Sono kōsoku* [The 1946 Constitution: Its Restraint], Bungei Shunjūsha, 1980, p. 12–15.

CHAPTER 2

Wartime Planning

On June 2, 1943, U.S. Secretary of War Henry Stimson received a letter from Byron Price, director of the U.S. Office of Censorship.[1]

It was only three days after the Japanese garrison on Attu Island had attempted a hopeless suicidal attack on U.S. troops. Some 150 surviving garrison members under the command of Colonel Yamazaki Yasuyo had taken the abortive action in the wee hours of May 30, after transmitting a report on the island's situation via the Imperial Navy's communication facility. While the Japanese troops succeeded in causing significant confusion among American soldiers at the U.S. military base, they all met their deaths. The Japanese side confirmed this through monitored U.S. military communication.

The last telegraph that Colonel Yamazaki sent was, however, a private message addressed to Lieutenant General Higuchi Kiichirō, commander of the Sapporo-based 5th Area Army. The telegraph said, "I wish to express my deepest gratitude for your unchanging kindness and my best wishes for Your Excellency's continued health and success."[2]

Around the same time in Europe, an air raid was about to be launched on the Italian fortress on Pantelleria. This was to be the preliminary skirmish of the Allied forces' invasion of Sicily. Pantelleria, an island situated midway between Tunis and Sicily, was a point of strategic importance that had been under the control of the Italian forces.

When the fleet carrying the Allied strike force approached the island on June 11, after a week-long series of air raids, the Italian fortress hoisted the white flag without any resistance. In the history of war, a military fortress rarely surrenders after air raids alone. What happened on Pantelleria presents a stark contrast to the British defenders on the island of Malta, who

---

1 JCS 873, May 24, 1944, Appendix A, The National Archives, RG218. Born in 1891, Byron Price worked for the Associated Press from 1912 until 1941, during which time he served as its executive news editor between 1937 and 1941. Price served as the U.S. Director of Censorship from 1941 through 1945.

2 Hattori Takushirō, *Daitōa Sensō zenshi* [Complete History of the Greater East Asian War], Tokyo: Hara Shobō, 1979. p. 435–436.

endured air raids by the Axis forces to the end.[3]

In any event, the successful operation left the road to Sicily—or, perhaps more appropriately, the road to Rome—wide open for the Allied forces.

As these events were unfolding, Byron Price was composing his letter to Secretary Stimson on the issue of implementing censorship in Allied-occupied areas. Anticipating that censorship would need to cover private correspondence, telegraphs, and telephones as well as newspapers and broadcasts, Price stressed to Stimson the need for a prompt investigation of censorship methods and the division of labor among the parties concerned.[4]

This was a highly meticulous and timely proposition, typical of Price. Prior to his appointment as director of the U.S. Office of Censorship by President Franklin D. Roosevelt, Price had been a seasoned journalist serving as executive news editor-cum-senior managing director for the Associated Press. During his more than twenty-year tenure in Washington, Price made the acquaintances of numerous government officials. Given his position, he was keenly aware of the need to pay constant attention to liaising with and coordinating between the U.S. Office of Censorship and such organizations as the Departments of State, War, and the Navy.[5]

On June 22, Secretary Stimson sent a response to Price's proposal. In a nutshell, there were two basic components to his reply. First, censorship of citizens of the occupied areas appeared to fall under the jurisdiction of the United States Army unit that controlled the area. Second, he wished to consult promptly with the Joint Chiefs of Staff in order to draw up a definite plan on the issue.[6]

Consequently, the Joint Chiefs of Staff immediately set out to formulate a plan for the censorship of citizens of the occupied regions. Three months later—by the time Italy surrendered on September 8—the plan was already complete and ready for execution. Seeing as the war situations in Europe and North Africa had changed so rapidly, the application of this plan was inevitably limited to the European-African battle front.[7]

Apart from this action by the Joint Chiefs of Staff, Price had already started consultations in June with the British Imperial Censorship Office

---

3 Katogawa Kōtaro, ed., *Dai 2-ji Sekai Taisen tsūshi* [Overview History of World War II], Tokyo: Hara Shobō, 1981, p. 258

4 JCS 873, May 24, 1944, Appendix "A," The National Archives, RG218.

5 *A Report on the Office of Censorship* (U.S. Government Printing Office, Washington, DC, 1945), p. 4–5.

6 JCS 873, May 24, 1944, Appendix B, The National Archives, RG 218.

7 Ibid., Appendix A.

and the Canadian Censorship Bureau. Parties to these consultations studied concrete ways to implement censorship strategies in Japan in anticipation of the situation after a German surrender.

In *A Report on the Office of Censorship*, which Price submitted to President Harry Truman (November 15, 1945), Price writes:

> . . . it appeared that the ideal situation, if it could be attained, would be to impose a universal communications blockade against Japan, thus making it possible to abandon virtually all other censorship once Germany was out of the war. At the Director's suggestion, the Secretary of State explored internationally the possibilities of such a blockade, but the replies from some nations indicated that there was no hope for the plan's success.[8]

Convinced that it would be impossible to carry out a worldwide information blockade vis-à-vis Japan, Price sent another letter to Secretary Stimson on September 14, 1943, pointing out that the Asia-Pacific front was absent from the censorship program formulated by the Joint Chiefs of Staff and suggesting that Secretary Stimson and the War Department authorities address the issue accordingly.[9]

In response, Stimson wrote the following on September 29.

> . . . You have noted that the agreement recently approved by the Combined Chiefs of Staff was limited to Euro-African areas; this was intentionally provided in order to meet certain problems peculiar to those areas. The War Department is now planning further agreements to apply to additional areas and particularly to the Pacific-Asiatic Theaters mentioned in yours of September 14, 1943. These agreements are being developed in collaboration with the Navy Department's Office for Occupied Areas, as there are spheres of operation in which the Navy may have a primary interest. However, even in such areas, the censorship interests would certainly best be served through the utilization, as far as practicable, of the censorship organization now being developed by the War Department.
>
> You will continue to be kept advised of the progress being made by the War Department in these matters. I wish to take this opportunity to thank you again for the valuable aid you and your organization are giving

8 *A Report on the Office of Censorship*, p. 15.

9 JCS 873, May 24, 1944, Enclosure, The National Archives, RG 218.

to the War Department. Our censorship interests are so closely aligned that continued close coordination will certainly remain invaluable.
Sincerely yours,

Henry L. Stimson
Secretary of War.[10]

The correspondence between Stimson and Price, then, harbored an embryo of the meticulous and stringent censorship that the U.S. occupation forces later conducted in Japan. The directive that was later transmitted to General Douglas MacArthur as JCS 873/3, as well as the related talking papers, all originated in the back and forth between Price and Stimson.

Around the time of the Stimson reply above, the Imperial Council convened in Tokyo for the first time since the start of the war to discuss an "outline of war leadership." After five hours of deliberation, beginning at 10 a.m. on September 30, 1943, the Imperial Council adopted an outline with two sections: one on policies and one on guidelines. The first guideline was formulated as follows.

> With the aim of establishing a strategic preparedness to counter American and British advances by mid-1944, no matter what the difficulties, we must capture and destroy enemy forces.
>
> The area that includes the Chishima and Ogasawara islands, the (mid and western) South Sea Islands (the present-day South Pacific Mandate) as well as western New Guinea, the Sunda islands, and Burma is defined as the sphere that absolutely must be held at any cost in the Pacific and Indian regions in order to execute the imperial war. Throughout the war, we must secure home sea traffic.[11]

This guideline was tantamount to the establishment of the so-called "Absolute Defense Line." The 51st Division of the Imperial Japanese Army, which had been stationed in Lae and Salamaua in eastern New Guinea outside the Absolute Defense Line, had already begun its retreat as early as September 15, allowing its soldiers to carry provisions for only ten days.[12]

A third letter written by Byron Price was addressed to Colonel A.J. MacFarland, secretary to the Joint Chiefs of Staff, and dated May 22, 1944—

10 Ibid., Appendix B.
11 Hattori (1979), p. 843.
12 Katogawa (1981), p. 248.

some eight months after Price's second letter to Stimson.

By that time, the wave of the Allied forces' counter-offensive in the western Pacific had been rushing toward Japan's Absolute Defense Line. On May 27, the massive forces of the U.S. Army 41st Infantry Division, under the direct command of Lieutenant General Robert Eichelberger, landed on Biak, a strategic spot in northwest New Guinea. Subsequently, on June 15, the 2nd and 4th Marine Divisions executed a landing operation on Saipan under the protection of fierce aerial assaults and naval bombardments.[13]

While Japan's Absolute Defense Line was on the verge of breaking in two spots, one in the south and the other in the north, Price still persisted in raising the issue of censorship in the occupied areas to the inner circle in Washington. His letter to MacFarland reads as follows.

> Dear Colonel McFarland:
>
> You will recall that nearly a year ago the Combined Chiefs of Staff (CCS/271) declared civil censorship in occupied areas in the Euro-African theaters to be a military responsibility.
>
> On September 14 last, I wrote the Secretary of State, the Secretary of War, and the Secretary of the Navy recommending that a similar directive be issued with respect to the Pacific-Asiatic Theaters. I enclose for your information copies of letters received in reply from Messrs. Stimson, Forrestal, and Berle. I would be glad to know whether any further progress has been made on this, since it occurs to me that the matter ought not to be lost sight of.
>
> Sincerely yours,
> /s/ Byron Price,
> Director.[14]

The secretariat of the Joint Chiefs of Staff forwarded this communique to the Civil Affairs Division of the Department of War on May 24. Upon receipt of the report from the Civil Affairs Division, the Joint Chiefs of Staff delivered the following response to Price on June 14.

> Dear Mr. Price:
>
> In reply to your letter of 22 May 1944 regarding civil censorship in occupied areas in the Pacific-Asiatic Theaters, the Joint Chiefs of Staff are pleased to be able to furnish the following information.

---

13 Ibid., p. 282.

14 JCS, 873, May 24, 1944, Enclosure, The National Archives, RG 218.

It is now a well-established and proven principle that the responsibility for censorship of civilian communications in areas occupied or controlled by armed forces must be the sole responsibility of the supreme commander of those forces. This rule will be applied to Pacific-Asiatic areas, just as it has been applied to Euro-African areas.

In his letter to you dated September 29, 1943, the Secretary of War advised that you would be kept informed of the progress being made in these matters. Until 19 May 1944, when a letter was dispatched to the Southwest Pacific Area, no directive had been issued with regard to civil censorship in Pacific-Asiatic areas, as it had been necessary to develop information from which guiding policies could be determined. The matter, however, has been constantly under study and is now taking a fairly definite shape.

The first step was to determine the areas that would be individually affected. This has been done, and presently four divisions have been made:

1. Southeast Asia (Burma, Malaya, Sumatra);
2. Southwest Pacific (Netherlands Indies, Philippines);
3. Central Asia (China, Thailand, French Indo-China);
4. Central Pacific (Japan and Japanese Dominions).

The initial planning in these areas is developing as follows (it should be stressed that this planning is tentative and subject to adjustment as occasion warrants):

1. Occupied areas in the Southeast Asia territory may be considered to be solely a British responsibility in view of the political status of Burma and Malaya. Sumatra, however, is an exception; and civil censorship planning for that territory must be correlated with civil censorship as provided for the rest of the Netherlands Indies under the Southwest Pacific Command.
2. Civil censorship in the Southwest Pacific Area will be the responsibility of the Commander in Chief, General MacArthur; and a missive has been addressed to that command outlining the situation. A copy of the missive referred to is appended for your information. This area may be of unusual interest to you as it includes the Philippine Islands in which area the Office of Censorship may have final responsibility following the period of military control.
3. The plans for civil censorship in Central Asia, particularly Thailand and French Indo-China, are still of a most tentative nature and require a further crystallization of conditions before they can be made more definite.

4. By far the largest civil censorship undertaking will be that required for Japan, both because of the complex nature of communications, including the language, and also because it is apparent that some type of military control including censorship will be required in Japan for a considerable time after her defeat.

A preliminary study of this problem has been prepared and is being processed in the War Department. A draft of the study was submitted to Colonel Carlson of your office and has received the benefit of his experience and advice, and a copy of the paper will be furnished to you as soon as it has been put in final form.

It would be sincerely appreciated if you would review the matters discussed herein. If you have any comments or suggestions, the Joint Chiefs of Staff would appreciate your passing them on directly to Major General Clayton Bissell, the Assistant Chief of Staff, G-2, WDGS, under whose jurisdiction this matter falls within the War Department.

For the Joint Chiefs of Staff.[15]
(emphasis added)

The missive to General MacArthur (dated May 19, 1944) that MacFarland referred to comprised two documents.[16]

One was an official letter from A.E. O'Leary, Adjutant General (Adjutant General's Office) at the Department of War, to General MacArthur. The other was a lengthy memorandum accompanying the official letter, titled "Censorship of Civilian Communications in Areas Occupied or Controlled by The Armed Forces."

O'Leary's official letter, after clarifying that the Supreme Commander for the Allied Powers was solely responsible for censorship of civil communications, pointed out the following seven points of contention.

First, censoring civil communications in the occupied areas would involve problems of a nature much more complicated than military censorship, which was confined to military personnel.

Second, the letter stressed that censorship of civil communications under the command of General MacArthur had to be an integral part of the worldwide network of Allied forces' censorship. Coordination with other related authorities, particularly with the U.S. Office of Censorship and the British Postal and Telegraph Censorship Department, would need to be maintained.

15 JCS 873/1, June 10, 1944, Appendix A, The National Archives, RG 218.

16 Ibid., Appendix B and Annex to Appendix B.

The same was true for constant, close liaison with the military commanders of other occupied areas.

Third, it would be the duty of civil censorship officers to conduct censorship of civil communications on behalf of the Supreme Commander for the Allied Powers. Civil censorship officers had to be experts in actual censorship operations and, fortunately, the U.S. Army had a stock of officers who had previously been seconded to the U.S. Office of Censorship, where they had gained the necessary experience. These officers could be transferred to General MacArthur's command. Because the appointment of civil censorship officers fell within the jurisdiction of the Department of War's Military Intelligence Division, the letter advised requesting the division to appoint appropriate officers.

Fourth, as far as the technical aspects of censoring civil communications were concerned, civil censorship officers were to have the authority to contact the assistant chief of staff for intelligence on the War Department General Staff directly—bypassing the military commander. General MacArthur was requested to immediately appoint civil censorship officers under his command and report their names and locations to the assistant chief of staff for intelligence at the War Department in Washington.

Fifth, the Department of War was prepared to provide the Southwest Pacific Area with information on the actual situation with regard to and future plans for censorship of civil communications that had gone into effect in northwestern Europe. Considering the involvement of the Dutch government in the matter, this information apparently related to the military operations in the Dutch East Indies.

Sixth, while censorship of civil communications was of a different nature than military censorship, theater censors would concurrently function as civil censorship officers in some regions. In these cases, deputies were to be appointed for each function.

Seventh, it was desirable that plans for the censorship of civil communications and their implementation be reported regularly to the War Department, which was mandated to coordinate all censorship organizations and their activities.

Concluding the official letter was a note saying that it was written "by order of the Secretary of War." The letter was signed by A.E. O'Leary, Adjutant General, Adjutant General's Office, Department of War.[17]

17 Ibid., Appendix B, "From the Adjutant General's Office, Department of War, to Commander-in-Chief, Southwest Pacific Area," May 19, 1944.

The "Censorship on Civil Communications in Areas under Military Occupation or Control" memorandum contained twelve items.

Of the various points in the document, the element meriting mention here is the emphasis on the inevitable duality inherent in civil-communication censorship. Censorship of civil communications served another, passive function—information collection. While information gathering was originally designed to help accomplish war goals, it was, at the same time, considered helpful in implementing the policies of the military and civilian authorities and, by extension, the governments of the Allied Powers in that the information gathered provided a means for accurately assessing the morale of the occupied citizenry. Information gathering, then, constituted a matter of urgency.

The censorship of civilian communications also performed the more active function of being a vanguard of governing policies in occupied areas. The objectives were to restrict the diffusion of any information going against the occupation policies in order to help stabilize economic activities in occupied areas and, at the same time, prevent the leakage of information to both the enemy side and underground resistance movements. It goes without saying that securing and maintaining communication lines represented the foundation of these activities.

Subsequently, the memorandum divided the period for censorship of civil communications into three stages: the battle stage, the occupation stage, and the transition-to-self-government stage.

During the battle stage, all civil communications would be shut off. While no actual censorship would take place at this stage, preparations for "carefully" censoring posts and other documents upon confiscation were part of the picture.

The occupation stage would involve censorship and the selective shut-off of civil communications on a concurrent basis. At the next stage, as governments were established by the citizens of occupied areas, censorship would be entrusted to these local governments. In order to protect the interests of the United States, liaison officers would be stationed in the local governments.

Needless to say, the memorandum's stipulations rested on the assumption that the Japanese mainland would certainly see battle. Recalling the actual censorship that took place during the occupation of Japan, however, one should note that, by far, the most noteworthy point in the memorandum was the sixth item:

> 6. In the case of enemy territory occupied by United States armed

forces and governed by a United States military administration there is little likelihood that an indigenous government will be set up prior to the signing of a peace treaty. During the period of occupation the only powers exercised by the inhabitants themselves will be those delegated to them by the military administration and will be concerned with the maintenance of public order and of the essential public utility services. Censorship control of civilian communications will be a function of the military authorities during the entire period of occupation. (emphasis added)

On the basis of this basic stipulation, the memorandum continued to identify five types of communication subject to censorship: postal, telegraphic communications, telephonic communications, travelers' documents, and films and photographs. The "postal" category for censorship included, in addition to first-class or sealed letters, second-class or printed papers, magazines and newspapers, parcels, and postal communications between civilians in the occupied territory and prisoners of war, as well as communications to enemy territory through licensed channels such as the International Red Cross. The telegraphs and telephone calls within the scope of censorship included land-wire, cable, and radio.

The memorandum set out the policy to minimize the mobilization of U.S. military personnel for censorship by employing local citizens as censorship examiners under the supervision of the occupation authorities. The document is among one of the earliest documents—and thus a precious piece of evidence—that gave a hint of the form of censorship for implementation in Japan.[18]

Meanwhile, offensives by the U.S. Navy and Army to penetrate Japan's Absolute Defense Line became increasingly fierce. It was on July 7, 1944, that the Japanese garrisons on Saipan attempted a final suicide charge, resulting in their annihilation. While the Imperial Japanese Army troops—the main force of the garrisons on Saipan—were 27,500 strong, the U.S. forces numbered around 71,000, mainly comprising two Marine Divisions. The firepower of the U.S. side, including naval cannons, was five times that of its Japanese counterpart, and the U.S. advantage in tank count was roughly threefold. American casualties in this battle ran to about 15,000.[19]

---

18 Ibid., Annex to Appendix B entitled "Censorship of Civilian Communications in Areas Occupied by the Armed Forces."

19 Katogawa (1981), p 284.

Subsequently, taking advantage of a weeks-long battery of brutal air raids and naval bombardments, U.S. troops resolutely carried out a landing on Guam on July 21. The Japanese garrison came in at around 18,500 troops, centered around the 29th Infantry Division and the 48th Independent Mixed Brigade, against some 55,000 U.S. troops, including the 3rd Marine Division, the 1st Provisional Marine Brigade, and the 77th Infantry Division. Learning a lesson from their experiences in Saipan, the U.S. forces reinforced their artillery by about seven times and tanks by about five times.

The Japanese garrison, which had shown formidable resistance against such overwhelming offensives, ceased its organized engagement on August 11. Casualties on the American side ran to about 7,000.[20] By that time, the Japanese garrisons on Tinian, an island separated from Saipan by a narrow strip of water, were also annihilated.[21]

What all this meant was that hardly a year since the confirmation of the Absolute Defense Line, a foothold for a U.S. invasion of the Japan mainland was firmly secured at the front inside the Line.

Just around that time, Byron Price once again began to call Washington's attention to the plan for censorship of civil communications in the Asia-Pacific region. In his August 9, 1944, letter to Major General Clayton Lawrence Bissell, assistant chief of staff for intelligence on the War Department General Staff, Price wrote:

> Dear General Bissell:
>
> I am gratified at the general tenor of your letter of August 5 with respect to planning for civil censorship in the Pacific-Asiatic areas. Pending further developments which you say are in prospect in the War and Navy Departments, I would like to make one suggestion.
>
> It seems to me that if a central advisory committee is created, the State Department should have representation along with the War and Navy Departments and the Office of Censorship. First or last, such a committee would be concerned more or less with large problems of international relationship overlapping into the period of peace after the conclusion of the war. I don't see how thoroughly sound conclusions could be drawn without the advice of the department primarily responsible for international relations.
>
> Perhaps it would help matters and insure quicker action if confer-

20 Ibid., p. 285.

21 Ibid.

ences were begun informally between State, War, and Navy and the Office of Censorship pending a decision as to whether a formal central committee is to be created. If you feel that such preliminary conferences are desirable, this office will, of course, be prepared to do its part.

Sincerely yours,
Byron Price,
Director[22]

The War Department, however, showed no response whatsoever to Price's proposal for over a month. Apparently irritated, Price decided to write directly to Fleet Admiral William D. Leahy, chief of staff to the Commander in Chief of the Army and Navy and chairman of the Joint Chiefs of Staff. In the letter, delivered to Fleet Admiral Leahy by a messenger on September 11, Price wrote:

Dear Admiral Leahy:

The Office of Censorship has received no recent news of developments in the matter of censorship of civilian communications in Pacific-Asiatic areas occupied or controlled by the United States authorities, other than temporary arrangements at San Francisco and Honolulu in respect to mails to and from the Marianas Islands.

In my letter of August 9, 1944, to Major General Bissell, copy enclosed, I suggested that some immediate benefit might result from a meeting of representatives of the State, War, and Navy Departments and the Office of Censorship in order to coordinate the pertinent efforts of each. Apparently this suggestion has not met with immediate favor, and it is thus necessary to ascertain what offices in the War and Navy Departments are authorized to discuss matters of policy, such as the following:

(a) The fundamental objectives of censorship in the Pacific, other than military security (It is noted that the War Department, in its secret letter of 19 May 1944 to the Commander-in-Chief, Southwest Pacific Area, enclosed a paper entitled "Censorship of Civilian Communications in Areas Occupied or Controlled by the Armed Forces." This paper gave specific information on a number of points, but it is not known whether similar or parallel instructions have been issued by the Navy Department).

---

22 JCS, 873/2, September 25, 1944, Appendix to Enclosure "B," The National Archives, RG 218.

(b) The coordination of civil censorship with the censorship net of the UNITED NATIONS, of which the United States Office of Censorship is a part.

(c) The extent to which this Office will be expected to participate in the censorship of communications with occupied areas. (It must be noted that the time is approaching when the United States Office of Censorship will cease to function, but it is assumed that this Office can render certain assistance prior to the complete cessation of hostilities.)

(d) The nature of press and broadcast censorship in the occupied areas (No reference to these items is noted in the War Department paper mentioned above).

(e) The status of the Office of Censorship with regard to reoccupied United States territory. (No answer has been received to my letter of August 29, 1944, on the subject of censorship in Guam. Also nothing further has been received on the subject of censorship in the Philippines, in which we may have an interest, according to the last sentence of subparagraph 2 of your letter of June 14 [aforementioned letter addressed to Colonel MacFarland]).

Recognizing the fact that the planning and preparation of civil censorship in the Pacific-Asiatic area is a tremendous undertaking, the consensus here is that it might be advantageous to accomplish all such planning in one operation, perhaps under the Joint Chiefs of Staff, rather than to burden the separate Theater Commanders not only with the task of planning and training, but with the necessity of coordinating their results in such a manner that the censorship in the entire area would be homogeneous in character. It is noted that an adequate program, designed along these lines, was inaugurated and is in operation in Europe.

Sincerely yours,
Byron Price,
Director.[23]

It appears that this rather harshly worded letter had an instant effect on the Joint Chiefs of Staff, as the following reply, drafted on September 25, suggests:

In reply to your letter of September 11, 1944, the Joint Chiefs of Staff wish to inform you that the Assistant Chief of Staff, G-2, War Depart-

23 Ibid., Enclosure B.

ment General Staff (Major General Clayton Bissell) and the Director of Naval Intelligence (Rear Admiral R.E. Schuirmann) are the officers in the War and the Navy Departments, respectively, who are authorized to discuss matters of policy regarding planning and preparation of civil censorship in Pacific-Asiatic areas.

Both Admiral Schuirmann and General Bissell will be glad to cooperate in every way possible with the Office of Censorship in planning and preparing to meet the problems outlined in your letter. It is hoped that you will feel free to consult them as necessary.[24]

The impact of Price's letter did not stop there. It was decided that the proposed liaison conference among the U.S. Office of Censorship and the Departments of State, War, and Navy would be convened with Bissell serving as moderator. Preparations were completed for making policy decisions on basic issues related to the censorship of civil communications, awaiting opinions from the commander of the occupied area (i.e., General MacArthur).[25]

Nevertheless, another seven weeks elapsed before the aforementioned directive JCS 873/3 was handed to MacArthur. It was on November 12, 1944, that the Joint Chiefs of Staff approved this directive concerning the censorship of civil communications in the areas under U.S. responsibility to be issued to the local military commander in the Asia-Pacific region.[26] By that time, MacArthur had already flung a massive force of 100,000 U.S. troops to Leyte, signaling the first step toward the recovery of the Philippines.[27]

The above correspondence and attachments delineate at least two important facts.

One was that, needless to say, the occupation authorities' censorship of civil communications in Japan was by no means an arbitrary act on the part of MacArthur's headquarters but was in compliance with U.S. Joint Chiefs of Staff directive JCS 873/3. Although I will discuss the directive in more detail later, let me point out here that censorship of civil communications in Japan took place at the order and will of the commander in chief of the United States Armed Forces—that is, President Franklin D. Roosevelt. This

24 Ibid., Appendix to Enclosure A.
25 Ibid., Enclosure A.
26 JCS 873/3, November 12, 1944, p. 29–42, incl., The National Archives, RG 218.
27 Katogawa (1981), p. 348.

statement is not only logically consistent but also factually verifiable. President Roosevelt himself had appointed Byron Price as director of the U.S. Office of Censorship. Roosevelt was highly appreciative of Price's talent and capability, and, as such, Price was the ideal representative for the president on the censorship issue.

The second important fact was the significance of Price's role in the issue. Accurately perceiving every turn of the war situation, Price tenaciously continued to send timely alerts to military leaders in Washington to prompt necessary actions. He consistently drove the issue until directive JCS 873/3 was finally issued.

It was Price himself, and not anyone in the U.S. military, who first raised the issue of the desirable nature of newspaper and broadcast censorship in the occupied areas, as his September 11, 1944, letter to Fleet Admiral Leahy shows. The fact that the Joint Chiefs of Staff ordered the censorship does not mean that the idea of censoring civil communications originated with the U.S. military or that the U.S. government had no active role in it—which could be seen as an alibi for the U.S. government, if you will.

On the contrary, the natural conclusion is that JCS 873/3 took shape through the consistent initiative of Price, a civilian director of the U.S. Office of Censorship. I might go so far as to say that, had there been no Price, the occupation forces' censorship of civil communications in Japan could have been quite different from what actually transpired.

A just, thorough assessment of Price requires an overview of the history of U.S. wartime censorship, a general survey of the American tradition behind the establishment of the U.S. Office of Censorship. The linguistic space that defined Japan's postwar days, after all, had ties to this historical evolution in the United States.

CHAPTER 3

Censorship's Justification

In the wee hours of December 8 (December 7, Hawaii time), 1941, only an hour after the Imperial Japanese Navy's attack on Pearl Harbor, the U.S. Navy's telecommunications-censoring posts in New York and San Francisco began to monitor all kinds of exchanges. Other posts in Miami, Los Angeles, New Orleans, and Seattle began their activities a few hours later.[1]

Censorship of the mail, which was assigned to the U.S. Army, had to wait a while longer. At midnight on December 11, the secretary of war issued a directive for the censorship of mail to begin within forty-eight hours.[2]

Prior to that, on December 8 (Eastern Standard Time), the day after the attack on Pearl Harbor, President Franklin D. Roosevelt had appointed J. Edgar Hoover, director of the Federal Bureau of Investigation, acting director of the U.S. Office of Censorship and instructed Hoover to promptly implement censorship by liaising and coordinating with the relevant parties until the necessary legislative measures were complete. It was actually upon the instruction of Acting Director Hoover that the secretary of war issued the order to censor the mail on December 11.[3]

On December 18, the United States Congress enacted the First War Powers Act, granting President Roosevelt the substantial authority necessary for waging war. The act included stipulations on censorship. Based on this wartime legislation, President Roosevelt signed Executive Order 8985, which stipulated that the "Director of Censorship shall cause to be censored, in his absolute discretion, communications by mail, cable, radio, or other means of transmission," the following day.[4]

At the same time, the executive order also stipulated the establishment of a Censorship Policy Board, with the postmaster general acting as chairman of the board, as well as a Censorship Operating Board to carry out liaison and coordination on a practical level among the relevant government agencies. Although the Censorship Policy Board convened only a few times, it nevertheless played a measurable role in deliberating on the rules applicable

1 *A Report on the Office of Censorship*. (U.S. Government Printing Office, Washington, DC, 1945), p. 3, 27.

2 Ibid., p. 4.

3 Ibid.

4 *Federal Register*, Vol. 6, No. 248, December 23, 1941, Executive Order No. 8985.

during wartime censorship of newspapers and broadcasts. The Censorship Operating Board comprised representatives from fifteen departments and agencies of the federal government, all of whom the director of the Office of Censorship selected. The Censorship Operating Board is credited with making significant contributions to the smooth operation of day-to-day activities.[5]

Incidentally, it was an interesting coincidence that Executive Order 8985 was issued on December 19, 1941. On that same day in Japan, the 78th extraordinary session of the Imperial Diet promulgated (to go into force on December 21) a Provisional Law for Control of Speech, Publications, Assembly and Association, a piece of wartime legislation similar in purpose to the executive order in the United States.[6]

Because it was abolished by order of GHQ after the war, the Provisional Law for Control of Speech, Publications, Assembly and Association came to be regarded as an evil law that suppressed the Japanese people's freedom. The law's maximum penalty was only one year's imprisonment, however. In contrast, Section 303 of the First War Powers Act stipulated that violators would be fined up to $10,000 or imprisoned for up to ten years, or both. In terms of the severity of the penalties, therefore, the American wartime legislation was much more stringent than Japan's was.[7]

It was against this backdrop that President Roosevelt appointed Byron Price, then the executive news editor and acting general manager of the Associated Press, director of the U.S. Office of Censorship. On this personnel decision, Roosevelt made the following special announcement in hopes of gaining the citizens' support:

> All Americans abhor censorship, just as they abhor war. But the experience of this and of all other nations has demonstrated that some degree of censorship is essential in wartime, and we are at war.
>
> It is necessary to the national security that military information which might be of aid to the enemy be scrupulously withheld at the source.
>
> It is necessary that a watch be set upon our borders, so that no such information may reach the enemy, inadvertently or otherwise, through the medium of the mails, radio or cable transmission, or by any other means.

---

5 *A Report of the Office of Censorship*, p. 5.

6 Nippon Kin-Gendaishi Jiten Henshū Iinkai, ed., *Nippon kin-gendaishi jiten* [Dictionary of Modern and Contemporary Japanese History], Tōyō Keizai Shinpōsha, 1978, p. 186.

7 *A Report on the Office of Censorship*, p. 4.

It is necessary that prohibitions against the domestic publication of some types of information, contained in long-existing statues, be rigidly enforced.

Finally, the Government has called upon a patriotic press and radio to abstain voluntarily from the dissemination of detailed information of certain kinds, such as reports of the movement of vessels and troops. The response has indicated a universal desire to cooperate.

In order that all of these parallel and requisite undertakings may be coordinated and carried forward in accordance with a single uniform policy, I have appointed Byron Price, Executive News Editor of the Associated Press, to be Director of Censorship, responsible directly to the President. He has been granted a leave of absence by the Associated Press, and will take over the post assigned him within the coming week, or sooner.[8]

It is noteworthy here that, even though the creation of the Office of Censorship was an open, public matter, it did not conduct any information propaganda activities whatsoever and remained a presence in the shadows, so to speak, leaving all propaganda activities to the Office of War Information established by Executive Order 9182 on June 13, 1942.[9] In the United States, then, the Office of War Information and the Office of Censorship supported the wartime information-control regime like two wheels of a cart with a clear division of duties. This scheme stood in stark contrast with the system in Japan, where the Cabinet Information Office concurrently functioned as a censorship authority. Furthermore, it was also interesting that this organizational arrangement—i.e., the Office of War Information conducting propaganda activities and the Office of Censorship attending to censorship—found its almost perfect reflection in the relationship within GHQ between the Civil Information and Educational Section (CI&E) and the Civil Censorship Detachment (CCD).

A detailed discussion of the CCD appears later in this book. Here, let me point out that the CCD's presence itself is powerful evidence that the prototype of the occupation forces' information-control regime in Japan had already taken shape, more or less, in Washington immediately after the eruption of the Pacific War.

Needless to say, a country's censorship of its own citizens and its pro-

---

8 Ibid., p. 5.

9 Elmer Davis and Byron Price, *War Information and Censorship*, Washington, DC: American Council on Public Affairs, 1943, p. 9.

paganda for and censorship of peoples of occupied territories are, by definition, different in terms of purpose and severity. For instance, while the U.S. Office of Censorship came about openly, via an executive order, the existence of the CCD in Japan remained undisclosed until the occupation ended. Still, censorship within the United States and censorship in Japan by the American occupation forces shared a tremendous similarity in that they both took place at the hands of American officials. It was the tendency of Americans, whom many believed to loathe censorship—as Roosevelt's statement intimates—to suppress that contempt when face to face with critical situations that might call for a resort to censorship.

For instance, Byron Price writes as follows in his *A Report on the Office of Censorship*.

> Censorship's public relations policies were shaped upon the thesis that it never would be possible, actually, to popularize censorship in a free country. To that end, the Agency at no time had a public relations department. On the rare occasions when it was necessary to issue public announcements, these announcements were mimeographed and given out directly from the Office of the Director.[10] (emphasis added)

The source of this psychological inclination is, needless to say, the thesis that the United States is a country of freedom. Behind this thesis is the First Amendment to the Constitution of the United States:

> First Amendment—Religion and Expression
> Congress shall make no law respecting an establishment of religion, or prohibiting the free exercise thereof; or abridging the freedom of speech, or of the press; or the right of the people peaceably to assemble, and to petition the Government for a redress of grievances.

Incidentally, one could liken the following four articles of the Constitution of the Empire of Japan to the First Amendment of the U.S. Constitution:

> Article 28. Japanese subjects shall, within limits not prejudicial to peace and order, and not antagonistic to their duties as subjects, enjoy freedom of religious belief.
> Article 29. Japanese subjects shall, within the limits of law, enjoy the

10 *A Report on the Office of Censorship*, p. 12.

> liberty of speech, writing, publication, public meetings and associations.
> Article 30. Japanese subjects may present petitions, by observing the proper forms of respect, and by complying with the rules specially provided for the same.
> Article 31. The provisions contained in the present Chapter shall not affect the exercises of the powers appertaining to the Emperor, in times of war or in cases of a national emergency.

A comparison of the two documents should readily reveal that, while freedom in the United States appears limitless at a glance, freedom in prewar Japan appeared subject to conditions regulating the liberties "within limits not prejudicial to peace and order," "[within limits] not antagonistic to their duties as subjects," "within the limits of law," and "by observing the proper forms of respect, and by complying with the rules specially provided for the same."

What would Americans do, however, if freedom, with its supposedly unconditional protections, had to be restricted "in times of war or in cases of a national emergency?" In other words, what would Americans do if the First Amendment temporarily applied conditions to people's freedom—allowing only liberties "not prejudicial to peace and order," "not antagonistic to their duties as subjects," and "within the limits of law?"

Should this actually happen, I am convinced that "freedom," which is in reality restricted and violated, would become some kind of taboo in the United States, and Americans would have to come up with a fiction that made it seem as if no violation of people's freedom were taking place. In other words, censorship would have to be conducted as if it were not being conducted at all—and, similarly, censorship of the media would have to be carried out as if such censorship did not exist.

What is noteworthy here is the probability of the emergence of a mechanism in the United States, "in times of war or in cases of a national emergency," that would make both civil censorship and news censorship a taboo—i.e., something that should not to be referred to or openly admitted—because, under the First Amendment, upholding the "fiction" would be an absolute necessity. In the United States, under these circumstances, the more freedom becomes an object of fetishism, the more civil censorship and news censorship become taboos. Therefore, even though the establishment of the U.S. Office of Censorship came by a public presidential announcement, it had to disguise its existence and activities as much as possible.

Nevertheless, one should remember that, throughout its history, the United States has often experienced "times of war" and "cases of a national emergency"—and each time, without fail, censorship has taken place. According to *War Information and Censorship* by Elmer Davis and Byron Price,[11] one of the few surviving public-relations documents pertaining to the Office of Censorship, there was a minority opinion against independence during the Revolutionary War. That sentiment, which colored some regional communities, was "invariably" suppressed even before the Constitution of the United States came to be.[12] In the War of 1812 against Britain, Major General Andrew Jackson himself became a censor. After his victory at New Orleans, Jackson became enraged with the *Louisiana Gazette,* which carried a critical article on him without official permission to print such news. In the end, Jackson had the writer of the article imprisoned. Moreover, he even forced a judge who had issued a writ of *habeas corpus* on behalf of the imprisoned writer to leave the city.[13]

As the book says, "In Baltimore, a mob wrecked the office of the *Federal American,* a newspaper which called the war unnecessary. After a month, the paper resumed publication, but one of its principals was killed by another mob."[14]

The Civil War produced many similar incidents. Mobs forced several Northern papers to suspend publication because of their stand against the war, while others had to display the American flag in their window.[15]

In August 1861, the Department of War set up censorship on telegraph lines, and the postmaster general denied mail service to certain papers accused of being disloyal to the Union cause.[16]

President Abraham Lincoln himself did not favor censorship and, when urged on one occasion to suppress the *Chicago Times*, did not approve it. In 1863, General Ambrose Burnside did suppress publication of the paper, claiming the publication's "repeated expression of disloyal and incendiary sentiments." It was thanks to appeals by prominent Chicago citizens and a resolution in the state legislature that President Lincoln authorized the *Times* to publish again.[17]

During the Spanish-American War, censors regulated the telegraph wires

---

11 Davis & Price (1943). See also note 48.

12 Ibid., p. 57.

13 Ibid.

14 Ibid., p. 57–58.

15 Ibid., p. 58.

16 Ibid.

17 Ibid.

at Tampa, Miami, and Jacksonville, but were apparently lenient. American newspapers with war correspondents ended up hiring small boats to carry dispatches across the water to Florida.[18]

While American troops were in the Philippines, meanwhile, critical reports of newspaper censorship—not about the military censorship itself, but rather the inequalities in its application—emerged.[19]

It was after the United States joined World War I in 1917, however, that large-scale, organized censorship began. On April 13, one week after the United States declared war, the secretaries of state, war, and navy urged President Woodrow Wilson to create a Committee on Public Information to exercise voluntary censorship over the American press and disseminate governmental information about the progress of the war. President Wilson, in response, appointed the three secretaries to the committee under the chairmanship of George Creel, a prominent figure in the world of journalism.[20]

One important point to note here is that the news censorship system in the United States at the time of World War I did not demarcate functions between censorship and propaganda, nor did it establish any division of labor between the two—akin to the organization of Japan's Cabinet Information Office at the time of World War II.

In fact, the Committee on Public Information (the "Creel Committee") is better remembered for its extravagant propaganda activities than its darker side of censorship. The Creel Committee's propaganda activities included the famous "Four Minute Men," who spoke to theater audiences, clubs, and other public groups, urging their listeners to buy Liberty Bonds and war savings stamps. According to Davis and Price, "the movies were mobilized, a bureau of war photographs was established, special work was done with the foreign language groups and with labor unions. And, as one of its major functions, the Committee took over the issuance of all Government news."[21]

For the purposes of censorship, the Creel Committee divided news into three categories: dangerous news, questionable news, and routine news. Editors were invited to submit any articles that they had doubts about. Committee-approved articles were stamped either "Passed by the Committee on

18 Ibid.

19 Ibid.

20 Ibid., p. 58–59. George Creel was born in Missouri in 1876. After serving *The Independent* (Kansas City), the *Denver Post*, and *The Rocky Mountain News* as an executive editorial writer, Creel was appointed to the head of the newly established Committee on Public Information in 1917, a post that he kept until 1919. He passed away in 1953. His publications include *Quatrains of Christ* (1907), *Wilson and the Issues* (1916), and *The People Next Door* (1926).

21 Ibid., p. 60.

Public Information" or "Authorized by the Committee on Public Information." The former indicated that an article could be published safely, but the committee did not guarantee its accuracy; the latter showed that an article had been investigated and officially approved by the committee.[22]

Regarding censorship of postal mail and cables in the United States during World War I, all wireless stations in the United States had been placed under the purview of the U.S. Navy in 1914. On April 28, 1917, cables and telegraph and telephone lines crossing the border were placed under the jurisdiction of the army and the navy. Meanwhile, the Trading with the Enemy Act and the Espionage Act were enacted, empowering the postmaster general to censor mail.[23]

It was under these circumstances that President Wilson established in October 1917 a Censorship Board aimed at integrating and coordinating censorship operations. The board consisted of the secretaries of war and navy, the postmaster general, the director of the War Trade Board, and George Creel. From that point on, censorship of the mail and cables fell under the jurisdiction of the board, and the Post Office Department paid the expenses and supplied a good share of the workers for the effort.[24]

As a result of the board's censorship, sources say, more than 250,000 persons had been on a list of censorship suspects at some time by the end of World War I. Court cases and prosecutions related to speeches, newspaper articles, pamphlets, and books that became targets of censorship ran to more than 1,900 in all.[25]

What these developments signify is that it was only after the United States joined an all-out war—that is, World War I—that Americans, on a national scale, had to come to grips with the fundamental contradiction between the First Amendment's guarantee of freedom of speech and the press and such censorship-related legislations as the Espionage Act, whether they liked it or not.

A few American intellectuals correctly recognized this issue and saw it as a crisis of the fundamental principles of the United States; Zechariah Chafee, Jr., professor of law at Harvard University, echoed that sentiment in

22 Ibid., p. 59.

23 Ibid., p. 60.

24 Ibid.

25 Ibid., p. 61. See also Zachariah Chafee, Jr., *Freedom of Speech*, New York: Harcourt, Brace & Howe, 1920, p. 1.

Freedom of Speech in 1920.[26] At the outset of the book, Chafee notes "over nineteen hundred prosecutions and other judicial proceedings during the war [World War I], involving speeches, newspaper articles, pamphlets, and books" and states that "it is becoming increasingly important to determine the true limits of freedom of expression, so that speakers and writers may know how much they can properly say, and governments may be sure how much they can lawfully and wisely suppress." (p. 1.)

This awareness penetrated the book. And thus, Chafee writes:

> It is already plain, I hope, that this book is an inquiry into the proper limitations upon freedom of speech, and is no way an argument that any one should be allowed to say whatever he wants anywhere and at any time. We can all agree from the very start that there must be some point where the government may step in, and my main purpose is to make clear from many different angles just where I believe that point to lie.[27]

The very fact that Chafee explicitly lays out his intention betrays the rather moderate stance that he took vis-à-vis the issue at hand. In subsequent lines, Chafee adds that he had no sympathy toward pacifists or antiwar advocates and confesses that, "The only one, I suppose, of all that number with whom I could sit down for half an hour's conversation without losing my temper is Mr. Bertrand Russell."[28]

Nevertheless, in Chafee's eyes, the censorship and other measures that the U.S. government took to restrict freedom of speech appeared to connote serious challenges to the First Amendment. Chafee felt this way because "[T]he free speech clauses of the American constitution are not merely expressions of political faith without binding legal force."[29]

What Chafee found particularly problematic was the contradiction between the First Amendment and the Espionage Act, which took effect on June 15, 1917, and underwent revision on May 16, 1918. Title 1, Section

---

26 Born in Providence, Rhode Island, in 1885, Chafee graduated from Brown University and the Harvard Law School. He practiced at the law firm of Tillinghast & Collins from 1913 to 1916. Chafee joined Harvard Law School as an assistant professor in 1916 and was promoted to full professor in 1919. He was appointed Langdell Professor of Law in 1938 and university professor in 1950. *Freedom of Speech* was his first book, which was later revised and renamed *Free Speech in the United States* in 1941. He was known as a liberalist jurist as well as an eloquent attorney. He published numerous books before his death in 1957.

27 Chaffee (1920), p. 1–2.

28 Ibid., p. 2.

29 Ibid., p. 3.

3 of the Espionage Act, which Congress enacted and vigorously enforced, stipulated that violators would be punished by a fine of up to $10,000 or imprisonment for up to twenty years, or both. The First Amendment, in contrast, stipulates that "Congress shall make no law abridging the freedom of speech, or of the press . . ." How can and should observers address this contradiction?[30]

It is true that, as Chafee writes, "thoughtful men and journals were asking how scores of citizens could be imprisoned under the constitution, which guaranteed freedom of expression, only for their open disapproval of the war as irreligious, unwise, or unjust." Still, even though the concept of all-out war had not yet been established, it had been widely perceived among officials in the United States—be they of the federal government or state governments—that the war (World War I) was totally different in nature from previous wars. In that sense, Americans had tacitly accepted General Erich Ludendorff's idea that wars were no longer won by armies in the field but by the morale of the whole people. As a matter of fact, before and during World War I, a substantial number of German agents sneaked into the United States and conducted activities to demoralize American citizens.[31]

Recognizing that the issue was a conflict between two vital principles—order and freedom—Chafee decided that a basis for reconciliation between the two principles would be crucial. He started his endeavor by rejecting two extreme views in the controversy. One was the view that the Bill of Rights was a peacetime document and, consequently, freedom of speech could be ignored in war. Chafee pointed out that the *Report of the Attorney General of the United States* in 1918 had officially repudiated this interpretation.[32]

At the other extreme was the belief that the First Amendment rendered unconstitutional any act, without exception, that abridged the freedom of speech or of the press; therefore, the reasoning followed, all speech was free, and only action could be restrained and punished.[33] Chafee found this view equally untenable, citing that provisions of the Bill of Rights could not be applied with absolute literalness and were subject to exceptions. For instance, Chafee argued, the prohibition of involuntary servitude in the Thirteenth Amendment did not prevent military conscription or the enforcement of a "work or fight" statute.[34]

---

30 Ibid., p. 6.

31 Ibid., p. 6–7.

32 Ibid., p. 7.

33 Ibid.

34 Ibid.

Having eliminated these two extremes, the true solution to the contradiction had to lie between them, Chafee felt. At this point, Chafee introduced two mutually inconsistent theories that had been especially successful in winning judicial acceptance and appeared frequently in Espionage Act cases.

One was the so-called "Blackstone's statement." It claimed that the government could not interfere via censorship or injunction before the words were spoken or printed, which would be tantamount to a violation of freedom of speech and expression, but could exact whatever punishment it saw fit after publication.[35]

Chafee announced that this Blackstonian theory had to be "knocked on the head once for all" because, in the first place, Blackstone was not interpreting a constitution, but simply describing the English law of his time (the eighteenth century).[36] Britain in those days had no censorship, but it did have extensive libel prosecutions. Even though Blackstone had a formidable influence on American judicial circles in those days, Chafee argued that his theory was invalid to begin with in interpreting the First Amendment's guarantees of freedom of speech and the press.[37] Chafee also argued that Blackstone's theory was "wholly out of accord with a common-sense view of the relations of state and citizen" and could go "altogether too far in restricting state action." For instance, the prohibition of previous restraint (pre-publication restraint) would make it impossible for the government to prevent a newspaper from publishing the sailing dates of transports or the number of troops in a sector, a limitation that would impose grave impediments on the execution of war operations.[38]

Chafee stated that Blackstone's definition gave very inadequate protection to the freedom of expression. He argued that instituting the death penalty for writing about socialism would be just as effective a form of suppression as censoring expression, even without any censorship system.[39]

Having thus criticized the Blackstone theory, Chafee subsequently introduced the second persuasive interpretation of freedom of speech under the First Amendment—that is, that the First Amendment protected the use of speech, but not its abuse. It was an argument for drawing the line between "liberty" and "license," which was easier to say than to do because "liberty" to the speaker could often become "license" to the government.[40]

---

35 Ibid., p. 8–9.

36 Ibid., p. 9.

37 Ibid., p. 8–9.

38 Ibid., p. 9–10.

39 Ibid., p. 10.

40 Ibid., p. 12–14.

Chafee's view on this issue, which touched on the historical significance of the U.S. Constitution, is worth noting. He posited that there were two different views of the relation between rulers and people, and the two views were in conflict. According to one view, the rulers were the superiors of the people and, therefore, were exempt from any censure that would tend to diminish their authority.[41] In this view, people could not make adverse criticism in newspapers or pamphlets; they could do so only through their lawful representatives in the legislature, who might be petitioned in an orderly manner.

Needless to say, eighteenth-century Britain fitted well with this view. As Blackstone had argued, liberty of the press under this regime, which prohibited direct criticisms of the ruler, was nothing more than the formal absence of censorship.[42]

In contrast, the other view held that the rulers were agents and servants of the people, who might therefore find fault with their servants and discuss questions of their punishment, their dismissal, and governmental policy.[43]

According to Chafee, the United States was the quintessential manifestation of this second view. Under the U.S. Constitution, the people—not the government—possessed absolute sovereignty, and the legislature as well as the executive branch had limited power. In this case, freedom of speech and expression should not be confined to freedom from previous censorship by the executive branch, as in the case of Britain, but should also include freedom from restrictive legislation by the legislature. In other words, the First Amendment, in principle, granted American citizens unlimited freedom to criticize the government and its policies.[44]

Based on these observations, Chafee argued, "The censor is the most dangerous of all the enemies of liberty of the press, and ought not to exist in this country unless made necessary by extraordinary perils."[45]

He continued, stating, "It is now clear that the First Amendment fixes limits upon the power of Congress to restrict speech either by a censorship or by a criminal statute, and if the Espionage Act exceeds those limits it is unconstitutional."[46]

41 Ibid., p. 19.
42 Ibid., p. 19–20.
43 Ibid., p. 20.
44 Ibid., p. 20–21.
45 Ibid., p. 32.
46 Ibid.

Nevertheless, Chafee's basic stance toward this issue, after all, did not deviate too much from moderate common sense. In his book, Chafee stressed that freedom of speech and press as protected by the First Amendment should not be assessed in terms of "proper use" versus "abuse" or "liberty" versus "license." Instead, a proper balance between individual interests and social interests was essential—and, if those interests conflicted, the question was which interests to sacrifice and which to protect under the circumstances.[47] Chafee contends:

> It is useless to define free speech by talk about rights. The agitator asserts his constitutional right to speak, the government asserts its constitutional right to wage war. The result is a deadlock. . . . To find the boundary line of any right, we must get behind rules of law to human facts.[48]

On the basis of the above observations, Chafee concludes:

> The true boundary line of the First Amendment can be fixed only when Congress and the courts realize that the principle on which speech is classified as lawful or unlawful involves the balancing against each other of two very important social interests, in public safety and in the search for truth. . . . In war time, therefore, speech should be unrestricted by the censorship or by punishment, unless it is clearly liable to cause direct and dangerous interference with the conduct of the war.
>
> Thus our problem of locating the boundary line of free speech is solved. It is fixed close to the point where words will give rise to unlawful acts. . . . And we can with certitude declare that the First Amendment forbids the punishment of words merely for their injurious tendencies.[49]

When we compare Chafee's sensible arguments with the reality of the massive, highly organized censorship system that subsequently developed in the United States, the irony is hard to deny. According to Chafee, restriction of speech and expression in wartime had to be limited to the minimum and imposed only when absolutely necessary. In actuality, however, censorship took place throughout World War II over a wide range of areas, including the mail, telegrams and telephones, publications, newspapers, and broadcasts. The operations took shape "without delay in perfect order" in accor-

47 Ibid., p. 34–35.

48 Ibid.

49 Ibid., p. 38–39.

dance with President Roosevelt's statement, which had stressed that "all of these parallel and requisite undertakings [should] be coordinated and carried forward in accordance with a single uniform policy." More than that, the censorship system was later exported to occupied Japan after the war and applied with similar efficiency. What it all tells us is that, over the course of two world wars, American society had been transformed into a society that could produce one of the world's most efficient censorship systems.

Perhaps Chafee's arguments and the American tendency to "disguise" the existence of censorship are simply two sides of the same coin. Zechariah Chafee, Jr., a jurist from the "good-old days" who naively believed in the American tradition of freedom, regarded the regulation of freedom of speech in the United States during World War I to be nothing more than a provisional measure. Although he found fault with any censorship overkill in the United States, Chafee still held hope that the First Amendment's classical freedoms would be resurrected in the linguistic space of American society.

It is obvious from the above that, even though Chafee regarded censorship as a necessary evil, he was convinced that, "[T]he censor is the most dangerous of all the enemies of liberty of the press." It seems needless to point out that the values of President Roosevelt, who stated that "all Americans abhor censorship, just as they abhor war," coincided with those of Byron Price when he confessed that "it never would be possible, actually, to popularize censorship in a free country." Both men held the view that censorship was indeed dangerous to the freedom of speech and expression.

In contrast to Chafee, however, both Roosevelt and Price were fully aware that this "evil" had metamorphosed into an indispensable, necessary evil. It might be that censorship was no longer an evil to tolerate only temporarily—instead, it may have become a "necessary evil" that, to a certain extent, had to remain in permanence.

Perhaps the classical freedoms of the United States that Chafee dreamed of might have died away with the end of the Monroe Doctrine. Because President Wilson decided to let the United States join World War I, thus leading the country out of isolation within the Americas and into the turmoil of international society, this "evil" may have inevitably became a "necessary evil." Since then, it appears that Americans have continued to suffer from an ever-present anxiety about the existence of their own country amid the conflicts of international society.

What kind of organization, then, did the U.S. Office of Censorship create under the leadership of Byron Price, and, specifically, what kind of activities did the organization conduct? The next chapter tackles these key questions.

CHAPTER 4

Inner Workings

It was indeed highly suggestive that the first task Byron Price tackled after being appointed director of the U.S. Office of Censorship was establishing a system of voluntary censorship of newspapers, broadcasts, and other communications.[1] The decision undoubtedly rested on an awareness among government officials that the voluntary censorship of newspapers and the press during World War I had been a failure that only spawned "many misunderstandings and much bitterness" among the relevant parties. Price, too, keenly shared this awareness.[2]

Price faced an additional challenge. Censorship during World War II had to deal with the new medium of radio, the merit of which was its ability to report information quickly. Unlike "postal and cable censorship [which] were already underway and were in the competent hands" of the U.S. Army and Navy, nothing had been done about this new medium. "The machinery for making decisions regarding . . . [radio] broadcasting had to be created from the ground up."[3]

At this point, Price wisely decided to discontinue the Office of Censorship's monopoly on distributing government-released news. George Creel's Committee on Public Information had held complete control over distribution during World War I, along with the censorship function. It appeared that Price intended to avoid entering a competition with private news agencies in news distribution because, even without rivals to deal with, it would be impossible for the Office of Censorship to be popular among American citizens. Price labeled this abstention from any propaganda activities whatsoever the "principle of appropriate authority."[4]

As I introduced in the previous chapter, when the United States Office of War Information was established under the directorship of Elmer Davis[5] in

1 *A Report on the Office of Censorship* (U.S. Government Printing Office, Washington, DC, 1945). p. 5–6.

2 Ibid., p. 32.

3 Ibid., p. 5–6.

4 Ibid., p. 32.

5 Elmer Holmes Davis was born in Aurora, Indiana, in 1890. Davis studied at the Universtity of Oxford from 1912 to 1914 as a Rhodes Scholar. Upon returning to the United States, he became a reporter with the *New York Times*. From 1939 on, he was a star radio commentator. When the United States Office of War Information was founded in 1942, Davis was appointed its director. Davis died in 1958.

June 1942, Price immediately concluded an agreement with Davis to establish a division of labor between their two organizations. Under the agreement, the Office of War Information would concentrate exclusively on the positive functions of news distribution and propaganda activities, abstaining from interference with the censorship operations. The Office of Censorship, meanwhile, would devote itself to the negative function of censorship to uphold the principle of appropriate authority.[6]

On December 26, 1941, Price appointed John H. Sorrells and J. Harold Ryan assistant director in charge of the Press Division and assistant director in charge of the Broadcasting Division, respectively. Sorrells, like Price, obtained a leave of absence from his post as executive news editor of the Scripps-Howard Newspapers and moved to Washington from New York City, where he had long resided, fully aware that his annual salary would drop. Ryan, from Toledo, Ohio, was vice president and general manager of Fort Industries. He agreed to the same conditions as Sorrells did when he accepted his appointment.[7]

This personnel decision to appoint an active journalist and a broadcasting executive to assistant directorships was a highly tactical maneuver on the part of Price, who wanted to secure the understanding and cooperation of the newspaper and broadcasting circles regarding voluntary censorship. The hiring move turned out to be a success. On the heels of those harbingers came more recruitment of mid-level executives from newspapers, broadcasting companies, and publishers by the Office of Censorship, quickly embroiling the entire American journalism circle in the wave of voluntary censorship.

On January 5, 1942, the headquarters of the Office of Censorship, which had initially operated out of a single room with borrowed clerical staff, moved to the Apex (Federal Trade Commission) Building at Sixth Street and Pennsylvania Avenue, NW, which today houses the United States Trade Representative (USTR).[8] By February 15 of the same year, the Office of Censorship had more or less completed its organizational setup. Its six divisions—Postal, Cable, Press, Broadcasting, Reports, and Administrative—were all swinging into operation, and its overall personnel had increased to more than 5,000. Of these, 3,100 were in the Postal Division and corresponding stations, while 1,819 were in the Cable Division and corresponding stations.[9]

---

6 *A Report on Office of Censorship*, p. 12.

7 Ibid., p. 8–9.

8 Ibid., p. 8.

9 Ibid.

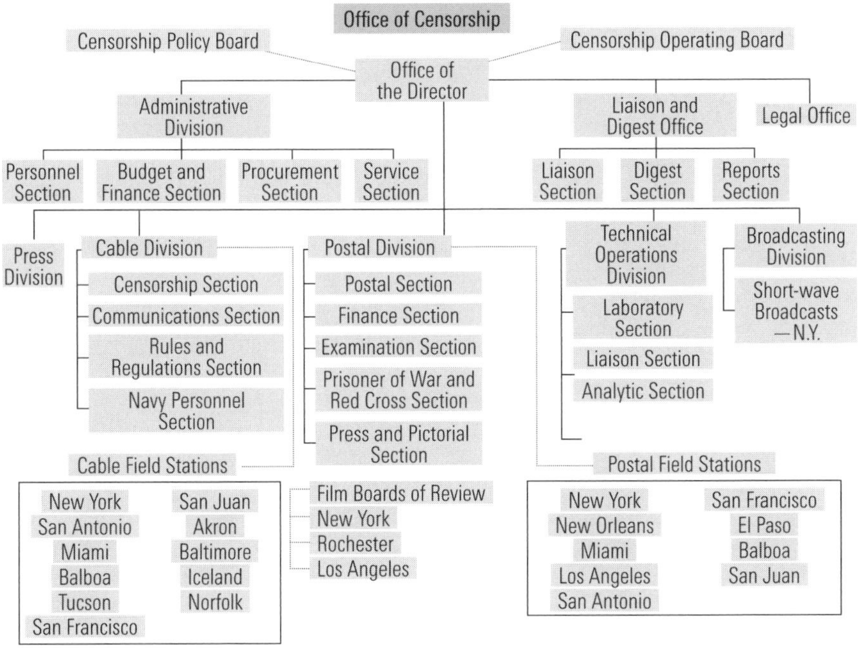

Figure 1. Organizational Chart of the Office of Censorship

The workforce continued to expand, peaking at 14,462 in January 1943. The organizational structure of the Office of Censorship also grew and reorganized into the framework in Figure 1.[10]

During the initial months of the Office of Censorship's operations, budget funding came from a $7,500,000 allocation from the Emergency Fund for the President. Subsequently, congress appropriated amounts of $26,500,000 for fiscal 1943, $29,600,000 for fiscal 1944, and $29,700,000 for fiscal 1945.[11]

On January 15, 1942, the first edition of the *Codes of Wartime Practices for the American Press* pertaining to the voluntary censorship of press and radio appeared. The document underwent four revisions until the issue of the fifth edition on May 15, 1945.[12] In addition, the Office of Censorship occasionally issued "special requests" as situations warranted. For instance, the request

10 Ibid.
11 Ibid., p. 10.
12 Ibid., p. 33.

for voluntary censorship of reports on movements of the U.S. president and other prominent Allied figures is a typical example.

The preamble of the June 15, 1942, edition of the *Code of Wartime Practices for the American Press* introduces the outline of the code.[13]

> This revision of the Code of Wartime Practices for the American Press is based on the experience of the Office of Censorship and of the Press during the weeks since the original Code was issued on January 15, 1942. But let it be repeated:
>
> It is essential that certain basic facts be understood. The first of these facts is that the outcome of the war is a matter of vital personal concern to the future of every American citizen. The second is that the security of our armed forces and even of our homes and our liberties will be weakened in greater or less degree by every disclosure of information which will help the enemy.
>
> If every member of every news staff and contributing writer will keep these two facts constantly in mind, and then will follow the dictates of common sense, he will be able to answer for himself many of the questions which might otherwise trouble him. In other words, a maximum of accomplishment will be attained if editors will ask themselves with respect to any given detail, "Is this information I would like to have if I were the enemy?" and then act accordingly.
>
> The result of such a process will hardly represent "business as usual" on the news desks of the country. On the contrary, it will mean some sacrifice of the journalistic enterprise of ordinary times. But it will not mean a news or editorial blackout. It is the hope and expectation of the Office of Censorship that the columns of American publications will remain the freest in the world, and will tell the story of our national successes and shortcomings accurately and in much detail.
>
> The highly gratifying response of the press so far proves that it understands the need for temporary sacrifice, and is prepared to make that sacrifice in the spirit of the President's assurance that such curtailment as may be necessary will be administered "in harmony with the best interests of our free institutions."
>
> Below is a summary covering specific problems. This summary repeats, with some modifications, requests previously made by various agencies of the Federal Government, and it may be regarded as superseding and consolidating all of these requests.

---

13 *Code of Wartime Practices for the American Press*, Edition of June 15, 1942 (U.S. Government Printing Office, Washington, DC, 1942), p. 1–2.

Obviously it is impossible to anticipate every conceivable contingency. The Office of Censorship will make special requests from time to time covering individual situations in order to round out this outline of newspaper and magazine practices which the Government feels are desirable for the effective prosecution of the war, and the security of American citizens.

Special attention is directed to the fact that all of the requests in the summary are modified by a proviso that the information listed may properly be published when authorized by appropriate authority. News on all of these subjects will become available from Government sources; but in war, timeliness is an important factor, and the Government unquestionably is in the best position to decide when disclosure is timely.

The specific information which newspapers, magazines, and all other media of publication are asked not to publish except when such information is made available officially by appropriate authority, falls into the following classes . . .

The first edition of the code also listed items for voluntary censorship, including information on: (1) general character and movements of troops, (2) ships, (3) planes, (4) fortification and coastal defense, (5) production, (6) weather, (7) photographs and maps, and (8) war damages (casualty lists, damage to military and naval objectives, etc.).[14] In the second edition, issued on June 15, 1942, the list grew to cover the following eleven items: (1) troops, (2) ship movements, cargoes, etc., (3) sunk or damaged ships, (4) attacks by air, (5) planes, (6) fortification defenses, (7) production, (8) weather, (9) rumors, (10) photographs and maps, and (11) war damages.[15] Furthermore, in the third edition, dated February 1, 1943, the list grew again to include as many as seventeen items.[16] The new additions to the list were (12) accredited military and naval correspondents (obligations of correspondents to submit to censorship), (13) sabotage, (14) combat zone interviews and letters, (15) military intelligence, (16) war prisoners, internees, and civilian prisoners, and (17) war news coming into the United States.

It seems beyond doubt that this increase of items subject to censorship accurately corresponded with the intensification of the war situation. February 1, 1943, was the day the Japanese garrison forces started withdrawing

---

14 *A Report on Office of Censorship*, p. 35–37.

15 *Code of Wartime Practices*, Edition of June 15, 1942, p. 2–6.

16 *Code of Wartime Practices*, Edition of February 1, 1943, p. 2–8.

from the island of Guadalcanal as well as the eve of the German surrender in Stalingrad. In the fifth edition of the code, issued on May 15, 1945, immediately after the fall of Nazi Germany, the number of items to be voluntarily censored decreased back to fourteen, reflecting the containment of the war to the battle with Japan in the Asia-Pacific arena.[17]

When war erupted between the United States and Japan, the United States was home to more than 2,000 daily newspapers, more than 11,000 weekly or semi-weekly newspapers, and some 900 commercial broadcasting stations. Additionally, 6,000 technical, professional, and scientific publications, 5,000 industrial, commercial, and financial publications, and 16,000 commercial house organs were also pumping out issues. Furthermore, there were thousands of church, school, fraternal, and educational publications. Thus, the Press Division and the Broadcasting Division of the Office of Censorship had the difficult task of familiarizing that multitude of media with the *Code of Wartime Practices* and encouraging them to conduct voluntary censorship.[18]

Price and his men handled this monumental task with characteristic finesse. The Press Division "established an Advisory Board composed of representatives of national and regional publishers and editors' associations. It also selected one editor in each state to act as a 'missionary' in spreading the gospel of voluntary censorship among his colleagues. These 'missionaries' came to Washington twice at their own expense to confer with Censorship officials." These "missionaries" subsequently returned to their home states, apparently, to continue the "spreading of the gospel" among their local colleagues.[19]

As for broadcasting, stations not only grappled with problems attendant to voluntarily withholding news that might aid the enemy, as the press did, but also had to discontinue playing songs on request and conducting man-in-the street interviews. Playing songs on request opened up the possibility that an enemy agent might send a secret signal to a colleague abroad through the simple ruse of having a station broadcast "Don't Sit Under the Apple Tree," dedicated to Cousin Sarah, at 7:45 p.m., January 23, for example. Similarly, in man-in-the street interviews, an enemy agent could get possession of a broadcaster's microphone in a seemingly innocuous interview and transmit a message with a hidden meaning.[20]

17 *Code of Wartime Practices for the American Press and Radio*, Edition of May 15, 1945, p. 2–4.

18 *A Report on the Office of Censorship*, p. 34.

19 Ibid., p. 34.

20 Ibid.

The report offers a wealth of other details. "The staffs of the Press and Broadcasting Divisions were on call 24 hours a day," it reads, "to answer inquiries and to provide counsel on borderline cases arising from Code requests." It was amazing that "never were there more than nine newspapermen and six radio men on the rolls in Washington."[21] There were no branch or regional offices, either, for divided authority would have split opinion on security in specific news stories. "A paper in Los Angeles, for example, might have been authorized to print facts that a regional office in St. Louis would have deleted." With that type of inconsistency, the efficiency and credibility of the censorship effort would inevitably suffer. As I will discuss later, this kind of confusion was frequent in the censorship by the U.S. occupation forces in Japan. Numerous pieces of evidence indicate that the inconsistencies were attributable to a failure to centralize and unify the authority of censorship.[22]

Price was proud when he boasted, "This small, cohesive organization cost the taxpayers approximately $100,000 a year." He called the operation "the best investment in security ever made in the United States Government."[23]

Along with consolidating the system for voluntary censorship of newspapers and broadcasts, Price had also poured time and energy into liaising and coordinating with his British and Canadian counterparts—that is, the British Imperial Censorship and Canadian Censorship offices. When Edwin S. Herbert (later Sir Edwin), director general of the British Imperial Censorship, arrived in Washington soon after the attack on Pearl Harbor, Herbert, Price, U.S. Department of State officials, and Canadian Censorship personnel held consultations that resulted in the signing of a tripartite agreement. In general, it was agreed that there should be a complete exchange of information among the three censorship authorities and, to whatever extent possible, that the work would be divided to avoid duplication. The British had been operating censorship arrangements for two years in many points around the globe, including Bermuda, Trinidad, and Jamaica. As a result of this agreement, it was decided that the U.S. Office of Censorship would function as a central clearinghouse of information.[24]

Out of this agreement emerged the Division of Records (later reorganized as the Liaison and Digest Office). While its main function was to ascertain various government agencies' needs for war information intercepted by the

21 Ibid.
22 Ibid.
23 Ibid.
24 Ibid., p. 7.

censorship offices of the three countries and distribute it accordingly, the organization adopted a policy of "What does not concern the war does not concern Censorship," a motto of British Imperial Censorship. Printed on the form used for distributing information to federal agencies was the following notice:

> The attached information was taken from private communications, and its extremely confidential character must be preserved. The information must be confined only to those officials whose knowledge of it is necessary to the prosecution of the war. In no case should it be widely distributed, or copies made, or the information used in legal proceedings or in any other public way without express consent of the Director of Censorship.[25]

Needless to say, the main source of this type of information was the censorship of letters, telegrams, and telephones. The army and navy personnel who had been censoring information even before the formal establishment of the Office of Censorship were formally transferred to the office on March 15, 1942. At that time, the Cable and Postal Divisions had been housed in Arlington, Virginia, across the Potomac River. But on May 13, 1942, they, too, moved to the Apex Building at Sixth and Pennsylvania to join the other divisions of the office.[26]

Not only did the U.S. Office of Censorship collaborate closely with British and Canadian censorship authorities, it also set up a censorship network with Latin American countries in accordance with the Pan-American agreements for the defense of the Western Hemisphere and sent liaison representatives to the corresponding organizations. Similarly, it also sent a representative to Services des Contrōles Techniques, the French censorship, which had first been located in Algiers but moved to Paris after the liberation of France.[27]

What this censorship network among the Allies across the European, American, and African continents constituted was—as I pointed out in Chapter 1—a communications blockade against Japan and Germany. The Casablanca Conference in January 1943 and the invasion of Normandy in June 1944 proved that the communications blockade could be very effective.

In the run-up to the Casablanca Conference, the Germans were aware that U.S. President Franklin D. Roosevelt and British Prime Minister Winston

---

25 Ibid.

26 Ibid., p. 8.

27 Ibid.

Churchill were planning to meet—but not of where the meeting would take place. They suspected London, on board a battleship, and Washington, but not once did they hit on Casablanca. Thanks to airtight information protection, the meeting between the two leaders was held in complete security.[28]

In the case of the Normandy mission, meanwhile, a tight media blackout had been in place for six months before the scheduled date of the invasion. During those six months, the U.S. Office of Censorship cooperated even more closely with its British and Canadian counterparts. One of the fruits of their cooperation was the secret conference that the U.S. Office of Censorship and British Imperial Censorship held in April 1944. With the censorship authorities in tight, interconnected formation, the *Code of Wartime Practices* was at its all-time strictest. When General Dwight D. Eisenhower's forces swarmed onto the Normandy beaches on June 6, it was clear that the enemy had indeed been completely in the dark about the time and place of the attack.[29]

The communications blockade did not function well, however, at the time of the Cairo Conference in November 1943, and Price blamed the British side for the shortcomings. At the time of the Teheran Conference, which united Roosevelt, Churchill, and Joseph Stalin immediately after the Cairo Conference, Reuters, the British news agency, carried a dispatch saying it was "known definitely" in Lisbon that the Cairo Conference was over and that Roosevelt and Churchill were on their way to meet Stalin in Iran. This report rendered the communications blockade ineffective from the beginning.[30]

The communications blockade proved most effective in maintaining confidentiality about the development of the atomic bomb. Details were completely withheld for more than two long years and finally disclosed to the entire world only after the atomic bomb was dropped on Hiroshima. To that end, the censorship authorities of the United States, Britain, and Canada worked closely together, exerting extreme caution.[31]

Of the various kinds of censorship that the U.S. Office of Censorship carried out, censorship of the mail required the largest number of personnel. In fact, *A Report on the Office of Censorship* revealed that the Postal Division required more than 10,000 employees at its peak.[32]

---

28 Ibid., p. 39.

29 Ibid., p. 15.

30 Ibid., p. 39.

31 Ibid., p. 41–42.

32 Ibid., p. 19.

Late in 1940, one year before the attack on Pearl Harbor, the authorities decided that Military Intelligence should pay special attention, and Major (later Brigadier General) W. Preston Corderman was detailed to investigate. Major Corderman brought in a reserve officer, Captain Gilbert C. Jacobus, as his assistant. In January 1941, Jacobus was dispatched to Bermuda to study British Censorship operations there.[33] In June of the same year, the Department of War promoted this small study unit (Corderman-Jacobus) to a Censorship Branch in its Military Intelligence Division. This move accompanied the approval of a general wartime-censorship program by President Roosevelt, who had foreseen U.S. participation in World War II. It was, naturally, Major Corderman who headed the Censorship Branch.[34]

Within two months of the establishment of the Censorship Branch, a censorship school opened on August 6, 1941. The first batch of trainees were nineteen reserve officers who were, upon graduation, assigned to the Corps Area Headquarters to begin recruiting and making detailed plans. Some of them were sent to British and Canadian censorship stations to acquire technical information and report on procedures. These officers had only had scant opportunities to make contact with local postmasters when the declaration of war came. Unlike the U.S. Navy, the U.S. Army assigned only officers to the Censorship Branch throughout the duration of the war.[35]

The army and navy personnel, who had been engaged in censorship even before the Office of Censorship came to be, were formally transferred to the Office of Censorship on March 15, 1942. Corderman, who now held the rank of colonel, became the first chief postal censor, and Captain Jacobus his deputy. The enormous task of recruiting postal censorship personnel fell principally to these two.[36]

A number of housewives, schoolteachers, and retired businessmen were recruited as civilian censorship personnel. Particularly noteworthy is that most of the civilian censors were women—the preferred demographic for the job. *A Report on the Office of Censorship* points out that women excelled in sustaining the intense concentration and attention to detail required to keep alert to breaches of security, even when the work was repetitive. Needless to say, applicants had to be investigated carefully to make certain of their loyalty to the United States.[37]

---

33 Ibid., p. 3.

34 Ibid., p. 3, 19.

35 Ibid.

36 Ibid., p. 3.

37 Ibid., p. 19–20.

Additionally, it was necessary to obtain translators in some 100 principal languages, given the unfeasibility of requiring all letters to be written in English. As for the training of the censors, the usual procedure was to give each recruit a week's basic training in the station, followed by two weeks of intensive work at special tables, before assigning them to posts on the examination floor. Censors who were to handle specialized material, such as business or financial mail, underwent additional training in courses in various specialties.[38]

As the war grew increasingly heated, the Postal Division of the Office of Censorship went through a major personnel overhaul. Toward the end of 1942, Colonel and Chief Postal Censor Corderman himself was recalled to the Department of War and replaced by Lieutenant Colonel Normal V. Carlson, and Major Jacobus was transferred to the post of European theater censor.[39]

Thus, during the last months of 1942, all but half a dozen of the 150 army officers in key positions at the Office of Censorship were slated for replacement. Officials launched a search for high-caliber executives from private business to become district postal censors and fill the newly vacated administrative positions at headquarters. This turn of events appeared to reflect Price's preferences well. A group of nearly 100 recruits received a month's training at the New York station, after which they filled positions throughout the organization.[40]

Out of the deluge of mail throughout the entire postal system, the percentage of letters opened by postal censors has been kept top secret; there is no indication that the number has ever been disclosed. However, as *A Report on the Office of Censorship* explains, not all letters were opened, and a system called a "watch list" was adopted.[41] Among the names on the list were those on the Proclaimed List of Certain Blocked Nationals—the government's official blacklist. All letters written by or addressed to watch-listed individuals were subject to unsealing and censorship. In Japan, too, the U.S. occupation forces would apply the same method.

The task of selecting letters subject to censorship in line with the watch list was called "flashing." Random samplings of letters were also unsealed to further expand and improve the watch list, as well. Of all the letters they read, postal censors generally found an extremely small percentage of material to delete. If the excisions would be too great, they often returned the

38 Ibid., p. 19–20.
39 Ibid., p. 8.
40 Ibid., p. 20.
41 Ibid., p. 11.

entire letter to the sender with a statement as to the reason for non-delivery—a measure taken only when the violation was attributable to the sender's carelessness. This practice was deemed helpful in educating the public and providing greater security in the long run. The U.S. occupation forces, however, did not adopt this practice in Japan for obvious reasons.[42]

More than a few spy incidents came to light through postal censorship. Although the Office of Censorship itself was not an investigative authority and intelligence activities lay outside its jurisdiction, its postal censorship provided helpful clues to investigators. The case of Velvalee Malvena Blucher Dickinson was a typical example.[43]

Mrs. Dickinson, born in California, graduated from Stanford University. She worked in a San Francisco brokerage house, specializing in Japanese accounts, and became a member of the Japanese American Society of San Francisco. She was welcomed in Japanese circles and was entertained aboard a Japanese warship in San Francisco Bay. When her husband died, she moved to New York and opened an exclusive doll shop on Madison Avenue, which proved popular and profitable.

Hints to the espionage plot involving Mrs. Dickinson emerged in her letters to an Axis spy residing in Buenos Aires, Argentina. Mrs. Dickinson posted five letters to a Señora Inez de Molinali, 2563 O'Higgins, Buenos Aires, using the names of various clients for her return addresses without their consent. While the letters were rife with flagrant misspellings, odd punctuation, and erratic statements, they were no more peculiar than hundreds of innocuous communications passing through the Office of Censorship daily and not the type that would arouse the suspicion of an examiner. Mrs. Dickinson committed two errors, however. The first was that the correct name of her "mail drop" was Molinari, not Molinali. The second error was that she used the wrong street address.

Bearing the wrong addressee and address, the letters naturally came back to the "senders" (return addresses) on the envelopes—the innocent clients of Mrs. Dickinson's doll shop—with a notice from the Argentinian post office. Puzzled by the forgery of their names on unfamiliar letters, two clients notified the Federal Bureau of Investigation of the suspicious activity. Mrs. Dickinson's name thus went promptly on the Office of Censorship watch list. Subsequent investigation revealed that, in those letters to Buenos Aires, Mrs. Dickinson was apparently attempting to convey information on the conditions and locations of Allied war vessels on the Pacific coast, which

42 Ibid., p. 21.

43 Ibid., p. 48–49.

she had visited frequently on business. The code in the correspondence with the Axis spies in Buenos Aires centered on replacing "doll" with "ship." She pleaded guilty to a charge of censorship evasion and received the maximum sentence of ten years in prison and a $10,000 fine.

As far as the censorship of motion pictures was concerned, Price utilized the Censorship Policy Board and Censorship Operating Board to set up the Censorship Boards of Review, a system to censor films leaving and entering the United States. There were three such boards: one in New York City to censor newsreels, one in Hollywood to censor motion pictures, and a third in Rochester, New York, to handle amateur stills and motion pictures.[44]

As I detailed in Chapter 2, it was between early June and late September of 1943 that Byron Price, director of the U.S. Office of Censorship, began to make suggestions on censorship plans for the occupied areas in the Asia-Pacific theater through letters to Secretary of War Henry Stimson. Soon after, Price reached out to the heads of twenty-eight government agencies that had been receiving intercepted material from the Office of Censorship. He wanted to consolidate the scope of censorship by identifying categories of information that would no longer be necessary upon the termination of hostilities with Germany, as the office would be turning its full attention to the continuing war against Japan.[45] Having received replies from those leaders, Price came up with a preliminary plan for post Victory-in-Europe Day (V-E Day), and he convened a Censorship Policy Board meeting on November 20, 1943. The meeting happened to occur on the eve of the U.S. mobile forces' amphibious attack on the atolls of Makin and Tarawa, which were located on the outer edge of Japan's Absolute Defense Line.

Based on discussions at the Censorship Policy Board, Price set out to consolidate a future plan by formulating and revising his preliminary plan. Price convened a major joint conference of district censors and division heads in Washington in the summer of 1944, producing the X-Plan—a detailed plan of operational realignment.[46] The X-Plan was to go into effect on X-Day—the day on which an armistice with Germany was signed or the occupation of Germany became substantially complete, whichever occurred first.

Price's letter to Major General Clayton Lawrence Bissell, assistant chief of staff for intelligence on the War Department General Staff (see Chap-

44 Ibid., p. 12.
45 Ibid., p. 15.
46 Ibid., p. 15–16.

ter 2), appears to have been written immediately after this joint conference in Washington. It seems only natural, then, to conjecture that the X-Plan adopted by the joint conference was behind the correspondence beginning with Price's letter to Bissel on August 9, 1944, and ending with the Joint Chief of Staff's reply to Price drafted on September 25.

In other words, Price thought that the end of hostilities with Germany should dictate the timing for shifting the focus of censorship activities from within the United States to the occupied areas. Essentially, the changeover would both relocate the censorship authority of the U.S. government from the Office of Censorship to the occupation forces in the occupied areas and move the location of censorship from the United States to German territory and occupied Japan. When Price announced that the Office of Censorship would turn its full attention to the continuing war against Japan after X-Day, therefore, he was envisioning the earliest transfer of the Office of Censorship's system (and accompanying expertise) to the U.S. military authorities in the occupied areas and the reduction and eventual liquidation of the Office of Censorship.

The significance of the role that Byron Price had played until the Joint Chiefs of Staff issued directive JCS873/3 on November 12, 1944, to General Douglas MacArthur, who had just launched the invasion of Leyte, is all the more obvious when one takes into account the chain of developments above. As I will discuss in more detail later, from that point on, the responsibility for censorship in occupied Japan was entrusted to General MacArthur, who was given the obligation as well as the authority to conduct censorship in Japan based on JCS873/3, which contained the system and know-how that the Office of Censorship had utilized. The directive was, essentially, a ball that Price threw to MacArthur.

When X-Day did arrive on May 8, 1945, Price promptly carried out the X-Plan according to plan and shrank the personnel of the Office of Censorship from 9,500 to 6,000 over the three months leading up to the end of the war against Japan. Prior to that, the Chicago Postal Station and some other postal stations had been closed down, and, on June 9, the Censorship Boards of Review, which had censored motion pictures, was disbanded.[47]

Along with these moves, Price also produced a V-J Book and distributed it to field stations and the divisions in Washington in July. Entitled *General Instructions for the Closing of Field Stations,* the booklet covered the four areas of things to be done at once, things to be undertaken on V-J Day and completed no later than three days thereafter, a description of personnel

47 Ibid., p. 17.

requirements and duties for liquidation, and a revised edition of the Instructions for Closing.[48]

The White House announced the Japanese acceptance of the Allied surrender terms at 7:00 p.m. on August 14, 1945 (EST), but the proclamation of V-J Day was postponed until Japan actually signed the terms. Price, nevertheless, decided that the war against Japan was essentially won and recommended to President Truman that the Office of Censorship immediately cease its censoring activities.[49]

At noon on August 15, 1945, President Truman signed the directive to give thirty days' notice to all employees of the Office of Censorship, except for a small group needed for liquidating the agency. Consequently, about 95 percent of the staff had left the Office of Censorship by mid-September. On September 28, President Truman signed Executive Order 9631, which formally abolished the Office of Censorship as of November 15, 1945.[50]

The presidential directive terminated *censorship within the United States* both in name and reality. It by no means meant, however, that *censorship by the U.S. government* was over. U.S. occupation forces had already been censoring civil communications not only in Germany but also in Japan, where the occupation had just started. The second revised version of the *AFPAC Basic Plan for Civil Censorship in Japan* issued to the concerned sections of the U.S. occupation forces in Japan on September 30, 1945, two days after the issuance of Executive Order 9631, reveals the presence of civil censorship in Japan most clearly.[51] This revised edition was a culmination of the quest for a basic plan on civil censorship in Japan, an effort that had roots in JCS 8773/3 and underwent repeated amendments as the war situation evolved. Before studying the *AFPAC Basic Plan for Civil Censorship in Japan,* however, one should look into JCS 8773/3 itself. After all, the entire scope of censorship by the U.S. occupation forces in Japan was directly based on this Joint Chiefs of Staff directive.

48 Ibid.

49 Ibid., p. 17–18.

50 Ibid., p 18. *Federal Register*, Vol. X, Tuesday, October 2, 1945, p. 12304.

51 *AFPAC Basic Plan for Civil Censorship in Japan*, Revised on September 30, 1945. The National Records Center, Suitland, MD, RG 331, Box 8568.

CHAPTER 5

The Language Factor

Directive JCS 873/3 consisted of four documents.[1]

The first was a memorandum co-signed by Colonels A.J. McFarland and E. D. Graves Jr. of the secretariat of the Joint Chiefs of Staff. The memorandum reported on the Joint Security Control's review of the conference joining representatives of the U.S. Office of Censorship and the departments of state, war, and navy, referencing a summary by the director of the Office of Censorship. According to the memorandum, the conference summary included two recommendations from Byron Price, director of the U.S. Office of Censorship. One suggested that the censorship organization to be set up in the Asia-Pacific area by the U.S. forces be consolidated into the existing censorship institution as an integral component. The second recommendation was that this new censorship organization in the Asia-Pacific area also participate in the system of information exchange on anti-enemy intelligence activities, which had actually been conducted by the censorship authorities of the United States, Britain, and Canada.[2]

The memorandum also disclosed the fact that, upon review of the conference summary, the Joint Security Control had submitted a report to the Joint Chiefs of Staff for its consideration. This report was simultaneously sent to the departments of state, war, and navy, as well as the Office of Censorship.

The report from the Joint Security Control was the second document in directive JCS 873/3.[3] Opening with a statement that its purpose was to request the Joint Chiefs of Staff's instructions on policies for adoption regarding civil censorship in Asiatic-Pacific areas under U.S. occupation and control, the report presented six basic facts related to the issues at hand.

First, the Joint Chiefs of Staff had already announced in JCS 873/1 that civil censorship in the occupied areas fell under the jurisdiction of the local supreme military commander.

1 National Archives, RG 218, Copy 59, Records of the United States Joint Chiefs of Staff, Declassified, 9-27-58.

2 Ibid., p. 28.

3 Ibid., p. 29–31.

Second, records showed that the Combined Chiefs of Staff had confirmed the above via CCS 271.

Third, the annex of the appendix to the report explained in detail that civil censorship was different in nature from military censorship, with the former being much more complicated than the latter.

Fourth, no directive had been issued before November 12, 1944, (the date on the memorandum) on a plan for or the implementation of civil censorship in the Asia-Pacific area.

Fifth, the appendix to JCS 819/4 specified the areas in the Asia-Pacific region that the Joint Chiefs of Staff had agreed to entrust to civilian jurisdiction. This designation had been revised at the 181st conference of the Joint Chiefs of Staff.

Byron Price's recommendations constituted the sixth basic fact. The document also emphasized that the integration and coordination of civil and military censorships along the lines of Price's recommendation had already begun in European countries.

Next, the report raised two issues for discussion. The first was that, in light of how interrelated censorship on civil communications and the civilian government generally were, it would be desirable for the Joint Chiefs of Staff to clarify areas of U.S. jurisdiction with regard to civilian government. Here, the report reiterated that a decision on the matter had already been made.

The second was that the U.S. Office of Censorship wished to exclude Guam and the Philippines from its jurisdiction, although censorship of civil communications normally fell within the office's domain. Pointing out that the office's censorship activities would take place only in wartime and that the office would be liquidated promptly upon the termination of the war, the report implied that the responsibility for censorship of civil communications in occupied areas fell entirely on the military.

Having touched on the above points and issues, the report presented the following conclusion:

> (Paraphrase) We believe the Joint Chiefs of Staff should adopt a policy and issue it to the concerned theater commanders in the form of a directive to clarify the jurisdiction concerning planning as well as implementation of censorship on civil communications within and toward the Asia-Pacific region.

At the end, the report requested the Joint Chiefs of Staff's sanction of the draft directive in the appendix of the report.

Titled “Civil Censorship in the Area of U.S. Responsibility in the Pacific-Asia,” this directive constituted the third part of JCS 873/3.[4] The seventh of the nine sections in the document presents the seven areas for which the United States was responsible:

a. Japan’s mainland, the southern half of Sakhalin island, Taiwan, and other Pacific islands that are the Japanese territories or mandated territories. But the interests of other Allied countries and their areas of responsibility would be taken into consideration before the areas of U.S. responsibility were finalized.
b. Korea. But the interests of other Allied countries and their areas of responsibility would be taken into consideration before U.S. responsibility was finalized. As an exception to the stipulations of the first article, planning for civil censorship in Korea would fall under the jurisdiction of the Commander in Chief, Pacific Ocean Areas (CINCPOA). It should be noted, however, that who would be responsible for implementation of civil censorship in the said area would be finalized at a later date.
c. Wake Island
d. The Philippine archipelago. Although censorship on civil communications in this area was within the jurisdiction of the U.S. Office of Censorship, the said Office announced that it was delegating the authority to the theater commander, and the theater commander has already accepted the responsibility. The theater commander may request assistance, when necessary, from the Republic of the Philippines government and other authorities stipulated by law.
e. Although censorship on civil communications in Guam normally falls under jurisdiction of the U.S. Office of Censorship, an agreement to delegate its authority to CINCPOA has already been reached.
f. Dutch East Indies (excepting Sumatra). The theater commander may request, when necessary, the local Dutch authority under its own command for assistance in conducting censorship on civil communications.
g. Portuguese Timor. The theater commander may request, when necessary, the local Dutch authority under its own command for assistance in conducting censorship on civil communications.

The first section of the directive stated that, as far as those seven areas were concerned, the theater commander was entrusted with the responsibility to plan and implement censorship of all civil communications in the liberated

4 Ibid., p. 23–35.

or occupied areas within the theater. It also noted the following, which Major General Charles Willoughby's memorandum[5] (quoted in Chapter 1) referred to.

> (Paraphrase) In addition, a theater commander is charged with the responsibility to collect, develop, and disseminate all kinds of information that is considered to be advantageous for the United States and other Allied Powers in the war effort and the quest for peace. For this purpose, civil communications must be censored after termination of the conduct of hostilities throughout the occupation period of the enemy territory.

The second section of the directive concerned the liberated areas. While censorship of civil communications in the liberated areas would initially be an initiative on the part of the U.S. military authority, the directive explained, the military commander could delegate responsibility for conducting the actual censorship—to the local government or other local authorities that the U.S. government had recognized, for example—in light of changes in circumstances. Nevertheless, as long as the area was under the theater commander's jurisdiction, the commander retained overall responsibility for supervising the censorship activities. In this case, the commander could recruit local personnel as deemed necessary and desirable.

Third came a section on censorship of civil communications in occupied enemy territories, which stipulated that censorship would officially be conducted by the theater commander through the organization under his direct control, but normally entrusted to the intelligence division under his command. When the occupied area regained a semblance of law and order, and if the situation allowed, the theater commander could attempt to disperse censorship functions and delegate implementation to a control board or military government institution. One notable stipulation was that as long as the area was under jurisdiction of the theater commander, he would never be relieved of his duty to oversee and control the overall process.

The fourth section, after pointing to the necessity to mutually coordinate censorship planning and implementation among theaters, touched on the following point:

> (Paraphrase) The Departments of War and Navy are prepared to provide

5 See note 11 in Chapter 1.

assistance to theater commanders in the formulation of censorship plans, the implementation of censorship manpower recruitment, and the procurement of facilities and equipment necessary to conduct censorship.

The fifth section was based on Price's recommendations. It stressed the need for coordination with the censorship authorities of other Allied countries in planning and implementing the censorship program. In exchanging information, the section read, the various theaters were to use the existing anti-enemy intelligence system and rely on the U.S. Office of Censorship for exchanges with other Allied countries.

Another statement from Charles Willoughby's memorandum appeared in section six, as follows.

> (Paraphrase) The censorship of civil communications instituted under the above stipulations may be mitigated at the discretion of the theater commander in terms of range and severity. Nevertheless, the censorship of civil communications can never be terminated in any district without prior permission from the Joint Chiefs of Staff.[6]

This important statement made it clear that the theater commander (MacArthur) had the discretion to mitigate censorship by the U.S. occupation forces in Japan but no authority to end it—and that had been the basis for the plan long before it went into operation. The body capable of terminating censorship in occupied areas was the Joint Chiefs of Staff, an organization under the direct command of the U.S. president.

Section seven has already been introduced, and section eight clarified that any area not specified in section seven lay outside the scope of U.S. responsibility. Should U.S. forces ever see activity in these areas, commanders were to consult with the Joint Chiefs of Staff concerning the extent of their involvement in the censorship of local civil communications.

Section nine explained the annex to the directive in the appendix.[7] A close study of the document, the fourth of the documents that constituted JCS 873/3, revealed that it was almost a carbon copy of the twelve-point memorandum accompanying the May 19, 1944, letter from A.E. O'Leary, senior adjutant, Adjutant General's Office, to General MacArthur. The title of the annex was "Censorship on Civil Communications in Areas under

6 National Archives, RG 218, Copy 59, Records of the United States Joint Chiefs of Staff, Declassified, 9-27-58, p. 34.

7 Ibid., p. 36–42.

Military Occupation or Control," exactly the same as that of the attachment to O'Leary's letter.

An important point to note, however, was that the annex included an additional subject to be censored: "publicity media," which did not appear in the 1944 document, is a revision with enormous implications.[8] I am convinced that the change was a result of sharp questioning by Price, director of the Office of Censorship, on the (paraphrase) "desirable nature of press and broadcast censorship in occupied areas" in his September 11, 1944, letter to Fleet Admiral William D. Leahy (chief of staff of the Commander in Chief of the Army and Navy and chairman, Joint Chiefs of Staff), which I introduced in chapter 2.

In my judgment, the two words "publicity" and "media" drastically changed the linguistic space of Japan after the defeat in the war. As new elements of section 7 (f) of the annex, these two words provided the legal basis for the second revision of the *AFPAC Basic Plan for Civil Censorship in Japan*, issued on September 30, 1945,[9] which forms the core of a closer analysis later in this book. It would be difficult to overstate the importance of fact that the Joint Chiefs of Staff—not MacArthur's headquarters—added "publicity media" as a subject for censorship to the meticulous U.S. occupation policies in Japan.

However, it was only in early August 1944 that the U.S. Army Forces Far East (USAFFE) under the command of General MacArthur, who had been in Hollandia in northern New Guinea planning the invasion of the Philippines at the time, made the first move toward civil-censorship planning.[10] Needless to say, the measure grew out of the messages in sections three and four of the May 19, 1944, letter from A.E. O'Leary to General MacArthur. In accordance with these messages, Brigadier General Elliott Thorpe, chief of counterintelligence under General MacArthur, requested the Department of War to dispatch officers to censor civil communications, upon which the war department dispatched Lieutenant Colonel (later Colonel) D.D. Hoover to Hollandia.[11] While the details of Lieutenant Colonel Hoover's background are unknown, the wording of the instructions suggest that Hoover had been seconded to the U.S. Office of Censorship earlier and gained experience there.

---

8 Ibid., p. 38, 7-f.

9 See note 51 in Chapter 4.

10 General Headquarters, Far East Command, Military Intelligence Section, General Staff, *Operations of Military and Civil Censorship, USAFFE/SWPA/AFPAC/FEC Intelligence Series*, Vol. X, p. 36.

11 Ibid., p. 36, note 1.

As soon as Hoover assumed his new post in Hollandia, he set to the task of producing the "USAFFE Basic Plan for Civil Censorship in the Philippines" in collaboration with Colonel Kendall, theater censor there, and saw the plan through to completion on November 1, 1944.[12]

By that time, General MacArthur had already launched the operation to recapture the Philippines. At noon on October 20, the more than 100,000 troops of the U.S. Sixth Army, under the command of Lieutenant General Walter Krueger, launched an amphibious attack on Leyte, assisted by naval bombardments from the U.S. fleet under the command of Admiral Jesse Barrett Oldendorf.[13] Lieutenant Colonel Hoover was transferred from Hollandia to Tacloban on Leyte Island and appointed the detachment commander for civil censorship on November 9, 1944.[14] Given the yet-unorganized nature of the detachment, however, Hoover had to borrow personnel and equipment from other units. Military censorship was initiated in Tacloban three days later, on November 12—exactly the same day that JCS 873/3 was issued in Washington.

The first thing that Hoover did in Tacloban was to open a censorship school to train civil censors. The basic plan predicted that, ultimately, 1,200 Filipino censors would be needed. The effort would involve twenty American censors, thirty-one U.S. Army officers and soldiers, and twenty-one U.S. Navy officers and sailors, the plan said, to oversee and manage the Filipino censors.[15]

On December 31, 1944, came the official decision to organize a Civil Censorship Detachment (CCD) under the command of Hoover. The CCD started activities on January 1, 1945.[16] Along with this development, the existing Censorship Detachment, USAFFE, was renamed the Military Censorship Detachment to prevent confusion.[17]

At the same time, a censorship division was added to General Staff Section 2 (G-2) in order to coordinate smooth communication between the civil and military censorship organizations, as well as to assist with operations, under the directorship of Colonel Kendall.[18] In other words, the CCD embodied the nature of a G-2 implementation unit under the command of

---

12 Ibid., p. 40, 41, note 6.

13 Katogawa Kōtarō, ed., *Dai 2-ji Sekai Taisen tsūshi* [Overview History of World War II], Tokyo: Hara Shobō, 1981, p. 348.

14 *Operations of Military and Civil Censorship*, p. 42, footnote 9.

15 Ibid., p. 40.

16 Ibid., p. 16, 42.

17 Ibid., p. 16.

18 Ibid., p. 16, note 31.

Major General Willoughby from its very inception—and the nature of the CCD did not change, even during the occupation of Japan.

On January 9, the four divisions of the U.S. Sixth Army under the command of Major General Krueger faced off against the enemy's two corps and pressed ahead with an amphibious attack at the Lingayen Gulf on Luzon. Prior to this, General Yamashita Tomoyuki of the Fourteenth Area Army of the Imperial Japanese Army had already moved his headquarters from Manila to Baguio on January 3.[19]

Despite General Yamashita's efforts to save Manila from war, the strike force of the U.S. Army's First Cavalry Division advanced into Manila on February 3, marking the beginning of about a month of intense street fighting. The battle ran up casualties of about 1,000 on the U.S. side and more than 10,000 on the Japanese side, while estimates put the number of Filipino deaths at roughly 100,000.[20]

On March 5, 1945, the battle of Manila ended completely. With that, the CDD closed down its headquarters in Tacloban on March 7 and moved into Manila the next day.[21]

On April 6, 1945, General MacArthur, then in Manila, received a confidential wireless message from the U.S. Department of War on a drastic change in organization of the U.S. forces in the Pacific and Asia. USAFFE was abolished as of that very date, and, in its place, the General Headquarters, United States Army Forces, Pacific (AFPAC) was established. The supreme commander of the new organization was, of course, MacArthur, who had just been promoted to general of the army by the U.S. Congress in December 1944[22] in a preparatory measure for the imminent Japan campaign. Although the General Headquarters, Southwest Pacific Area (SWPA) was still the nominal command center of the Allied forces, it was publicly acknowledged that the mission of the U.S. Army and Navy was to invade the Japanese mainland.[23]

In fact, an amphibious attack had already taken place on March 26 on Okinawa's Kerama Islands. On April 1, a great fleet of some 1,300 naval vessels advanced close to the main island of Okinawa. After heavy naval bombardments, U.S. troops on 150 large vessels and 60 smaller vessels

19 Hattori (1979), p. 771.

20 Katogawa (1981), p. 351.

21 Hattori (1979), p. 1063, *Operations of Military and Civil Censorship, USAFFÈ/SWPA/AFPAC/FEC* Documentary Appendices (II), p. 45.

22 Ibid., p. 3, note 8.

23 Ibid., p. 4.

started landing on the Kadena coast that same day. At the heart of the mission on the U.S. side was the Tenth Army, operating under the command of Lieutenant General Simon Buckner Jr.[24]

On the Japanese side, in the afternoon of April 6, when General Mac Arthur received the radio message from Washington, the battleship *Yamato*—a symbol of the glory of the Imperial Japanese Navy—sailed out of Tokuyama Bay, accompanied by a flotilla of one light cruiser and eight destroyers, and headed south toward the waters off Okinawa in preparation for a "Surface Special Attack."[25]

Going back to the reorganization of the U.S. forces, the new alignment also affected the internal composition of G-2, part of General Headquarters/United States Army Pacific (GH/USARPAC). Taking the place of the censorship division within G-2 was a Counter Intelligence Section, which operated under the supervision of the General Headquarters' chief of counterintelligence along with the military and civil censorship detachments.[26]

Having faced formidable resistance from the Japanese forces on Okinawa, the U.S. forces launched an all-out assault on all battle fronts on April 19. While the Japanese 62nd Army fought desperately against invading U.S. forces on April 20, General MacArthur offered a striking opinion to the Department of War via a wire from Manila. "There would be an anticipated deficiency of some 36,000 hospital beds," his message read, "even counting everything then available in the Pacific, should [both Operations] Olympic and Coronet be adopted."[27]

The overall plan for the final conquest of Japan, which had been in the planning at the Joint Chiefs of Staff, was called Operation Downfall.[28] Operation Olympic[29] was its first phase, which would involve an amphibious assault by the Sixth Army under the command of Major General Krueger against southern Kyushu to secure the necessary beachhead. During this operation, the Sixth Army's I Corps would land in Miyazaki, the XI Corps in Shibushi Bay, and the V Corps in the vicinity of Kushikino on the western coast of the Satsuma Peninsula.

The second phase, Operation Coronet,[30] was a plan to land a massive

24 Hattori (1979), p. 803.

25 Katogawa (1981), p. 366.

26 *Operations of Military and Civil Censorship*, p. 4.

27 *Reports of General MacArthur*, Vol. 1, Supplement, p. 1, note 6.

28 Ibid., p. 1, note 5.

29 Ibid., Katogawa (1981), p. 371.

30 *Reports of General MacArthur*, Vol. 1, Supplement, p. 1, note 6, Katogawa (1981), p. 371.

force directly on the Kanto Plain on March 1, 1946, and attack Tokyo in one fell swoop. More concretely, the Eighth Army under Lieutenant General Eichelberger would make a landing from Sagami Bay and rush toward Kumagaya and Koga, spearheaded by its armored cavalry, to isolate Tokyo from behind. The First Army, led by Major General Courtney Hodges, would land on Kujūkuri beach and divide into two segments, with one division advancing toward Tokyo and the other advancing southward on Bōsō Peninsula to command the mouth of Tokyo Bay; eventually, the second segment would advance toward Yokohama with a division of the Eighth Army.

Needless to say, the forces to be mobilized for these two operations would have been the largest amphibious assault force ever assembled. The U.S. Joint Chiefs of Staff recognized that, while Operation Olympic was possible with the forces already in the Pacific theater, Operation Coronet would require a redeployment of U.S. troops and equipage from the European theater.[31]

On April 20, 1945, the same day that MacArthur wired his opinion on the two operations to the Department of War, Brigadier General Elliott Thorpe, chief of counterintelligence, approved a "Basic Plan for Civil Censorship in Japan."[32] The basic plan was the original version of what would undergo three revisions, but it should be obvious from the strategic developments above that the plan's conception had roots in the premise of an imminent invasion of the Japanese mainland. Reading through the twenty-page basic plan, it quickly becomes clear that the document gave detailed consideration to all the foreseeable problems in implementing civil censorship.

Before touching on these considerations one by one in subsequent chapters, I need to underscore one very characteristic issue that permeated the basic plan: the dearth of personnel proficient in the Japanese language. The GH/USARPAC had suffered from this problem during its preparation for invading the Japanese mainland. Although personnel for the Pacific theater with competence in Japanese came mainly from the Allied Translators and Interpreters Section (ATIS), demand had constantly exceeded supply. And it was none other than the Military Intelligence Service Language School (MISLS) in Fort Snelling, Minnesota, that had been the supplier of personnel with Japanese-language capabilities.[33] The school began its operations on November 1, 1941, before the eruption of war between Japan and the

31 Katogawa (1981), p. 370.

32 *Operations of Military and Civil Censorship*, Documentary Appendices (II), p. 41.

33 *Operations of Military and Civil Censorship*, p. 47.

United States, as the Fourth Army Intelligence School.[34] Both Lieutenant Colonel (later Brigadier General) John Weckerling and Captain (later Colonel) Kai Rasmussen, who had been working at the Fourth Army Intelligence School, had spent some time in Japan earlier. When war erupted against Japan, they predicted that Japanese-language speakers would be indispensable for the U.S. military. Nonetheless, there were few Caucasian personnel proficient in the Japanese language in those days—and training them in a short period of time represented a daunting challenge.[35]

Consequently, an initiative to recruit second-generation Japanese-Americans as Japanese-fluent personnel began. This was, obviously, a risk-taking venture that went against the general atmosphere in contemporary American society, where people were suspicious of Japanese-Americans and their allegiance to the United States. When a language examination was actually administered to some 3,700 Japanese-Americans, however, the results astonished Lieutenant Colonel Weckerling and Captain Rasmussen. Only 3 percent of all examinees were found to be sufficiently proficient in the Japanese language, while 4 percent were above the required standard, another 3 percent were deemed employable only after lengthy training, and the remaining 90 percent were found utterly unusable.[36]

The results go to show that, contrary to popular belief in the United States, second-generation Japanese-Americans had assimilated more thoroughly to American society than many expected. As Marcus Hansen said, "What the son wishes to forget, the grandson wishes to remember"; among second-generation Japanese-Americans and, generally, all migrants alike, the second generation resents their fathers' and mothers' attachments to their former home countries and makes extra efforts to become "American" in the abstract sense of the word.[37] Nevertheless, American society in the 1940s harbored a die-hard prejudice that Hansen's "third-generation principle" would not apply to second-generation Japanese-Americans. Ironically, the result of the language proficiency examination ended up shattering this prejudice.

Realizing, belatedly, that even second-generation Japanese-Americans had to receive language training to be useful, Weckerling and Rasmussen requested the Department of War to open a school for Japanese-language instruction. Their request found little support among the top echelon of the

34 *MISLS Album* (U.S. Military Intelligence Language School, Fort Snelling, MN, 1946), p. 9.

35 Ibid., p. 8.

36 Ibid., p. 8.

37 Will Herberg, *Protestant, Catholic, Jew: An Essay in American Religious Sociology*, Garden City, NY: Doubleday, 1955, p. 186.

military. Permission to open the school finally came on November 1, 1941, but the institution was not a war department school—rather, it was an institution attached to the Fourth Army, headquartered in San Francisco. The budget for the endeavor was only $2,000.[38]

When war with Japan broke out, then, the Fourth Army Intelligence School had just opened in a refurbished old hangar near the Fourth Army headquarters at the Presidio of San Francisco. Officers had to mimeograph teaching materials and run around to look for low-budget typesetting shops to print textbooks.[39] The inaugural class had sixty students, of which fifty-eight were second-generation Japanese-Americans and two were Caucasian Americans with some experience in the Japanese language. Seeing as fifteen of them soon dropped out due to their inadequate performance, only forty-five students completed the course to become the school's first graduates.[40]

All eight instructors were second-generation Japanese-Americans. The school's assistant principal, John F. Aiso, had been a private (E-2) in the U.S. Army but entered reserve duty as soon as he started working at the school and became a private citizen. Similar measures were taken with other second-generation Japanese-Americans in the military. One should note, however, that some rejoined the military register and eventually attained promotions to commissioned ranks; examples included John Aiso, who became a major, and Arthur Kaneko, who became an Army first lieutenant.[41]

The old hangar was divided into two, with one half a classroom and the other half a barracks. The eight instructors all lived under the same roof with the students. Because the classroom was devoid of chairs, orange crates served as makeshift chairs. Neither did the classroom have desks or other necessities—all of which had to be improvised. Everything else, from typewriters to paper and other office supplies, had to be borrowed from other offices.[42]

This misfortune was partly due to the obscure status of the Fourth Army Intelligence School, an unlicensed school, technically; as such, it did not receive appropriations from the federal budget as a U.S. Army special training program.[43] The special training program designation was instituted to contract out special training in the Japanese language to various universities in the United States. The Japanese-language school at the Presidio, however, did not receive that designation.

---

38 *MISLS Album*, p. 28.

39 Ibid., p. 31.

40 Ibid., p. 9.

41 Ibid., p. 9.

42 Ibid., p. 31.

43 Ibid., p. 28.

The *MISLS Album,* a summary history of the Military Intelligence Service Language School, provides no explanation of the exclusion. I conjecture that it had to do with the school's function: in substance, it served a concurrent role as a war-relocation camp for second-generation Japanese-Americans.

On January 29, 1942, U.S. Attorney General Francis Biddle issued an instruction that a security belt zone should be set up along the Pacific coast of the United States and that all descendants of enemy nations should be moved out of that zone.[44] On February 13 of the same year, members of the U.S. Congress from the Pacific Coast states jointly sent a letter to President Roosevelt to request immediate removal of all people of Japanese descent, whether they were American citizens or not, from the three states of California, Oregon, and Washington.[45]

On February 19, President Roosevelt signed Executive Order 9066, which stipulated the forced eviction of people of Japanese descent.[46] On March 2, Lieutenant General John L. DeWitt, commanding general of the Western Defense Command, ordered the expulsion of all people of Japanese descent from the western half of the three Pacific states and southern Arizona.[47] This order affected as many as 110,000 of the approximately 126,000 people of Japanese descent then residing in the United States.[48]

The first group of people of Japanese descent from the Los Angeles area was transported to the War Relocation Center in Manzanar, California, on March 22, 1942. Altogether ten relocation camps were opened in barren lands in California, Arizona, Idaho, Wyoming, Colorado, Utah, and Arkansas, one after another. The relocation of people of Japanese ancestry was complete by November 3 of the same year.[49]

Therefore, unless one was serving in the military or enrolled in the Fourth Army Intelligence School either as a teacher or a student, second-generation Japanese Americans were sooner or later transported to one of the ten relocation camps. Whether they served in the military or resided at relocations camps, people of Japanese ancestry had to be segregated from American society.

MISLS Album contains a few photos depicting the daily life of the Japa-

---

44 Harry H. L. Kitano, *Japanese Americans,* Prentice-Hall, 1976, p. 71.

45 Ibid., p. 71.

46 Ibid., p. 71–72.

47 Ibid.

48 Ibid.

49 Ibid.

nese language students at the Presidio. One of them has a caption saying, "Places to go were few in town" and the explanation that, because all their friends had been evacuated from the West Coast, the YMCA was one of the few places to meet. In the photo were six uniformed students and one person in plain clothes. One of the seven might have been a Caucasian soldier. Four stood with their backs to the photographer, and the profiles of two others were barely visible, the photo being taken from behind at a diagonal. The only face clearly visible belonged to the plainclothes person. Bathed in the winter sun, the seven cast long shadows, which contributed to the gloomy and lonely feel of the photo.[50]

Of the forty-five first graduates from the school, thirty-five were immediately sent to the Pacific theater and assigned to the Guadalcanal or Alaska areas. Despite being Army personnel, the thirty-five were given no official military rank. It was about one year later that they received "special promotions" to private (E-1) after division and army commanders recognized their contributions to the victory in the battle of Guadalcanal.[51] While the *MISLS Album* attributed this phenomenon to the absence of a system for recognizing language personnel with the rank of specialist in those days,[52] I find the explanation hard to accept. In my judgment, the personnel must have encountered discrimination even within the military. They must have been confined, so to speak, in an invisible relocation camp.

The Fourth Army Intelligence School closed on June 1, 1942. In its place, the Military Intelligence Service Language School (MISLS) opened at Camp Savage in Minnesota,[53] operating directly under the Department of War. This development was attributable, for one thing, to an increase in the number of students, which the old hangar at the Presidio could no longer accommodate, and to the war department's belated recognition of the importance of personnel proficient in the Japanese language.

Camp Savage had originally been a nursing home for low-income elders run by the state of Minnesota; the war department had purchased it and converted it into a language school. While there were only nine classes accommodating 200 students at the time of the school's opening, it expanded to offer twenty-three classes in the summer of 1943, forty-one classes in the autumn of the same year, and forty-six classes toward the end of the year.[54]

50 *MISLS Album*. p. 32.
51 Ibid., p. 9.
52 Ibid., p. 9.
53 Ibid., p. 9.
54 Ibid., p. 10, 36.

The third group of students who entered the school in the summer of 1943 included thirty-five Caucasian cadets. Many of those thirty-five had trained in an ad hoc Japanese-language school at the University of Michigan, and some had spent some time in Japan. Upon finishing their language training at Camp Savage, they were immediately promoted to the rank of second lieutenant. The third group also included ten naval officers who had trained at the U.S. Navy's Japanese-language school at the University of Colorado, as well as nine commissioned officers and seven noncommissioned officers in the Canadian Army.[55]

MISLS received the fourth cohort of students in January 1944, by which time the school had expanded to offer fifty-two classes and employ twenty-seven civilian teachers and sixty-five noncommissioned officer instructors. The total enrollment reached 1,100, of which 107 students were Caucasian cadets, including those slated to undergo special training to become Office of Strategic Services (OSS, present-day Central Intelligence Agency) personnel.[56]

By the autumn of 1944, the school at Camp Savage had trained a total of 1,600 noncommissioned officers, 42 cadets, and 53 commissioned officers.[57] Needless to say, Camp Savage had already transformed itself drastically from its earlier setup, akin to a war relocation camp, to a full-scale military facility complete with not only classrooms but also a dormitory, mess hall, theater, lecture hall, gym, and officers' dining hall.[58]

The nearby U.S. Army base at Fort Snelling attended to the procurement for and management of the school. Eventually, the decision was made to transfer the school itself to Fort Snelling. By the time of commencement for the ninth group of students in November 1944, the transfer of the U.S. Army Intelligence Language School to Fort Snelling was complete.[59]

As the end of war in Europe became imminent and, in contrast, the war against Japan heated up, the administration slashed the training periods at Fort Snelling. What used to be taught in six to nine months was now taught in six to eight weeks. Lessons were given day and night and even on Saturdays, which were normally reserved for examinations. Teachers took turns teaching, even at night, and offered separate tutorials.[60]

On the actual battle front, the Japanese-language specialists of the Mil-

55 Ibid., p. 10.
56 Ibid., p. 10–11.
57 Ibid., p. 11.
58 Ibid.
59 Ibid., p. 11–12.
60 Ibid., p. 12.

itary Intelligence Service—graduates of the language schools—performed such feats as recovering the operational plans of the Imperial Japanese Navy in the naval battle off the Philippines from the crashed plane of Marshal Admiral Koga Mineichi, commander in chief of the Imperial Japanese Navy's Combined Fleet, and deciphering the entire battle strategy.[61] The Imperial Japanese Navy's devastating defeat in the Battle of the Leyte Gulf a half year later was brought about by none other than the MISLS graduates.

On the accomplishments of the MISLS graduates, Major General Charles Willoughby said:

> We used them even on Bataan. They collected information on the battlefield, they shared death in battle, and when one of them was captured his fate was a terrible one. In all, they handled between two and three million documents. The information received through their special skills proved invaluable to our battle forces.[62]

Joe Rosenthal, Pulitzer-winning press cameraman, reminisced:

> They work so close to the enemy on these missions that with danger of being killed by Japs, they run the risk of being shot, unintentionally, by our own marines. . . Many have paid with their lives. They have done an outstanding job, and their heroism should be recognized. It has been recognized by the marine commanders where I saw them in action at Guam, Peleliu and Iwo.[63]

It was only natural that the GH/USARPAC, which had been planning the invasion of Japan's mainland, wanted to recruit MISLS graduates working for ATIS as censors when the organization began planning the first "Basic Plan on Civil Censorship in Japan." Article 6 of Section 1-c on manpower read:

> (Paraphrase) The shortage of manpower proficient in the Japanese language can only be solved by transferring at least fifty commissioned officers capable of reading, writing, and speaking in Japanese and about the same number of noncommissioned officers with similar capabilities from the ATIS detachment on top of (or in lieu of) the personnel trained by the Department of War. It is believed that the

61 Ibid., p. 15.

62 Ibid., p. 115.

63 Ibid.

> language proficiency required of censorship personnel must be considerably higher than in other cases.[64]

In actuality, however, GH/USARPAC had to consider relying on Japanese citizens in the occupied area if it wished to conduct civil censorship as planned. For instance, Article 3 of Section 1-c on manpower of the basic plan contained the following statement.

> (Paraphrase) It will be necessary to recruit a considerable number of Japanese civilians as translators and assign them to positions that allow them to handle important documents.[65]

And Article 7 of c: Second Stage of Section 2: Stages of Censorship Implementation stipulated:

> (Paraphrase) The majority of the U.S. military and civilian personnel are to be assigned to supervision and management positions. It is imperative to organize a team of Japanese citizens with the ability to read and speak in English and have them translate all correspondence into English so documents can be forwarded to censorship before their dispatch. Another team of Japanese translators stationed at receiving stations should translate the above English translations back into Japanese before the documents are delivered to the destinations. The delay in delivery incurred by this process is not worth any consideration at all. Those among the translators who attempt to bypass censorship shall be sentenced to imprisonment.[66]

Clearly, the U.S. Pacific Army authorities had already established the basic policy of using Japanese manpower in civil censorship in Japan from an early stage of the planning effort.

---

64 *Operations of Military and Civil Censorship*, Documentary Appendices (II) 41, p. 5.

65 Ibid., p. 4.

66 Ibid., p. 7.

CHAPTER 6

The Basic Plan

The Basic Plan for Civil Censorship in Japan, first issued on April 20, 1945,[1] consisted of eight sections: (1) overview, (2) stages of censorship implementation, (3) watch list and special communications investigation, (4) transmission of intelligence acquired through censorship, (5) postal mail censorship, (6) telephone and telegram censorship, (7) censorship of documents carried by tourists, and (8) conclusion.

Overview A stipulated the function and authority of civil censorship in Japan and explicitly grounded the censorship procedures in the basic policies of directive JCS 873/3.

Concrete policy decisions regarding the implementation of censorship fell under the jurisdiction of the Supreme Commander of the United States Army Pacific (General MacArthur), while the Civil Censorship Detachment (CCD) was to serve as the implementation force. One should note, though, that the CCD was put under the supervision of General Staff Section 2 (G-2) of the General Headquarters/United States Army Pacific (GH/USARPAC), and it was stipulated that the CCD, when conducting censorship, would follow the instructions of the General Headquarters/Southwest Pacific Area (GHQ/SWPA), GH/USARPAC, U.S. Department of War, U.S. Joint Chiefs of Staff, and General Headquarters, Joint Chiefs of Staff of the Allied Forces.[2]

The complexity of this chain of command was only in appearance—at its heart, the system was not especially complex. The nominal complexity was attributable to the two hats that General MacArthur wore: Supreme Commander of GHQ/SWPA and Supreme Commander of GH/USARPAC.

Given that the invasion of the Japanese mainland was the exclusive responsibility of the U.S. forces, as I explained earlier, GHQ/SWPA and the Joint Chiefs of Staff of the Allied Forces of the above five supervising institutions were simply nominal additions. The actual chain of command was a fixed, linear connection from the U.S. Joint Chiefs of Staff (Department of War) on the top to GH/USARPAC, General Staff Section 2 (G-2), and the Civil Censorship Detachment at the bottom. What this means is that the cen-

1 *Operations of Military and Civil Censorship, USAFFE/SWPA/AFPAC/FEC* Documentary Appendices (II) Vol. X, Intelligence Series, Appendix 41.

2 Ibid., p. 1.

sorship in occupied Japan was the work of the U.S. government via the U.S. forces from beginning to end—it was by no means censorship by the Allies.

When Japan signed the Potsdam Declaration, one of MacArthur's two hats—that of Supreme Commander of GHQ/SWPA—assumed a new name: Supreme Commander for the Allied Powers. MacArthur now wore that hat alongside the hat of the Supreme Commander, GH/USARPAC, making the role's function and authority somewhat obscure.[3]

As far as censorship went, however, MacArthur's authority did not exceed even an inch of the authority in the hands of a U.S. military theater commander. Overview A-3 explicates the facts of the matter:

> 3. This preliminary plan has been prepared as the basis of discussion by the Civil Censorship Officer, with the War Department and the U.S. Office of Censorship, and may be expanded or revised to include prior planning in the War Department or in other theatres. However, the basic stringency of the plan will not be altered without reference to the Theater Commander. The directive of the Joint Chiefs of Staff to which reference is made in Par. 1 above, states:
> . . . The War and Navy Departments are prepared to assist Theater Commanders in planning, in the procurement of technical censorship equipment as they may desire.[4]

Overview A-4, meanwhile, clarifies the background of the decision in A-3 as follows.

> 4. As of 30 June 44, the War Department view on planning responsibility for Japan was set out as follows in a letter to the Commanding General, USAFICPA from the AC of S, G-2, WDGS.
> "In consultation with the Joint Chiefs of Staff and the Navy Department it has been decided that the War Department will take the initiative in this matter. It is contemplated that a small planning group will be organized without delay to make a study of this problem and make recommendations for the organization of civil censorship in Japan and for the procurement and training of the required personnel. It is further contemplated that when the required organization has been developed

3 Etō Jun, ed., *Senryō shiroku: Dai 1-kan: Kōfuku bunsho chōin keii* (Occupation History Record: Vol. 1: Background of Japan's Signing of the Surrender Document), Tokyo: Kōdansha, 1981, p. 27.

4 *Operations of Military and Civil Censorship*, Documentary Appendices (II), Appendix 41, p. 1.

> to the necessary degree it will be turned over to the theatre commander to be employed by him for discharging his responsibilities in connection with civil censorship."[5]

The Basic Plan was delivered immediately after the exchange of letters between Byron Price, who, on May 22, 1944, requested facilitation of civil-censorship planning in the Asia-Pacific area, and Colonel A. J. MacFarland, secretary to the Joint Chiefs of Staff, who replied on June 14.[6] The long shadow of Byron Price looms large here. He not only paved the way for the issuance of JCS 873/3 but must have also prompted the not-so-insignificant involvement of the U.S. Department of War, Department of the Navy, and Office of Censorship in civil censorship in Japan.

The areas under the jurisdiction of GH/USARPAC enumerated in Overview A-5 included Japan's mainland, southern Sakhalin, all the Pacific Islands that were Japanese territories or under Japan's mandate, Taiwan, and Korea. The list did not include Wake Island, Guam, Portuguese Timor, the Dutch East Indies, and several others.[7]

Worth noting here is the inclusion of southern Sakhalin. The Yalta Agreement, signed by heads of the American, British, and Soviet governments two months and ten days earlier on February 11, 1945, had stipulated that "the southern part of Sakhalin as well as all the islands adjacent to it shall be returned to the Soviet Union" in its Article 2 (a). This discrepancy—an inconsistency in possession—gives the impression that GH/USARPAC, which included southern Sakhalin in the areas subject to the "Basic Plan on Civil Censorship in Japan," may not yet have been aware of the existence of the Yalta Agreement as of April 20, 1945.

Nevertheless, item 4 of D: Third Phase of the Phases of Censorship Operation of the Basic Plan states:

> 4. Treatment of civilian communications between the American sphere of Japan and any Russian sphere will depend upon future directives from superior command organizations and in liberated countries will be determined by agreements at the international policy level.[8]

This is a rather delicate statement that appears to reflect the preamble of the

---

5 Ibid., p. 1.

6 See notes 14 and 15 in Chapter 2.

7 *Operations of Military and Civil Censorship*, Documentary Appendices (II), Appendix 41, p. 2.

8 Ibid., p. 8.

Yalta Agreement, which said, "The leaders of the three Great Powers—the Soviet Union, the United States of America and Great Britain—have agreed that in two or three months after Germany has surrendered and the war in Europe has terminated the Soviet Union shall enter into the war against Japan on the side of the Allies on condition that . . ."

In any event, it is curious that this first Basic Plan included southern Sakhalin as part of the area subject to civil censorship, but also presupposed the presence of "areas occupied by U.S. forces and areas occupied by Russian forces" within Japan. At a glance, the logic appears to be contradictory. Overview A-6 makes the following important censorship policy statement:

> 6. In preparing a Japanese Plan, the planning of G-2 Division, SHAEF, for Germany has been studied and some of its concepts are contained herein, inasmuch as the objective in both Axis centers will be the same. The plan proposed for Japan, however, is <u>considerably more strict than that proposed for Germany</u>.[9] (emphasis added)

The term "strict," as used here, echoed the term "stringent" used in Overview A-3. But the statement that the censorship program in Japan would be markedly stricter than that in Germany was full of weighty implications. The statement, it would appear, candidly reflected the fundamental difference between the U.S. occupation policy toward Japan and its approach to handling Germany. Incidentally, the term "stringency" made another appearance in the conclusion of the Basic Plan:

> Specific details in the foregoing over-all civil censorship plan are subject to change to meet the requirements of the situation in Japan. . . . It is not anticipated that such deviations as are necessary will be of a major nature, however, and the plan herewith presented shall serve as the basis of all operations in Japan without alteration of its stringency.[10]

I hasten to add here that, as Overview A-2 indicated, censorship of newspaper transmissions and broadcast manuscripts was not within the jurisdiction of the CCD at the time of the first Basic Plan. In the Asia-Pacific theater, censorship of newspapers and broadcasts had traditionally been under the jurisdiction of GH/USARPAC officers in charge of public relations; it appears that the same

9 Ibid., p. 2.
10 Ibid., p. 20.

practice remained in place under the Basic Plan.[11]

Section B: Mission of the Overview stressed at the outset the important role civil censorship would play in collecting information necessary to enforcing the conditions of surrender in Japan and restoring legal and economic order.[12] The Mission also underscored the idea that censorship authority in the Pacific area inevitably had to be self-reliant after the German surrender—even the U.S. Office of Censorship was to be liquidated after the defeat of Japan. On that basis, the document enumerated the following four missions for civil censorship in Japan:[13]

a. To help theater commanders maintain military security by conducting censorship and supervision of civil communications (postal mails; wireless messages; radio, telegram, and telephone; documents carried by tourists; and all others);
b. To obtain from post-occupation communications useful secret information on military operations and liberation as well as military and civilian governments in areas under occupation or supervision. From pre-occupation communications that the advance team of the censorship detachment should confiscate, secret information on military operations and related matters should be obtained;
c. To block transmission of any information that could provide aid and comfort to the enemy; and
d. To prevent communication channels from being used by underground resistance and other subversive organizations.

In order to accomplish the mission, the Basic Plan called for special attention to two points: adhering to the principle of censoring all civil communications, without exception, and presenting information acquired through censorship to organizations authorized by the theater commander.

Item 5 of B: Mission of the Overview stipulated that the process of conducting censorship should abide by the following objectives and, for that purpose, keep the military and civil government institutions of the concerned Allied members constantly informed.[14]

---

11 Ibid., p. 1.
12 Ibid., p. 2.
13 Ibid., p. 3.
14 Ibid.

a. Destruction of Japanese or other enemy organizations.
b. Disarmament of Japan and prevention of re-armament.
c. Detection of underground military, quasi-military and political bodies.
d. Prevention of disorder.
e. Detection and recovery of loot.
f. Enforcement of military and economic terms of the surrender instrument.
g. Control and stabilization of currency, including prevention of transactions in prohibited currencies.
h. Prevention of communications between Japanese and parties of whatever nationality abroad who are known to Allied intelligence agencies to have been sympathetic to the Axis cause or to have given aid or comfort to Axis nationals.

I have already touched on the issue in C: Manpower of the Overview—the dearth of personnel proficient in the Japanese language.[15] While the Basic Plan stated that the total number of censor personnel would be determined in consultation with the U.S. Department of War, it nevertheless estimated that, on top of the current 31 army officers, 126 army noncommissioned officers, 21 naval officers, 20 naval noncommissioned officers, and 20 civilian members of the U.S. Office of Censorship, the following reinforcements would, at the minimum, be necessary.[16]

Army personnel: 45 commissioned officers and 260 noncommissioned officers
Navy personnel: 109 commissioned officers and 192 noncommissioned officers

Section D of the Overview discussed supplies and stipulated that GH/USARPAC should issue a request to the Department of War or the Office of Censorship for the necessary equipment for censorship and, considering that all the supplies would need to be transported from the United States, prompted GH/USARPAC to take the requisite action immediately.[17]

15 See Chapter 5.
16 *Operations of Military and Civil Censorship*, Documentary Appendices (II), Appendix 41, p. 4
17 Ibid., p. 5.

Section A: Evolution of Organization of (2) Phases of Censorship Operation of the Basic Plan laid out the following basic policy.

Establishment of stringent censorship control in Japan will proceed according to phases, in a pattern proved workable and satisfactory in the Philippines and in other theaters. It will be maintained as long as deemed necessary by the Theater Commander to the accomplishment of his mission.[18]

Subsequent stages labeled "B: First Phase," "C: Second Phase," and "D: Third Phase" nearly mirrored the three stages in the May 19, 1944, letter from A.E. O'Leary (Adjutant General, Adjutant General's Office, Department of War) to General MacArthur. As I noted in Chapter 2, the three stages in the letter were (a) the battle stage, (b) the occupation stage, and (c) the stage after the establishment of a government by the citizens in the occupied areas.[19] Particularly noteworthy about the Basic Plan is that item 6 of C: The Second Stage proposed issuing the following ordinance in the name of the theater commander.[20]

Figure 2.

CENSORSHIP RESTRICTIONS
Any communication containing mention of the following will be destroyed.
Troop movements Criticism of Allies Codes Politics Rumors Any subject disturbing public tranquility
Violation of the above will be punished by Military Tribunal.

This was the first form of the thirty censorship policies that were to be adopted after Japan was officially occupied.[21] Although the presence of censorship in occupied Japan was kept secret and thus no such ordinance was ever issued, as I will explain later, the intention of the occupation forces' censorship authority apparent in the ordinance remained as is after the cancellation of the Olympic and Coronet Operations upon Japan's acceptance of the Potsdam Declaration—nothing changed.

Section (3) of the Basic Plan, Watch List and S/W Check of Communications, revealed for the first time that the watch list system, which had been

18 Ibid.

19 See notes 17 and 18 in Chapter 2.

20 *Operations of Military and Civil Censorship*, Documentary Appendices (II), Appendix 41, p. 7.

21 Etō Jun, *Ochiba no hakiyose* [Sweeping up Fallen Leaves], Bungeishunjū, 1981, p. 284–286.

Figure 3.

DISTRICT NUMBER & AREA		LOCATION	RECORDING PREFIX
I	Eastern HONSHU	TOKYO	JP/TOK
II	Western HONSHU	OSAKA	JP/OSA
III	KYUSHU	NAGASAKI	JP/NKI
IV	SHIKOKU	TAKAMATSU	JP/TKY
V	HOKKAIDO	HAKODATE	JP/HKD
VI	TYOSEN (Korea)	KEIJO	JP/KEJ
VII	TAIWAN (Formosa)	TAIHOKU	JP/TKU
VIII	RYUKYU ISLANDS	NAHA	JP/NAH
IX	KARAFUTO (Sakhalin)	TOYOHARA	JP/TOY
X	TISIMA (Kuriles)	TOMARI	JP/TOM

In the above prefixes, the first two letters indicate the Civil Censorship Group of origin ("JP" for Japan and the three-letter group indicates the station ("TOK" for Tokyo).

adopted on the United States mainland since World War I and effectively utilized by the U.S. Office of Censorship during World War II, was also to be a component of the civil-censorship program in occupied Japan.

The Basic Plan stipulated that the master watch list—the basis for the watch list system—had to include a comprehensive list of individuals to watch, compiled through submissions by the counterintelligence division of G-2, local military and civilian organizations in Japan, the U.S. Office of Censorship, and other sources. The Plan called for stringent censorship of the master watch list entries, including both incoming and outgoing communications.

Aside from this master watch list, the Basic Plan also called for a local watch list for each of the occupied areas and a review of the names of the people on each list every thirty days. Names of blacklisted individuals in local watch lists could be transferred to the master watch list only when approved by deputies of civil censorship officers.[22]

Broadly speaking, the message of item IV. Dissemination of Intelligence Obtained through Censorship under the Basic Plan did not far exceed the range stipulated in the Overview's B: Mission section. It did, however, make reference to a "comment sheet" that the CCD would produce and distribute among concerned parties. As soon as the occupation of Japan began, this comment sheet began to run rampant in various circles.[23]

22 *Operations of Military and Civil Censorship*, Documentary Appendices (II), Appendix 41, p. 8.

23 Ibid., p. 9.

This section also included Figure 3, which was about censor zoning.[24]

Section V. Postal Censorship gave a detailed account of the information on domestic postal operations in Japan (as of March 1941) that the U.S. Department of War possessed in accordance with the above zoning. The following statements merit special attention.

> The manual of standard operating procedures now in use in the Philippines will be followed in Japan, except that more emphasis will be placed on re-examination in the third phase of operations, where for the first time an extensive aggressive censorship organization will be required.[25] (Section 3 of A. Organization, emphasis added)

And:

> 1. As previously stated in this plan, civil censorship in Japan will be severely restrictive. It is designed to draw a ring around the Japanese-controlled area which will reduce the possibility of communications getting out of that area during the first and second phases and will facilitate the gathering of intelligence during the third phase.[26] (Section 1 of C. Theory of Operation, emphasis added)

And:

> 2. If an effective censorship net is to be drawn around Japan, the question of liaison with other foreign censorships, particularly Russian and Chinese, arises. The proposed rigid censorship should alleviate the many previous difficulties encountered with Chinese censorship. During the whole of the war, it is understood there has been leakage of information between Japanese-occupied and unoccupied China. Related also is the question of civil censorship in such parts of the Chinese theater as North China and Manchukuo, which have long been dominated by the Japanese.[27] (Section 2 of C. Theory of Operation, emphasis added)

The echoes of Byron Price's proposition for a universal communications blockade, as already introduced in Chapter 2, ring clear in these excerpts.[28]

The Basic Plan proposed that, first, Japan should be enclosed by an effec-

24 Ibid.
25 Ibid., p. 10–11.
26 Ibid., p. 12.
27 Ibid., p. 12.
28 See note 8 in Chapter 2.

tive net of censorship that would isolate its linguistic space completely from the outside world. Henceforth, this closed linguistic space would be transformed at the will of the occupation authority through a broad censorship offensive.

The U.S. government had already given similar treatment, albeit on a much smaller scale, to the ethnic Japanese in the United States, as evidenced by the isolation of Japanese-American residents in the Pacific Coast states in war-relocation centers.[29] The Basic Plan, however, was proposing to conduct a similar information shutout and transformation of the linguistic space on an incomparably larger scale vis-à-vis the Japanese as a nation.

This unprecedented enterprise, which had seemed an impossible task in June 1943 even to Price himself, was starting to seem feasible by April 1945. More than just approaching feasibility, it was set for implementation in half a year, at the latest, by GH/USARPAC.

I have nothing particular to add regarding sections (6) Telephone and Telegram Censorship and (7) Censorship of Documents Carried by Tourists of the Basic Plan, except to say that the document placed telephone and telegram censorship under the jurisdiction of the U.S. Navy.[30] The gist of (8) Conclusion of the Basic Plan, which repeatedly stressed the strictness of the censorship at hand has been addressed earlier in this chapter.

The first draft of the "Basic Plan on Civil Censorship in Japan" was approved by Lieutenant General Richard K. Sutherland, chief of staff in the South West Pacific Area on April 30, 1945.[31] On that very day, a 200-plane-strong air-raid squadron of B-29s and P-51s flew over the Kanto Plain and carried out random bombings.[32] In Berlin, meanwhile, the Soviet army seized the German parliament building and hoisted its flag in victory. It was reported that Hitler had committed suicide at the Reich Chancellery that same day.[33]

Lieutenant Colonel Donald Hoover, officer in charge of civil censorship for GH/USARPAC, flew from Manila to Washington, carrying with him the Basic Plan that had just been approved by the chief of staff in the South

---

29 See notes 49 and 50 in Chapter 5.

30 *Operations of Military and Civil Censorship*, Documentary Appendices (II), Appendix 41, p. 18.

31 *Basic Plan for Civil Censorship in Japan*, dated July 10, 1945, The National Records Center; Suitland, Maryland, RG 331, Box No. 8568, File No. 211, p. 1.

32 Hattori (1979), p. 1065.

33 Tōyō Keizai Shimpōsha, ed., *Sakuin seiji keizai dai-nenpyō: Jōkan nenpyō hen* [Indexed Chronological Table of Politics and Economy, Vol. I, Chronological Table], Tōyō Keizai Shimpōsha, 1971, p. 1424.

West Pacific Area in early May.[34] The first thing Lieutenant Colonel Hoover did in Washington was to have a lengthy consultation with the special overseas program section of the Department of War. The discussion with the overseas section, which had been in charge of planning civil censorship in the occupied areas, fleshed out the Basic Plan substantially. Subsequently, Hoover also had consultations with the U.S. Office of Censorship as well as the Departments of War and Navy, during which he voiced various requests, particularly concerning securing manpower for the CCD.[35]

By this time, Germany had already surrendered unconditionally. With its entire territory overrun by the Allied forces, its führer dead, other government leaders having either committed suicide or fled the country, and no new central government to take over from Nazi rule, the Third Reich crumbled in total anarchy.

On May 7, 1945, General of the Infantry Alfred Josef Ferdinand Jodl, representing Admiral Karl Dönitz (commander in chief of the German Navy and Hitler's successor as head of state with the title of "President of Germany and Supreme Commander of the Armed Forces), met General Dwight Eisenhower, supreme commander of the Allied Expeditionary Force, in Reims and signed the instruments of unconditional surrender. On May 8, the official signing of the instrument took place in Karlshorst, Berlin. The Allies had completely conquered the German state, which vanished from the earth.[36]

Upon the signing, the Japanese government abrogated all agreements with Germany, including the Anti-Comintern Pact and the German-Italy-Japan Tripartite Pact.[37]

It was around that time that a secret initiative to explore possibilities for a new military operation was about to begin stirring at GH/USARPAC in Manila: Operation Blacklist, which would involve military deployments in case of the sudden collapse or surrender of the Japanese government before the implementation of the Olympic and Coronet Operations. Operation Blacklist formed on the basis of secret intelligence suggesting that the Japanese government had begun considering the possibility of securing peace

34 *Operations of Military and Civil Censorship*, Volume X, p. 52, note 34.

35 Ibid., p. 52, note 34.

36 Tōyō Keizai Shimpōsha, ed., *Sakuin seiji keizai dai-nenpyō: Jōkan nenpyō hen* [Indexed Chronological Table of Politics and Economy, Vol. I, Chronological Table], Tōyō Keizai Shimpōsha. 1971, p. 1425.

37 Hattori (1979), p. 886.

through the Japanese embassy in Moscow.[38] Operation Blacklist called for the progressive occupation of fourteen major areas in Japan and from three to six areas in Korea, an arrangement enabling the Allied forces to exert undisputed military, economic, and political control. The initial primary missions of Operation Blacklist were the disarmament of the Japanese armed forces and the establishment of communications control.[39]

The operations would deploy twenty-two divisions and two regimental combat teams in addition to air and naval elements, utilizing all the U.S. forces available in the Pacific Theater at the time. According to the plans, the main forces behind the initiative would be 251,800 troops from the Sixth Army under the command of General Walter Krueger and 308,700 troops from the Eighth Army under Major General Robert Eichelberger.[40] On July 20, the first draft of Operation Blacklist was submitted for deliberation to the U.S. Army and Navy joint conference in Guam. The final editions of the Blacklist plan were dated August 8, 1945.[41]

The first revised edition of the "Basic Plan on Civil Censorship in Japan," dated July 10[42]—a revision based on Hoover's consultations with the Departments of War and Navy and the U.S. Office of Censorship in Washington—only marginally reflected the Operation Blacklist scheme. The relative insignificance of Operation Blacklist's influence on the plan was most readily obvious in the fact that the authority for censorship of newspaper communications and radio broadcasting manuscripts fell not under the jurisdiction of the CCD but rather to officers in charge of public relations at General Headquarters.[43]

While the Basic Plan of April 20 had been divided into eight sections across twenty pages, the first revised edition of July 10 was divided into nine sections across twenty-three pages. The most noteworthy changes are as follows.[44]

First, the purposes in section B: Missions of the Overview expanded from eight items to thirteen items. Newly added were:

38 *Report of General MacArthur*, Vol. I, Supplement, p. 2.

39 Ibid., p. 2, 10.

40 Ibid., p. 6.

41 Ibid., p. 12, note 30.

42 *Basic Plan for Civil Censorship in Japan*, dated July 10, 1945, The National Records Center; Suitland, Maryland, RG 331, Box No. 8568, File No. 211.

43 Ibid., p. 1.

44 Ibid., p. 2–3.

a. To defeat the enemy which continues to resist the Allied forces;
e. To arrest and convict war criminals;
j. To obtain complete knowledge on Japan's intelligence activities and counterintelligence organizations;
k. To block communications between Japanese nationals abroad; and
l. To assess Japan's overseas propaganda activities and the activities of overseas associations of Japanese nationals.

In addition, "confirmation of the location of overseas Japanese assets" was added to purpose (g) "To control and stabilize currency" in the original plan.[45]

Second, section C: Manpower of the Overview took on a new level of detail. Manpower reinforcements were significantly increased, and timetables for the predicted arrival of reinforcements at the front line by seasons were also included. The revised reinforcements were:[46]

Army manpower: 203 commissioned officers and 420 noncommissioned officers and soldiers
Navy manpower: 288 commissioned officers and 305 noncommissioned officers and marines

Section C of the Overview, referring to the excellent technical skills of the U.S. Navy in the field of telephone and telegram censorship, stipulated that censorship in this field was to be to the exclusive domain of naval personnel.[47]

I also find it interesting that, aside from the Military Intelligence Service Language School (MISLS) at Fort Snelling, the document also lists the University of Michigan, the University of Colorado, Stanford University, and the University of Chicago as Japanese-language training institutions for censors.[48]

The third major change was in section A: Organizational Development of (2) Stages of Censorship Implementation. While the item had had only two sections in the original plan, the revision brought it to eight sections, an expansion that must have been a reflection of the Operation Blacklist scheme.[49]

45 Ibid., p. 2.
46 Ibid., p. 4.
47 Ibid.
48 Ibid., p. 5.
49 Ibid., p. 7–8.

While the first revised version of the Basic Plan was supplemented with a condition for the implementation of censorship—when a phased conquest of Japan is deemed necessary—the revised version still upheld the three-step approach comprising the First Phase (battle stage), Second Phase (transition to stability), and Third Phase (stability stage). The draft proclamation to be issued at the Second Stage was revised as follows.[50]

(Paraphrase) Figure IV

CENSORSHIP RESTRICTIONS
Letters should be written in *kaisho-tai* [square-block style]. *Gyosho-tai* [semi-cursive style] or *sosho-tai* [cursive style] are not allowed to be used in letters. Any communication containing mention of the following will be banned: Troop movements Criticism of Allies Codes Politics Rumors Any subject disturbing public tranquility Violation of the above will be punished by Military Tribunal.

The fourth change in the revised Basic Plan was a specific reference to "civil censorship organizations in Japan" in chapter 3, which had been titled "Watch List Special Communications Investigation" in the original plan. According to the new chapter 3, the national headquarters would be in Tokyo, operate under the supervision of U.S. military officers in charge of civil censorship, and have the following sections aside from an administrative division:[51]

a. Postal mails division
b. Telephone and telegram division
c. Documents carried by tourists division
d. Special activities division
e. Information records division

These divisions, the revision said, would operate on the principle of "small but highly skilled work forces." It was also stipulated that army or naval officers who had received training at the U.S. Office of Censorship would

50 Ibid., p. 9.

51 Ibid., p. 10.

receive appointments as division directors.

Of these five divisions, the special activities division would engage in the detection of secret ink and the deciphering of codes. The Department of War's special overseas planning section and the U.S. Army Signal Intelligence Service at Arlington Hall, Virginia, had collaborated in the organization and development of the special activities division.[52]

The information records division would help collect secret information obtained through censorship and disseminate the results to the relevant organizations. Preparation and maintenance of the master watch list would also fall under this division's jurisdiction.[53]

A glance at the organizational chart of the Civil Censorship Detachment should make it obvious that it was faithful to the organizational chart of the U.S. Office of Censorship (see Fig. 1 in Chapter 4). Byron Price's philosophy shone through not only in the configuration of the organization but also in the adoption of the principles of "small but highly skilled work forces" and meritocracy.

The fifth change was the revision of censorship zoning by location of regional headquarters. The ten zones in the original plan were reduced to nine, and Korea, Taiwan, the Ryukyu Islands, Sakhalin, and the Kuril Islands were excluded from the target of censorship. The influence of the Yalta Agreement is perceptible in the new zoning:[54]

Figure V

DISTRICT NUMBER	LOCATION	RECORDING PREFIX
I	Sapporo	JP/SAP
II	Sendai	JP/SEN
III	Niigata	JP/NII
IV	Tokyo	JP/TOK
V	Nagoya	JP/NAA
VI	Osaka	JP/OSA
VII-VIII	Hiroshima	JP/HIR
	Okayama (substation)	JP/OKA
IX-X	Fukuoka	JP/FUK
	Nagasaki (substation)	JP/NAG

The sixth change in the revised Basic Plan of July 10 was the addition of the following statement, appearing as the third paragraph of the Conclusion:

52 Ibid., p. 10, 22.

53 Ibid., p. 10, 20–22.

54 Ibid., p. 21.

> (Paraphrase) As mentioned, there still remains a possibility that civil censorship may continue even after the termination of military control. One of the objectives for the director of counterintelligence, thus, is to build up a permanent censorship organization that can be directly transferred to the kind of Japanese institution responsible for control that the Joint Chiefs of Staff envisions.[55]

On July 27, 1945, the first revised edition of the Basic Plan of July 10 received official approval from Major General Richard J. Marshall, deputy chief of staff, GH/USARPAC.[56] The seal of approval came one day after the proclamation of the U.S.-Britain-China joint declaration on Japan—the Potsdam Declaration—which defined eight conditions for Japanese surrender on July 26. The tenth article of the Potsdam Declaration read as follows.

> We do not intend that the Japanese shall be enslaved as a race or destroyed as a nation, but stern justice shall be meted out to all war criminals, including those who have visited cruelties upon our prisoners. The Japanese Government shall remove all obstacles to the revival and strengthening of democratic tendencies among the Japanese people. Freedom of speech, of religion, and of thought, as well as respect for the fundamental human rights shall be established.[57] (emphasis added)

At 8:15 on the morning of August 6, 1945, a B-29 bomber, the U.S. Strategic Air Force's *Enola Gay*, dropped the world's first battle-use atomic bomb on Hiroshima.[58] At 5:00 p.m. on August 8 (local time), Japanese ambassador to the Soviet Union Satō Naotake visited the Soviet foreign ministry at the invitation of Foreign Minister Vyacheslav Molotov. Giving Ambassador Satō, who had requested Soviet mediation in peace negotiations with the United States and Britain, no chance to speak, Foreign Minister Molotov himself read aloud a declaration of war against Japan and handed it to Ambassador Satō. Before dawn on August 9, Soviet troops began invading Manchuria en masse.[59] At 12:01 p.m. on the same day (local time), the B-29

55 Ibid., p. 23.

56 *Operations of Military and Civil Censorship*, Vol. X, p. 53–54.

57 Ministry of Foreign Affairs, ed., *Shūsen shiroku 4* [Historical Record of the End of the Pacific War, Vol. 4]. Tokyo: Hokuyōsha, 1977, p. 10–11. (https://www.ndl.go.jp/constitution/e/etc/c06.html last visited on November 22, 2017).

58 *Sakuin seiji keizai dai-nenpyō: Jōkan nenpyō hen*, p. 1437.

59 Ministry of Foreign Affairs, ed., *Shūsen shiroku 4*, p. 75–76.

The Great Artiste, another plane in the U.S. Strategic Air Force, dropped an atomic bomb on Nagasaki.[60]

In order to cope with these developments, the first Imperial Council (a conference in the presence of the Japanese emperor) convened at 11:50 p.m. on August 9 in a chamber inside the Imperial Palace's bomb shelter. The gathering yielded Japan's first response to the Potsdam Declaration, which included the statements below, which were conveyed to the Allied countries via Minister-Counselors Kase Shun'ichi (Switzerland) and Okamoto Suemasa (Sweden) on August 10.

> The Japanese Government are ready to accept the terms enumerated in the Joint Declaration which was issued at Potsdam on July 26th, 1945, by the heads of the Governments of the United States, Great Britain and China, and later subscribed by the Soviet Government, with the understanding that the said Declaration does not comprise any demand which prejudices the prerogatives of His Majesty as a sovereign ruler.[61]

Upon receipt of the above, U.S. Secretary of State James Byrnes delivered a response on August 11 via the acting Swiss ambassador to the United States. The response included the following wording.

> From the moment of surrender the authority of the Emperor and the Japanese Government to rule the state shall be subject to the Supreme Commander of the Allied Powers who will take such steps as he deems proper to effectuate the surrender terms.[62]

At 6:40 p.m. on August 12, Byrnes's reply was forwarded to the Ministry of Foreign Affairs in Tokyo by Minister-Counselor Kase in Switzerland.[63] The next day, the Supreme Council for the Direction of the War met at 8:30 in the morning to discuss Byrnes's reply. Although the meeting lasted all day, with the only interruption being a cabinet meeting, it failed to reach any conclusion.[64] At that point, Prime Minister Suzuki Kantarō proceeded to the Imperial Palace to consult with Kido Kōichi, the Lord Keeper of the

---

60 *Sakuin seiji keizai dai-nenpyō: Jōkan nenpyō hen*, p. 1438.

61 *Shūsen shiroku 4*, p. 163–164. (https://www.ndl.go.jp/constitution/shiryo/01/010/010tx.html#tc006 last visited on November 25, 2017).

62 Ibid., p. 215–217. (https://www.ibiblio.org/pha/policy/1945/1945-08-11a.html last visited on November 25, 2017).

63 *Shūsen shiroku 5*, p. 3.

64 Ibid., p. 3–4.

Privy Seal of Japan, and petitioned the emperor to sanction the immediate convening of the Imperial Council. The resulting Imperial Council meeting convened at 10:50 in the morning, after which the Imperial decision was given to accept the Potsdam Declaration, and concluded at around noon.[65]

At 11:00 p.m. on August 14, the Ministry of Foreign Affairs wired a "Communication of the Japanese Government of August 14th, 1945, addressed to the Governments of the United States, Great Britain, the Soviet Union and China" to Minister-Counselor Kase in Switzerland. The emergency wire included the following statements.

> 1. His Majesty the Emperor has issued an Imperial Rescript regarding Japan's acceptance of the provisions of the Potsdam Declaration.
> 2. His Majesty the Emperor is prepared to authorize and ensure the signature by His Government and the Imperial General Headquarters of the necessary terms for carrying out the provisions of the Potsdam Declaration. His Majesty is also prepared to issue his commands to all the military, naval, and air authorities of Japan and all the forces under their control wherever located to cease active operations, to surrender arms, and to issue such other orders as may be required by the Supreme Commander of the Allied Forces for the execution of the above-mentioned terms.[66]

The United States government interpreted the above communication of the Japanese government as a full acceptance of the Potsdam Declaration and Byrnes's reply of August 11.[67]

General MacArthur, for his part, communicated the following message to Japan's Imperial Headquarters at 10:35 p.m. on August 15 via Chongqing Radio:

> (Paraphrase) I have been appointed supreme commander of the Allied forces by the United States of America, the Republic of China, the United Kingdom, and the Soviet Union and granted the authority to make an agreement directly with Japanese government officials to terminate the conduct of hostilities at the earliest possible timing. . . . May we request you to acknowledge receipt of this telegram.[68]

---

65 Ibid., p. 47–49.

66 Ibid., p. 75. (https://www.ndl.go.jp/constitution/shiryo/01/010/010tx.html#tc006 last visited on November 29, 2017)

67 Ibid., p. 177.

68 Etō (1981), p. 27.

Demanding close attention here is the fact that the Japanese government's acceptance of the Potsdam Declaration inevitably constrained civil censorship, which the U.S. occupation forces were to conduct in Japan later, whether they liked it or not—the principle of freedom of speech and expression, which were akin to the stipulations of the First Amendment to the U.S. Constitution. Needless to say, this was precisely because Article 10 of the Potsdam Declaration stipulated that "Freedom of speech, of religion and of thought as well as respect for the fundamental human rights shall be established."[69]

As I explained in Chapter 3, the First Amendment stipulates that "Congress shall make no law respecting an establishment of religion, or prohibiting the free exercise thereof; or abridging the freedom of speech, or of the press . . ."[70] A cursory reading is enough to notice that Article 10 of the Potsdam Declaration relied heavily on the wording of the First Amendment, almost word for word.

Regarding the Potsdam Declaration, the U.S. Department of State issued a *Comparison of the Proclamation of July 26, 1945, With the Policy of the Department of State,*[71] which offered the analysis that "The proclamation is a statement of terms addressed to Japan (par. 1) and to the Japanese government (par. 13) which if accepted would constitute an international agreement subject to interpretation by the usual canons of international law," and, as such, the Declaration would be binding on both parties.

If that were indeed the case, the civil censorship that the U.S. occupation forces were about to conduct in Japan would inevitably come into head-on conflict with the principle of freedom of speech and expression that Article 10 of the Potsdam Declaration guaranteed. These two stances were inescapably contradictory and inconsistent. More than that, the U.S. government strictly ordered General MacArthur to enforce civil censorship as a part of the Japan occupation policies in JCS 873/3. The only way to resolve this contradiction would be to conduct civil censorship in accordance with the orders of the Joint Chiefs of Staff and, at the same time, continue to hide the presence of the censorship itself.[72]

---

69 *Shūsen shiroku 4*, p. 8, 10–11.

70 The Japanese Association for American Studies, ed. & translated, *Genten Amerika-shi: Dai 2-kan kakumei to kenkoku* [American History in Original Texts, Vol. 2. Revolution and Nation Building], Tokyo: Iwanami Shoten, 1951, p. 27. (https://constitution.findlaw.com/amendment1.html last visited on November 30, 2017.)

71 *Foreign Relations of the United States, 1945 Conference of Berlin* (USGPO), p. 1284–1289. (https://history.state.gov/historicaldocuments/frus1945Berlinv02/d1254 last visited on November 30, 2017.)

72 Etō Jun, *1946-nen kenpō: Sono kōsoku* [1946 Constitution: Its Constraints]. Tokyo: Bungei Shunjū, 1980, p. 13.

Throughout the occupation period, the presence of not only the CCD but also of all the other censorship organizations of the occupation forces thus remained under wraps. The fundamental reason behind the ban on references to censorship lies somewhere between this Article 10 of the Potsdam Declaration and JCS 873/3—hidden in the structure of contradiction itself.

Needless to say, what soon emerged was a perplexing, incongruous situation in which such values as "democracy" and "freedom of speech and expression" became profoundly idolized while the actual linguistic space, in contrast, became strictly restrained, increasingly constrained, and infinitely closed.

Had Zechariah Chafee Jr., author of *Freedom of Speech* (see Chapter 3), witnessed this situation, he would have been shocked to find that Americans—who should have stood firmly on the principles that had been stipulated by the First Amendment to the U.S. Constitution—could create such a mystifying linguistic space once they themselves had turned into the occupation authorities. After all, the linguistic space was so stringent and miserably isolated that neither Chafee's theory, the Blackstone theory, nor the theory on "use" versus "abuse" (see Chapter 3) could convincingly explain it.

It is not clear, however, how much Colonel Hoover (date of promotion to colonel unknown) and staff members of the CCD, charged with the task of creating this closed linguistic space, were aware of the significance of their mission. What was clear, though, was that their Basic Plan literally fell into chaos in the face of Japan's unexpectedly early and abrupt acceptance of the Potsdam Declaration.[73] Almost all the implementation manuals and guidebooks for censors that had been in preparation based on the first revised edition of the Basic Plan of July 10 had to be scrapped. The abrupt shift forced the abandonment of Operation Blacklist, not to mention Operation Downfall.[74]

Although Colonel Hoover himself departed Manila by air on August 25, together with some members of the advance team, he was forced to spend a few days in Okinawa due a typhoon off Shikoku that night. It was on or about September 1, 1945, that Hoover and his team at last arrived in Yokohama—and that arrival officially initiated the Civil Censorship Detachment's activities in Japan.[75]

On September 3, the day after the signing of the Japanese Instrument of Surrender on board the USS *Missouri*, the core of the CCD advance party

73 *Operations of Military and Civil Censorship*, Vol. X, p. 55.

74 Ibid., p. 57.

75 Ibid., p. 55. There is no official record on the arrival of Colonel Hoover in Yokohama.

landed at Yokohama together with the Eleventh Army.[76] The Instrument explicitly indicated in its second and sixth paragraphs that it was based on the Potsdam Declaration.[77]

On the same day, Brigadier General Elliott Thorpe, chief of counter-intelligence, GH/USARPAC, decided that censorship of local newspapers and broadcasts would fall under the jurisdiction of the Civil Censorship Detachment.[78] There had been a few twists and turns behind this decision. The original Basic Plan, both its initial plan as well as the first revised plan, had actually assigned censorship of newspapers and broadcasts to army officers in charge of public relations. Backing up the public-relations officers was the United States Office of War Information (OWI), whose members had all been eager to engage in the task. Unfortunately, however, they did not have enough manpower; if they were to censor newspapers and broadcasts, they would have had to borrow censors from the CCD. Given the situation, Brigadier General Thorpe decided to unify the implementation of civil censorship in order to prevent organizational confusion, taking his cue from Byron Price.[79]

One important point to emphasize here is that the genesis of the eventual feud between the Civil Information and Educational Section (CI&E) and the CCD, which persisted throughout the entire occupation period, was indeed this decision by Brigadier General Thorpe. In any event, the decision added the important task of censoring mass media, including newspapers and broadcasts, to the mission of Colonel Hoover. Hoover, on his part, immediately launched the second revision of the Basic Plan.

As I mentioned earlier, the second revision of the *AFPAC Basic Plan for Civil Censorship in Japan* was completed on September 30, 1945.[80] By that time, however, Hoover and his CCD had already launched the task of vigorously creating the closed linguistic space in Japan. While the visible war had ended, an invisible war to annihilate Japan's thought and culture was about to begin—on a unilateral basis.[81]

---

76 Ibid.

77 *Shūsen shiroku 5*, p. 198–199.

78 *Operations of Military and Civil Censorship*, Vol. X, p. 58.

79 See notes 4, 5, and 6 in Chapter 4.

80 See note 51 in Chapter 4.

81 See notes 1 and 2 in Chapter 1.

PART
II

How the United States Conducted Censorship in Japan

CHAPTER 7

An Invisible Cage

In September 1945, the Japanese people were cloaked in a stony silence, almost to the point of eeriness, as they watched U.S. troops putting Japan under occupation day by day.

Russell Brines, an Associated Press reporter who arrived in Japan as a member of the first press corps of the Allied powers, later confessed that he was astonished by how calm the entire population of Japan was.[1]

Brines was not the only one. As a matter of fact, every member of the occupation forces was suspicious about the possibility of a "gigantic trap" underneath Japan's calm façade.[2] They were fearful that someday, the silence would abruptly end and bloodshed commence, annihilating the entirety of the U.S. forces.

As if to endorse this fear, the Intelligence Series appendix to the Operation Blacklist directive carried the warning:

> . . . General intelligence problems will be enormously magnified, in contact with a fanatical population; there are no docile natives, as on New Guinea, or a pro-American population, as in the Philippines; every Japanese national is a potential enemy; all intelligence may become operational intelligence; sabotage and under-ground resistance are doubly menacing because of complicated language and race psychology. All intelligence agencies must face this sinister background and re-orient their general activities; an acute shortage of language personnel requires close coordination of functions in the language field. II-1-1[3] (emphasis added)

The prevailing perception was that all Japanese people were "potential enemies" and that Japan, where these potential enemies resided, was an evil country at its core. This notion continued to linger in the minds of U.S. military authorities even long after the cancellation of Operation Blacklist.

1 *The Asahi Shimbun*, September 14, 1945.

2 *Operations of Military and Civil Censorship, USAFFE/SWPA/AFPAC/FEN Intelligence Series*, p. 57–58.

3 *Operations of the Civil Intelligence Section GHQ, FEN & SCAP*, Vol. IX, Intelligence Series (I), p. 8. "Blacklist," Annex 5d, Sec. 1, par. 2.

In fact, the notion continued to permeate the common consciousness until it became a kind of filter that activated automatically virtually any time a member of the authorities saw Japan or the Japanese.

The authorities could detect no sign of any remorse among the eerily silent Japanese for their evilness. Private letters unsealed by U.S. military censors teemed with messages like the following.

> I was shocked by this abrupt development. Even though our government is now in the worst possible shape, I, for one, pledged to fight the holy war to the end and do not wish to die in vain. Our enemy openly advocates humanism and internationalism, but look at the brutality it has shown to our people. I want U.S. to remember the countless war casualties on our side. And I cannot help but feel hatred toward the enemy.
>
> (Dated August 16)

> I saw them for the first time when I went to Isezaki-chō yesterday. They were triumphantly driving cars and walking about.
>
> A sentry on the bridge was sitting on the parapet, chewing gum with his rifle dangling from his shoulder. It was so disheartening to remember that we were beaten by such sloppy soldiers.
>
> (Dated September 9)

> We are all aware that the Greater East Asian War ended miserably. Nowadays, you cannot avoid seeing those hateful American soldiers on your way to school or anywhere else. This afternoon, I saw several of them entering a barber shop near my school.
>
> American soldiers also came to my school and looked around. What a gross bunch! Even a small child like myself felt anger toward them, when I wondered what our fallen soldiers would have felt to see this.
>
> (Dated September 29)[4]

The letters dated August 16 and September 29 appear to be addressing the senders' fathers or brothers stationed overseas. Judging from the correspondence, it did not seem as if the contemporary Japanese people attributed the miseries of war and defeat to their "evil nature" at all.

In their minds, the countless war casualties had accumulated not because

4 *G-2 Daily Intelligence Summary* No. 45, Nov. 4, 1945, p. 6.

of the evil nature of Japan but because of the carnage and destruction by the enemy—that is, the U.S. forces. Their prime target of hatred, it followed, was the destroyers, not the Japanese government or the military. This was, without a doubt, how the Japanese people in those days normally perceived the situation. If one sees the situation from that angle, the Japanese people—even elementary school pupils—must have felt the presence of dead soldiers looming in the background, seeing what they were seeing. The dead and the living, in their minds, were witness to the same reality.

Needless to say, the censorship of civil communications was just a lead line, so to speak, that the occupation authorities cast into the sea of the Japanese people's silence. Authorities had to destroy the emotion and values that saturated the silence and tear the living away from the dead. If the operation failed to launch promptly, there was no knowing when all the occupation forces would fall into that "gigantic trap" and face annihilation themselves. For the authorities, it was literally a race against time.

While the act of combat as defined by international law was terminated with the signing of the Instrument of Surrender on the USS *Missouri,* an extralegal, invisible war had commenced in its place. Civil censorship in Japan was this invisible war—and figured to deliver a crippling blow with a power comparable to that of the atomic bomb.

Brigadier General Elliott Thorpe, director of intelligence under General MacArthur and the official in charge of the censorship operation, arrived in tranquil Japan on September 4 and immediately headed for Tokyo with Lieutenant Colonel Galloway, commander of the 441st Squadron.[5] Brigadier General Thorpe was also accompanied by Arthur S. Komori, a second-generation Japanese American interpreter and a member of the Counter-Intelligence Corps (CIC). Komori, one of the second-generation Japanese-American spies trained by the Federal Bureau of Investigation (FBI), had been sent from Hawaii to a Japanese residential area in the Philippines, from which he later escaped.

The idea of having second-generation Japanese-American spies hole up in the Philippines prior to the eruption of war with Japan had apparently come from Major General Charles Willoughby, General MacArthur's chief of intelligence, or G-2. In any event, Komori became the first CIC spy to arrive in Tokyo.[6]

Brigadier General Thorpe's first task in Tokyo was a thorough secu-

5 *Operations of the Civil Intelligence Section*, p. 5.

6 Ibid., p. 5, note 15.

rity checkup in preparation for transfer of the General Headquarters of the Supreme Commander for the Allied Powers (GHQ/SCAP). There was no room for any negligent oversight whatsoever, from the personal backgrounds of the Japanese citizens to be hired as local staff to the inspection of confiscated facilities, including the Dai-ichi Sōgo Building, where GHQ/SCAP was to be housed.[7] To accomplish this mission, Brigadier General Thorpe had two implementation forces under his command. One of them was the CIC, which had first operated out of the Dai-Ichi Sogo Building but later transferred to the Teikoku Sogo Building.

The 441st Squadron, whose members were fanned out all over Japan to engage in intelligence activities as the eyes and ears of the CIC, was headquartered at the former Military Police Corps headquarters in Takebashi. Pre-equipped with soundproof interrogation chambers and detention facilities, as well as wireless communications and photo processing capabilities, this former military police headquarters proved useful for the activities of the 441st.

In contrast to the CIC, which had commenced operations immediately with the start of the occupation, the Civil Censorship Detachment (CCD), the other implementation force under Thorpe's command, lagged one step behind.[8]

As I mentioned in the first part of this book, Colonel Donald Hoover, commander of the CCD, and his party arrived in Yokohama around September 1, 1945. Immediately upon arrival, Hoover set up a provisional headquarters inside the Yokohama Customs building. However, the main contingent of the headquarters staff had been delayed; the only group at Hoover's immediate disposal was the second advance party of the CCD under the command of the Eighth Army's 11th Legion, which had arrived in Yokohama on September 3.[9] Yet in front of Colonel Hoover was a copy of the directive that Brigadier General Thorpe had asked Lieutenant General Richard K. Sutherland to approve on September 3. The second section of the directive reads: "Censorship of newspapers and broadcasts is to be conducted by the Civil Censorship Detachment of the United States Army Pacific (USARPAC) based on policies stipulated by the supreme commander" under the direction of the commander of the Counter Intelligence Corps.

Needless to say, this instruction was tantamount to another revision of

---

7 Ibid., p. 5.
8 Ibid., p. 7.
9 Ibid., p. 16.

the first revision of the "Basic Plan on Civil Censorship in Japan" dated July 10, 1945. Previously, the Plan had stipulated that censorship of newspapers and broadcasts was to fall under the jurisdiction of the public relations officer (PRO) instead of the CCD. Moreover, the U.S. military authority had never conceived of occupying a Japan where, even under heavy bombardments, the mass media—including newspapers, broadcasts, and publishing—remained functional.

Brigadier General Thorpe's instruction stipulated:

1. In accordance with verbal instructions, I have assumed responsibility for local press and radio censorship in Japan. Approval is requested of the plan outlined herein.
2. Censorship of local newspapers and radio will be conducted by Civil Censorship Detachment, AFPAC, under direction of the Chief of Counter-Intelligence, along policy lines determined by the Supreme Allied Commander.
3. Censorship of the press will be conducted on a post publication basis; i.e., the newspapers will be notified of subjects which cannot be discussed and all publications will be read after publication to ensure that these prohibitions have not been violated. Prohibitions will be few; violations will be punished by suspension from publication for the length of the time merited by the offense.
4. In order to provide a simple, easily understood "code," the following Imperial Rescript is suggested, the phraseology to be that used in such announcements:

    The Supreme Commander for the Allied Powers has decreed that there shall be a minimum of restrictions upon freedom of speech. Freedom of discussion of matters affecting the future of Japan is encouraged by the Allied Powers, with the exception that nothing will be permitted that disturbs public tranquility. The Supreme Commander will suspend any publication or radio station which disseminates information that disturbs public tranquility and thus harms the efforts of Japan to emerge from its defeat as a new nation entitled to a place among the peace-loving nations of the world.

5. While "information that disturbs public tranquility" is a vague definition, it nevertheless is one which will enable suppression of any publication or radio station violating censorship and at the same

time carries a connotation of primary interest in Japanese welfare.

6. The "scrutinizers" of newspapers and other publications must perforce be Japanese or Japanese-speaking persons available on the ground, until arrival of linguist personnel from the states. They will be schooled carefully in what constitutes "information that disturbs public tranquility," which in the last analysis will be subjects the Supreme Commander does not desire discussed.
7. Closer control will be exercised over Domei News Agency, with every article disseminated by that agency being censored rigorously by officers stationed in the agency. Material will be passed without censorship if it originates with the Public Relations Officer, OWI, PWB, and MGS here Local Press and Radio Censorship or in the United States, or in the Department of State. Matter issued by other Allied Powers will be censored to the degree desired by the Supreme Commander.
8. Radio broadcasting initially can be controlled by Censorship Advance Detachments accompanying the various occupying forces, under provision of the Imperial Rescript. It is regarded as probable that a spot-check of broadcasts will suffice after the broadcasters have been made familiar with censorship requirements.
9. On approval of the plan outlined, it is proposed to call a meeting of representatives of publishers and broadcasters in Tokyo to outline the subjects generally falling within "subjects disturbing public tranquility." Domei agency facilities will be used to inform outlying communities of censorship restrictions.
10. The policy outlined herein is believed to be one which will meet with approval of American newspaper leaders who advocate freedom of the press in all countries and should lead to a favorable public opinion at home on this subject.[10]

Obvious at a glance was that the instruction was a provisional directive on the assumption that there would be an extreme dearth of manpower with the necessary Japanese-language proficiency. The document also included items on which the occupation authority used highly political discretion to forgo their implementation. For instance, the proposal to issue the *Codes of Wartime Practices* as an Imperial Rescript never came to fruition. Colonel Hoover also had to face unexpectedly staunch resistance from Japanese

10 *Operations of Military and Civil Censorship*, Documentary Appendices (I), Vol. X, Intelligence Series, Appendix 23.

media organizations. It was only until October 8, 1945, that the CCD could carry out ex-post censorship. After this date, major newspapers became subject to pre-censorship.[11]

As a result of this provisional instruction of September 3, Colonel Hoover nonetheless had to establish a new section in the CCD to take charge of censoring newspapers, radio, and other mass media. This was on top of the three administrative sections and five program divisions (postal mails division, telephone and telegram division, documents carried by tourists division, special activities division, and information records division) that the Basic Plan had prescribed. In addition, short of an Imperial Rescript, Colonel Hoover needed to present the occupation authority's censorship policy one way or another.

The Press, Pictorial, and Broadcast Division (PPB) was set up on the spot in response to the first of the two instructions above. After commencing activities on September 10, the division quickly grew into the largest organization within the CCD.[12]

The second of the two instructions—presenting the censorship policy—was carried out on September 10 in the form of the Supreme Commander for the Allied Powers Directive to the Imperial Japanese Government (SCAPIN-16). The directive was issued instead of an Imperial Rescript. Considered in conjunction with a series of directives issued in the latter half of September, the decision to issue the document instead of an Imperial Rescript was an extremely important one. In short, SCAP GHQ adopted a policy of bypassing the Japanese government completely when managing Japan's linguistic space.

> SCAPIN-16 reads:
> OFFICE OF THE SUPREME COMMANDER FOR THE ALLIED POWERS
> SCAPIN-16 10 September 1945
> MEMORANDUM FOR THE IMPERIAL JAPANESE GOVERNMENT
> THROUGH: YOKOHAMA LIAISON OFFICE
> FROM: The Supreme Commander for the Allied Powers
>
> 1. The Japanese Imperial Government will issue the necessary orders to prevent dissemination of news, through newspapers, radio broad-

11 *Operations of the Civil Intelligence Section*, p. 24.

12 Ibid., p. 59.

casting or other means of publication, which fails to adhere to the truth or which disturbs public tranquillity.

2. The Supreme Commander for the Allied Powers has decreed that there shall be an absolute minimum of restrictions upon freedom of speech. Freedom of discussion of matters affecting the future of Japan is encouraged by the Allied Powers, unless such discussion is harmful to the efforts of Japan to emerge from defeat as a new nation entitled to a place among the peace-loving nations of the world.
3. Subjects which cannot be discussed include Allied troop movements which have not been officially released, false or destructive criticism of the Allied Powers, and rumors.
4. For the time being, radio broadcasts will be primarily of a news, musical, and entertainment nature. News commentation and informational broadcasts will be limited to those originating at Radio Tokyo studios.
5. The Supreme Commander will suspend any publication or radio station which publishes information that fails to adhere to the truth or disturbs public tranquillity.

For the SUPREME COMMANDER:
s/ Harold Fair
t/ HAROLD FAIR
Lt Col, AGD
Asst Adjutant General[13]

The Japanese government forwarded this "Freedom of Speech and Press Directive" to all district commandants and prefectural governors on September 11. Japan's mass media did not show any sign of compliance with this directive, mostly because the Dōmei News Agency, which was the core figure among Japanese media, continued to outscoop other, overseas news agencies in the coverage of Japan's news.

It was none other than Dōmei News Agency that got the scoop on the details of the transfer of the occupation forces to Tokyo, for example, and even on the arrival time of General MacArthur in Tokyo on September 8. At the outset of the occupation period, the *New York Times* had relied almost solely on shortwave radio transmissions by the Dōmei News Agency for Japan-related news. When General MacArthur banned all broadcasts in for-

13 Ibid., Documentary Appendices (I) Appendix 22.

eign languages on September 3, the Dōmei News Agency's English-language program nonchalantly recited MacArthur's order and went on with its normal program as if nothing had happened.[14]

It was only natural that Dōmei's actions would rankle correspondents from American news agencies, including the Associated Press (AP), the United Press (UP), and the International News Service (INS), which had been under strict military censorship. They confronted Lieutenant Colonel Richard Powell, assistant to GHQ's PRO.

Meanwhile, Allied correspondents were protesting vigorously to SCAP that Dōmei was "scooping" them on Occupation news despite General MacArthur's order. They said the infamous Japanese news agency was not only filtering all the Occupation news to the public, but also still was broadcasting to the United States in violation of orders. The Allied reporters insisted it was unfair that they should have to operate under strict censorship regulations while Dōmei functioned freely. Lieutenant Colonel Richard Powell, assistant public relations officer at SCAP, told the correspondents that his staff had no authority to regulate Dōmei, that this was the job of the counter-intelligence staff, which had not yet been set up in Tokyo. Powell said there was yet no way to stop the Japanese government from passing General MacArthur's orders on to its newsmen. He said the broadcasts being heard in the United States actually were domestic broadcasts which were of such high power that they could be heard abroad.

This unlikely explanation overlooked the fact that Japan's domestic broadcasting network operated on a very low frequency, as well as the fact that some of the broadcasts were in English–hardly for domestic consumption.

One harassed correspondent commented: "We are being made the laughing stock of the world for getting beaten on our own news."[15]

The Dōmei News Agency was the most prominent news agency in Japan in those days. Having received approval for incorporation, with various daily newspapers in Japan and the Nippon Hōsō Kyōkai (NHK: Japan Broadcasting Corporation) as its participating members, in November 1935, the agency commenced operations in January 1936.[16] It was established through a government-backed merger between Nihon Shimbun Rengōsha (Associated Press, or "Rengō") and Nihon Dempō Tsūshinsha (Japan Telegraphic

---

14 William J. Coughlin, *Conquered Press, The MacArthur Era in Japanese Journalism*, Palo Alto, CA: Pacific Books, 1952, p. 16–19.

15 Ibid., p. 18.

16 Nippon Kin-Gendaishi Jiten Henshū Iinkai, ed., *Nippon kin-gendaishi jiten* [Dictionary of Modern and Contemporary Japanese History], Tōyō Keizai Shimpōsha, 1978, p. 461.

News Agency, or "Dentsū"), which had been in competition. Although it took the organizational form of a nongovernmental membership association, it was, in effect, a government-run news agency—and the foremost news handler in the Far East.[17]

Dōmei had contracts with the world's leading news agencies, including the AP, Reuters, the Central News Agency (China), Russian News Agency TASS, and Agence Havas (France), to form a formidable network. After the eruption of the war, DNS (Germany) and Agenzia Stefani (Italy) became primary news sources for Dōmei.[18] The agency maintained as many as sixty-eight branch offices within Japan, twenty-one in China throughout the war, and six in Europe. It also dominated news-service activities in Malay, Singapore, Sumatra, and North Borneo. More important, however, was the fact that overseas wireless communications and international shortwave radio were designated to be exclusive operations of Dōmei. As the above conversation between Lieutenant Colonel Powell and correspondents from the U.S. media suggests, Dōmei's signal was so powerful that it easily reached the Pacific Coast of the United States.[19]

It was self-evident that Byron Price's vision of a universal communications blockade against Japan would remain infeasible as long as the function of Dōmei, which boasted a worldwide communication network and maintained branch offices even in such neutral countries as Switzerland, Sweden, and Portugal, remained intact. Dōmei was thus destined to be the first target of the invisible censorship war.

In addition, Dōmei's shortwave radio not only got scoops on movements of the occupation forces but also gave detailed reports on the specific activities of the forces' officers and soldiers. For instance, even before the signing of the Instrument of Surrender on the USS *Missouri,* an act of sexual assault committed by a member of the U.S. Marine Corps was promptly reported worldwide. After the incident, reports of misconduct by members of the U.S. military continued to surface almost daily. When it was reported that a girl working at a licensed red-light establishment was abducted and raped by twenty-seven U.S. soldiers, the U.S. Army and Marine Corps authorities were unable to ignore the report and had to make an announcement that it was a groundless allegation.[20]

---

17 *Operations of the Civil Intelligence Section*, p. 23.

18 Ibid., p. 23.

19 Ibid., p. 23–24.

20 Coughlin (1952), p. 16.

Japanese media organizations were able to keep that brand of hard-hitting, daring journalistic activity because the Japanese media, including the Dōmei News Agency, were firmly convinced that Japan and the Allied powers were on equal footing, that relations between the two were reciprocal, and that the contract between the two was guaranteed by the Potsdam Declaration and the Instrument of Surrender. In other words, Japanese media interpreted, quite appropriately, that it was only the Japanese armed forces that had surrendered unconditionally, as article 13 of the Potsdam Declaration stipulated, and that the Japanese government and the Japanese people surrendered only after they accepted the terms of the Potsdam Declaration.

In fact, there is evidence that even General MacArthur, supreme commander for the Allied powers, shared a similar interpretation for a time at the beginning of the occupation and believed that the Potsdam Declaration tacitly stipulated a certain restraint on U.S. conduct. MacArthur's comment in his response to the draft of SWNCC 150/4, which later came to be known as the "Initial Post-Surrender Policy for Japan," that he sent via confidential wire to General George C. Marshall (chief of staff of the army) on September 3 offers a clue as to his thinking. MacArthur expressed concern that the directives he had been given unofficially seem to deviate significantly from the principles stipulated by the Potsdam Declaration in several important ways.[21] Seeing as even MacArthur himself had misgivings about the arrangement, it was only natural that the Japanese side, both officially and privately, interpreted that its fall was a defeat by agreement and never a defeat by conquest.

If it was indeed a defeat by agreement, the defeated side, Japan, would have the right to reserve the freedom to criticize the winner, the United States. Article 10 of the Potsdam Declaration also said, "Freedom of speech, of religion, and of thought, as well as respect for the fundamental human rights shall be established." Given that stipulation, there was indeed no reason that the Japanese media should collude with illegal misconduct on the part of occupation forces by not reporting it.

This was more or less the basic stance of the Japanese media organizations at the time. At 4:15 p.m. Eastern War Time (EWT, or 3:15 a.m. Eastern Standard War Time) on September 10, SCAPIN-16: Freedom of Press and Speech 1945/09/10 took effect. According to a UP shortwave reception station that picked up Dōmei's overseas radio signal, Dōmei continued to transmit shortwave for more than four hours after SCAPIN-16 entered into

---

21 National Archives, Washington, DC, RG 165, Record of the War Department, General and Special Staffs, War Department Message Files.

force. At 7:40 a.m. EWT, Dōmei reported a plan that would transfer about 10,000 U.S. troops to the Tokyo area in a few days.

SCAPIN-16: Freedom of Press and Speech 1945/09/10, issued by the supreme commander of the occupation forces, was completely ignored by the Japanese media. Dōmei continued to report on movements of the U.S. Army and Navy as well as misconduct by U.S. military personnel. Then, at noon on September 14, Dōmei's signal went silent.[22]

The Agency had received an order to immediately terminate its overseas broadcasting programs in English, French, Spanish, and Chinese. At 5:29 p.m. that day, Dōmei received a strict order, once again, to terminate all of its operations on the grounds that it had transmitted news that "was disturbing to the public tranquility."[23] This was, indeed, CCD's first strike of the hatchet against Japan's media organizations.

The next morning, Colonel Donald Hoover, commander of the CCD, summoned leaders of the Japanese news organizations—including Furuno Inosuke, president of the Dōmei News Agency; Ōhashi Hachirō, president of the Japan Broadcasting Corporation (NHK); Kawai Tatsuo, chief of the Cabinet Information Bureau; and Tōgasaki Kiyoshi, managing director of the *Nippon Times*—to GHQ and made the following announcement.[24]

> You have been called together to receive instructions regarding censorship of news distributed in Japan through press and radio.
>
> The Supreme Commander is not satisfied with the manner in which the Japanese government, the press and radio have observed the directive of 10 September on the subject.
>
> General MacArthur has decreed that there should be an absolute minimum of restrictions upon the freedom of speech and discussion of matters affecting the future of Japan. His limitations were that this discussion would not be untrue, that it would not disturb public tranquillity and that it would not be harmful to the efforts of right-thinking Japanese to help their nation emerge from its defeat. Freedom of the press is very dear to the Supreme Commander, and it is one of the freedoms for which the Allies have fought.
>
> You have demonstrated that the latitude provided in the directive cannot be entrusted to you. You have not met this responsibility cooperatively. In the days since your surrender, you have revealed your

22 Coughlin (1952), p. 20.

23 Ibid.

24 *The Asahi Shimbun*, September 17, 1945.

lack of good faith in handling the news. Therefore, the Supreme Commander has directed a more severe censorship. Domei News Agency was suspended yesterday at 17:29 hours for the dissemination of news disturbing to the public tranquillity.

Any other media which violate the directive will be similarly suspended.

General MacArthur desires that it be clearly understood that the Allied Powers do not regard Japan as an equal in any way. It is a defeated enemy which has not yet demonstrated a right to a place among civilized nations. The tone of the colored news which you have been presenting to the public gives the impression that the Supreme Commander has been negotiating with the Japanese government. There are no negotiations, and the public should not be permitted to gain a false idea of the position of the Japanese government in relation to the Allied Powers.

The Supreme Commander will dictate orders to the Japanese government . . . He will not negotiate with it. Negotiations take place among equals . . . and the Japanese are not to be led to believe that they already have regained the respect of the world or the status whereby they can "negotiate" over orders of the Supreme Commander. This slanting of news must be discontinued immediately.

You are upsetting the public tranquillity in that you do not give the truth to your people; you are creating an inaccurate picture of the true status of Japan.

You have known that many of the statements you published were untrue. All matter going to the Japanese people will be more strictly censored from now on. One hundred percent censorship of press and radio will continue to be enforced. No more false statements, no misleading statements will be permitted; no destructive criticism of the Allied Powers. The government will take steps immediately to assure that this policy is carried out. If it does not do so, Supreme Headquarters will.[25]

Domei News Agency may return to the status of a national Japanese news service as of 12 noon today. This service will be limited to Japan only, utilizing the telephone, radio and telegraph for internal distribution, subject to 100 percent censorship by United States representatives in Domei. The ban on overseas broadcasts will continue and news from overseas bureaus of Domei will be subject to this prohibition.

---

25 *Manual of Press, Pictorial, and Broadcast Censorship in Japan*, September 30, 1945, p. 3–4.

This announcement by Colonel Hoover touched on an extremely important point in two senses. The first had to do with the occupation forces' basic policy toward Japan. The other was about censorship policy, which played an important part in the basic policy.

As for the basic policy toward Japan, Colonel Hoover's announcement was an outright denial of the reciprocal and mutually binding relations between Japan and the Allied powers that the Potsdam Declaration had stipulated. In other words, Hoover's statement was a universal negation of the notion of defeat by agreement and a unilateral declaration of Japan's defeat by conquest. Therefore, the announcement also negated General MacArthur's intimation on September 3 that the aforementioned draft of SWNCC 150/4, which had been unofficially announced, deviated markedly from the principles stipulated by the Instrument of Surrender and the Potsdam Declaration in several points.

It is simply unthinkable for Colonel Hoover, a mere commander of an implementation force, to have made such an important announcement on his own. The statement must have had a deeper, more official grounding. A closer look suggests that he made the above announcement to Japanese media leaders based on JCS 1380/6, which President Truman issued to General MacArthur on September 6.

Incidentally, the first paragraph of the memorandum stipulated that, "Our relations with Japan do not rest on a contractual basis, but on an unconditional surrender." Furthermore, the third paragraph stated that "the statement of intentions contained in the Potsdam Declaration . . . will not be given effect, however, because we consider ourselves bound in a contractual relationship with Japan as a result of that document" but "because the Potsdam Declaration forms <u>a part of our policy</u> stated in good faith with relation to Japan."[26] (emphasis added)

It bears mentioning that in July 1945, about six weeks before the memorandum was issued, the U.S. Department of State had expressed a view on the Potsdam Declaration that was totally opposite to what JCS 1380/6 implied. This State Department document has already made an appearance in the first part of this book, but the context here calls for a closer reading of several paragraphs. The document is normally referred to as Department of State Memorandum No. 1254 (Foreign Relations of the United States: Diplomatic Papers, The Conference of Berlin, 1945, Volume II) under the title

26 Etō Jun, ed., *Senryō shiroku: Dai 4-kan* [Occupation History Record: Vol. 4], Tokyo: Kōdansha, 1982, p. 366. (https://www.ndl.go.jp/constitution/e/shiryo/01/023/023tx.html#t002, last visited on December 12, 2017)

"Comparison of the Proclamation of July 26, 1945, With the Policy of the Department of State." Even though no date was given, its footnote states, "This memorandum, prepared in the Office of Far Eastern Affairs, was considered at the 152d Meeting of the Secretary's Staff Committee, July 30. It is attached to the minutes of the 151st Meeting of that Committee."[27]

To quote its first three sections:

> I. Question—To what extent is the proclamation of July 26, 1945, consistent with the policy of the Department of State?
>
> II. Discussion—
>
> 1. The proclamation is a statement of terms addressed to Japan (par. 1) and to the Japanese government (par. 13) which if accepted would constitute an international agreement subject to interpretation by the usual canons of international law. Under international law ambiguous terms in an international agreement have been interpreted favorably to the state which accepted them. The state which proposed them should express its intention clearly. (See Harvard Research, Draft Convention on Treaties, American Journal of International Law, Supp., 1935, vol. 29, p. 941, citing several arbitral awards.)
>
>   The Department's policy has interpreted unconditional surrender as contemplating a unilateral surrender with no contractual elements whatever.
> 2. The contractual character of the surrender contemplated by the proclamation together with the allusion to "good faith" in paragraph 13, suggests that to some extent the execution of the terms is to be left to the good faith of the Japanese Government.
>
>   The Department's policy has assumed that all requirements would during the first stage be carried out by Allied forces without any reliance upon the good faith of any Japanese authorities.
> 3. The proclamation interprets unconditional surrender as applying only to "all Japanese armed forces."
>
>   The Department's policy has interpreted unconditional surrender as applying to Japan, thus covering not only the armed forces, but also the emperor, the government and the people.

This goes to show that the Department of State had an almost identical view

27 Ibid., p. 367–370. (https://history.state.gov/historicaldocuments/frus1945Berlinv02/d1254 last visited on December 12, 2017.)

of the Potsdam Declaration as did the Japanese side. It was a reciprocal and mutually binding contract and, as such, when accepted, it would require the State Department to change its policy drastically. Moreover, the Declaration would be adopted into the Instrument of Surrender and form a basis governing the relations between Japan and the Allied powers.

To put it differently, the State Department at that time was fully and accurately aware that the Potsdam Declaration could never be confined merely to "a part of our [the United States'] policy" and that it would, conversely, restrict all American policies toward Japan. The Potsdam Declaration was accepted by Japan, of course, and did become a document of agreement that actually constrained the very foundation of the U.S. occupation policy toward Japan.

It should be obvious by now that JCS 1380/6 was nothing short of a unilateral declaration of United States' intention to forcibly throw off this constraint by using the start of occupation and demobilization of the former Imperial Japanese Army and Navy personnel as leverage. As censorship is inherently situated at the junction between power and language, Colonel Hoover of the CCD was the first to exercise the "power" element in the form of his announcement. After all, power loses its requisite elements without the ability to influence language or alter its paradigm.

For instance, Colonel Hoover announced to the Japanese media leaders in attendance that they had failed to disseminate truth to the Japanese people, had thus disturbed public tranquility, and had described Japan's true position inaccurately. The "truth" that Colonel Hoover referred to here was the truth for the United States or the occupation forces, not necessarily the truth for the Japanese media organizations. For the Japanese side, it was "truth" that Japan and the Allied powers were essentially on equal footing; it was this truth that had made negotiations possible. It was an untruth merely for the occupation forces.

When two mutually contradictory "truths" collide, those in a position to make judgments freely must choose one, the other, or the third position—that neither one is truth. Censorship, however, does not allow people to make such free judgments; instead, it coerces people to accept as truth what represents a truth for one party and not the other—an inversion of the paradigm of language and the destruction of identity based thereon. That was precisely what the CCD's censorship activities consistently intended over the subsequent four years. CCD censorship was an attempt to reform "evil" Japan and the Japanese people by means of thought and language. More than that, it was a scheme to make Japan a country or a region that was not Japan, the Japanese a nation that was not Japanese.

In order to realize that vision, the occupation authorities had to confine the Japanese people into a gigantic, invisible cage ahead of the strike of that big hatchet. Following the ban on the Dōmei News Agency's overseas operations on September 14, GHQ ordered the confiscation of the properties and documents of the Japanese legations in neutral countries on October 25 and the severance of Japan's official relations with legations of neutral countries in Japan. At this point, Japan's linguistic and information space became completely closed both officially and privately.[28]

In contrast to the Manzanar War Relocation Center for people of Japanese descent, a location surrounded by barbed-wire fences and watchtowers during World War II,[29] there was no comparable symbol denoting the prisoners' domain in defeated Japan—the battlefield of this invisible war. The activities of both the CIC and the CCD—which were to play the role of observation posts—were all carefully concealed.

After the announcement to Japanese media leaders on the morning of September 15, Japanese newspapers never again covered the activities of Colonel Hoover. As for his successors, including Colonel Wadsworth, Colonel Putnam, Lieutenant Colonel Sykes, and Colonel Grove, not even their names appeared in the Japanese media.[30]

---

28 Etō Jun, ed., *Senryo shiroku: Dai 2-kan* [Occupation History Record: Vol. 2], p. 307, 315.

29 Harry H. L. Kitano, *Japanese Americans: The Evolution of a Subculture*, Prentice-Hall, 1976, p. 72.

30 *Operations of Military and Civil Censorship*, Documentary Appendices (I), p. i–ii.

CHAPTER 8

Press Censorship

Despite its hard-line tone, the announcement made by Colonel Donald Hoover was received in Japan only as just another announcement. There was no shortage of Japanese newspapers and magazines that continued to show resistance. The Civil Censorship Detachment (CCD) had to cope with the ongoing pushback by banning and confiscating publications.

As a matter of fact, on September 18, only three days after Hoover's announcement, the Supreme Commander for the Allied Powers issued the following directive. Needless to say, it was drafted by none other than Colonel Hoover.

> Office of the Supreme Commander for the Allied Powers
> AG 000.76 (18 Sep 45)   18 September 1945
> (SCAPIN - 34)
> Memorandum for: Imperial Japanese Government
> Through: Central Liaison Office, Tokyo
>
> Subject: Suspension of Tokyo Newspaper Asahi Shimbun
>
> 1. The Japanese Imperial Government will issue the necessary orders to suspend publication of the Tokyo newspaper *Asahi Shimbun*.
> 2. This suspension is to be effective as of 16:00 hours this date (18 September 1945) and to continue until 16:00 hours 20 September 1945.
>
> FOR THE SUPREME COMMANDER:
> s/ Harold Fair
> t/ HAROLD FAIR
> Lt Col, AGD
> Asst Adjutant General[1]

Two articles that appeared on September 15 and September 17 prompted the banning of the *Asahi Shimbun*. The September 15 issue carried a discourse

1 *Operations of Military and Civil Censorship*, Documentary Appendices (I), Vol. X, Intelligence Series, Appendix 22.

by Hatoyama Ichirō, a member of the House of Representatives who later became prime minister. Replying to a question on desirable policies for the postwar restoration of Japan, Hatoyama said:

> Because the United States has declared that "right is might," it can by no means deny that the use of atomic bombs, the annihilation of innocent civilians, assaults on hospital ships, or the use of poisonous gas were serious violations of international laws and constituted war crimes. We must devote our efforts to making Americans aware of their obligation to compensate the victims of their conduct and their responsibility to aid in Japan's recovery. We should candidly admit that Japan alone cannot possibly accomplish its restoration and show Americans that Japan's democratic resurgence and participation in international trade would not contradict the United States' national interest or the welfare of the world. We should by all means induce Americans to play an active, cooperative role in Japan's reconstruction.[2]

The September 17 issue carried an article titled "We Demand an Explanation from the U.S. Forces: Japanese People's Reaction to the Disclosure of the Japanese Soldiers' Assaults on Filipino People." The article read:

> . . . The fourth point concerns the true intentions of the U.S. forces behind the abrupt disclosure of this incident today. Some suspect a connection between today's reports of misconduct by Japanese soldiers in the Philippines and the sexual assault incidents that have occurred frequently since the arrival of the Allied forces in Japan. These latter incidents, though, recently dwindled after being reported repeatedly by newspapers and after the U.S. military authority's pledge to crack down on such conduct. Needless to say, heinous conduct driven by abnormal psychology in the midst of fierce battle and rapes committed during a peaceful occupation, like those occurring in today's Japan, should not be discussed in the same breath. Nevertheless, it was pointed out by an American news reporter that the brutal conduct of the Japanese military on the Philippine islands had been a major cause behind Japan's failure to gain the confidence of local people. Despite the difference in circumstances, the same can be said about the effects of the conduct of the occupation forces in Japan today. It is sincerely

2 Hatoyama Ichirō, "Shintō kessei no kōsō (jō)" [A Scheme for a New Political Party: Part 1] in *The Asahi Shimbun*, September 15, 1945, p. 1.

hoped that, at the restart of a new, peaceful Japan, the Allied forces would behave properly from a thoroughly humanist perspective.[3]

The forty-eight-hour ban on the publication of the *Asahi Shimbun* was followed by a twenty-four-hour ban on the publication of the *Nippon Times* on September 19. The bans were issued by a Supreme Commander for the Allied Powers Directive to the Imperial Japanese Government (SCAPIN-37).[4] The ban on the *Nippon Times* was enforced owing to a violation of procedure on the part of the newspaper—a failure to submit an editorial for pre-publication censorship—rather than because its content was found censorable.[5]

Furthermore, the CCD issued SCAPIN-79 on October 1, ordering the confiscation of the September 29, 1945, issue of the *Tōyō Keizai Shimpō* as follows:

Office of the Supreme Commander for the Allied Powers
AG 000.76 (1 Oct 45) CI
1 October 1945
(SCAPIN - 79)
Memorandum for: Imperial Japanese Government
Through: Central Liaison Office, Tokyo
Subject: Confiscation of September 29th *Toyo Keizai Shimpo*

1. The Japanese Imperial Government will issue the necessary orders to effect the confiscation of all distributed copies of the 29 September 1945 issue of *Toyo Keizai Shimpo.*
2. Confiscated copies will be submitted to Press, Pictorial, and Broadcast Division, Civil Censorship Detachment, 6th Floor, Radio Tokyo Building, for disposition.

FOR THE SUPREME COMMANDER:
s/ Harold Fair
t/ HAROLD FAIR
Lt Col, AGD
Asst Adjutant General[6]

3 "Motometai gun no shakumei/Hitō no bōkyo happyō e kokumin no koe" [We Demand the U.S. Forces' Explanation: Japanese People's Reaction to the Disclosure of the Japanese Soldiers' Assaults on Filipino People], *The Asahi Shimbun*, September 17, 1945, p. 1.

4 *Operations of Military and Civil Censorship*, Documentary Appendices (I), Appendix 22.

5 Coughlin (1952), p. 22.

6 *Operations of Military and Civil Censorship*, Documentary Appendices (I), Appendix 22.

That day's editorial, titled "Sexual Assaults by U.S. Occupation Forces Personnel Would Prevent Construction of World Peace," was the reason for the measure. The editorial reads:

> I must profusely apologize to readers for my failure to detect the presence of delinquent elements within the U.S. occupation forces, who have committed a variety of assaults.
>
> As soon as it was known that the troops of the Allied forces would occupy key locations in Japan, local residents became deeply agitated. They were worried because there was no knowing what kind of misconduct those troops might commit in their communities. In fear of the occupation troops, some local officials went so far as to instruct local women and children to evacuate their hometowns and schools for girls to close. I have felt bitter every time I heard about these things.
>
> Unlike enemy troops landing in battlefields during what was called the homeland defense war, the Allied forces are advancing peacefully into Japan as the result of the ceasefire agreement, to say nothing of the fact that the entire world is watching their conduct. How, then, could they possibly do violence to Japanese citizens? Thus, fear of the arrival of the occupation troops is all due to the ignorance and low moral standards of the Japanese people. Or so I thought.
>
> I became convinced that the Japanese people should refrain from uncivilized reactions, and I shared my conviction with the readers of the *Tōyō Keizai Shimpō.* To my regret, however, my conviction has been, at least partially, betrayed by facts that prove that the judgment of local officials, which I had criticized for its absurdity, was actually sound. This is why I must profusely apologize to my readers.
>
> Needless to say, assaults by the occupation troops have been committed by a relatively small number of ill-behaved soldiers, and this by no means indicates that the U.S. military leadership has adopted such a vulgar policy against the Japanese people. So far, the assault cases have not been numerous. Thus, if I am allowed to justify my earlier judgment, I wish to say that this degree of misconduct is really inevitable under these circumstances. But I know this is nothing but just an excuse, and as such is not an answer that truly satisfies my readers. It is lamentable that there have been soldiers so arrogant as to commit acts of violence, no matter how small the number thereof.
>
> In the United States, our Imperial Japanese troops have recently come to be criticized frequently for their outrageous behavior in overseas military arenas. Their torture of prisoners of war has also been

denounced. It has been insisted that offenders should be punished as war criminals. I feel remorseful about the alleged misconduct of Japanese military personnel in foreign lands—they must have been possessed by an evil spirit. If the allegations are indeed true, those criminals must be punished severely at the hands of the Japanese.

Comparing the conduct of the U.S. troops in Japan today with the behavior of the Imperial Japanese troops, some may claim that they are more or less the same in terms of their immorality. If that is so, then American criticism of the conduct of Japanese soldiers during World War II is a case of the pot calling the kettle black. How should we—or how can we—refute the argument that the behavior on both sides is more or less the same? Particularly in light of the atrocities that the Soviet Union, now a nation friendly to the United States, has been reported to have perpetrated, how should we rebut these arguments?

Needless to say, it is not my intention to aimlessly condemn the U.S. military or to excuse the conduct of Japanese soldiers. What worries me deeply is the negative impact of the U.S. military's failure to secure the trust of a war-defeated nation for the construction of future peace. The United States has claimed that it should aim at not only the physical disarmament of Japan, but also the psychological disarmament of the Japanese people. In other words, the United States has declared that it will accomplish the mission of embedding a pacifist philosophy in Japan. As a prerequisite, however, this calls for the U.S. military or the United States as a whole to be an agent suitable for the mission at hand. Otherwise, how could they step into the spirit of a foreign national? In the past, the United States devastated pacifists in Japan and prompted the rise of militarists in Japan by enacting foolhardy immigration laws in its home territory—laws that formed one of the remote causes of the recent war in the Far East. This is a view that has been accepted by Americans themselves. This reporter, therefore, hopes that Americans, both officials and private citizens, will sincerely reflect on their conduct.[7]

"This reporter," the author of the above reproach of U.S. military conduct, was likely Ishibashi Tanzan, president and editor in chief of the *Tōyō Keizai Shimpō* at that time. Interestingly, the Japanese people later chose both

7 "Shinchū-beigun no bōkō/sekai no heiwa kensetsu o samatagen" [Violent Conduct of the U.S. Occupation Forces/It Could Hamper Construction of World Peace] in *Tōyō Keizai Shimpō*, September 29, 1945, p. 2–3. The author quotes the text, which is in the possession of the publisher of the magazine.

Hatoyama Ichirō, whose monologue appeared in the September 15 issue of the *Asahi Shimbun*, and Ishibashi Tanzan, whom many believe penned the above editorial, as their prime ministers after the San Francisco peace treaty became effective—even though the CCD evidently found both men to be problematic.

Prior to the ban on the two publications above, Colonel Hoover had issued a Press Code for Japan (SCAPIN-33) on September 19.[8] The document, which formed a pair with the Radio Code for Japan (SCAPIN-43 of September 22, 1945), made its way to the Japanese press and publication circles on September 21.

SCAPIN-33, which would restrict Japan's linguistic space for six and a half years in place of SCAPIN-16, issued on September 10, reads as follows:

> General Headquarters
> United States Army Forces, Pacific
> Assistant Chief of Staff, G-2
> Civil Censorship Detachment
>
> 21 September 1945
>
> Code for Japanese Press
>
> In accordance with the Supreme Allied Commander's objective of establishing freedom of the press in Japan, a Press Code for Japan has been issued. This PRESS CODE, rather than being one of restrictions of the press, is one which is designed to educate the press of the Japanese in the responsibilities and meaning of a free press. Emphasis is placed on the truth of news and the elimination of propaganda. This Press Code will cover, in addition, all publications printed in Japan.
> 1. News must adhere strictly to the truth.
> 2. Nothing should be printed which might, directly or by inference, disturb the public tranquility.
> 3. There shall be no false or destructive criticism of the Allied Powers.
> 4. There shall be no destructive criticism of the Allied Occupation and nothing which might invite mistrust or resentment of those troops.
> 5. There shall be no mention or discussion of Allied troops movements unless such movements have been officially released.
> 6. News stories must be factually written and completely devoid of editorial opinion.

---

8 *Operations of Military and Civil Censorship*, Documentary Appendices (I), Appendix 22.

7. News stories shall not be colored to conform with any propaganda line.
8. Minor details of a news story must not be over-emphasized to stress or develop any propaganda line.
9. No news story shall be distorted by the omission of pertinent facts or details.
10. In the make-up of the newspaper no news story shall be given undue prominence for the purpose of establishing or developing any propaganda line.[9]

Considering that it was not until September 20 that Lieutenant Colonel C. W. Wadsworth and the rest of the core of the Civil Censorship Detachment, which had been stationed in Manila, joined Colonel Hoover, it is obvious that Colonel Hoover drafted the Press Code for Japan in a very short period of time, relying only on the assistance of the few available personnel.

It was thus only natural that this hastily compiled code later caused a number of practical problems. For instance, *Operations of Military and Civil Censorship*, USAFFE/SWPA/AFPAC/FEC, an internal document of the United States Army Forces in the Far East compiled in September 1950 after the dismantlement of the CCD, contains the following:

> Possibly the greatest censorship weakness lay in the realm of policy. The Civil Censorship Detachment functioned in Japan under the direction of documents, pertinent to the surveillance of the mass media of communication, that were nebulous and abstract to the point of providing little or no direction. The Press Code, for instance, on which the Radio and Pictorial Codes were based, ostensibly informed the Japanese Government of the contents of printed matter that would violate censorship. Yet, an analysis of the Code shows that <u>its ten points</u>, with the exception of the fifth, relative to the discussion of Allied troop movements, <u>serve as a catch-all designed to cover, and forbid, any news item whose suppression was desired, for whatever reasons.</u> The probable reason for this lack of specificity was that the Code was devised less than nine days after PPB had been established, and at that time the objectives of mass media censorship had not yet been clearly delineated. However, the fact that the Code was not subsequently modified and changed to bring its provisions into line with realistic

9 http://hittitemongolwomen.blogspot.jp/2015/07/press-code-for-japan-to-understand-fake.html (last visited on January 11, 2018).

editorial thought, was a policy weakness that caused many hardships to PPB personnel. . . . Point two is an extremely good example of this: "Nothing shall be printed which might, directly or by inference, disturb the public tranquility." This is, at the least, badly phrased. All news items are designed to prick and disturb "public tranquility." Any news item that did not do so would not be read. Perhaps the addition of the word "inflammatory," in some connotation, would have clarified this point.[10] (3. Criticism in Chapter 6: Overview, emphasis added)

The document continues with the following proposal in 4. Recommendations:

> Any future Press Code should be concise and explicit. It should constitute a policy more rigid than elastic, and one that is adhered to with no exceptions.[11]

Looking back from as objective a viewpoint as possible, however, the Press Code for Japan, which "serve[d] as a catch-all designed to cover, and forbid, any news item whose suppression was desired, for whatever reasons," must have been an extremely convenient tool for the CCD as a policy if not in terms of practical application.

Moreover, the code faithfully complied with a rather cynical observation: "While 'information that disturbs public tranquility' is a vague definition, it nevertheless is one which will enable suppression of any publication or radio station violating censorship," found in Brigadier General Thorpe's September 3 directive. Even though this code was, thus, a hastily compiled composition, it was not abolished or even revised until the end of the occupation of Japan on April 28, 1952—a circumstance attributable to the obscurity of the code, which allowed its flexible application.

While the Press Code for Japan and the Radio Code for Japan aimed for the direct restriction of Japan's press and journalism sector, the CCD also attempted to wedge itself between the Japanese government and news organizations through indirect restrictions. SCAPIN-51, dated September 24 and titled "Disassociation of Press from Government," was its first attempt.

> Office of the Supreme Commander for the Allied Powers
> AG 000.76 (24 Sep 45) CI 24 September 1945
> (SCAPIN - 51)

---

10 *Operations of Military and Civil Censorship*, p. 216–217.

11 Ibid., p. 217–218.

Memorandum for: Imperial Japanese Government
Through: Central Liaison Office, Tokyo
Subject: Disassociation of Press from Government

1. In order further to encourage liberal tendencies in Japan and establish free access to the news sources of the world, steps will be taken by the Japanese government forthwith to eliminate government-created barriers to dissemination of news and to remove itself from direct or indirect control of newspapers and news agencies.
2. No preferential treatment will be accorded to any news service now existing or which may be created. Foreign news services of all nations will be permitted to serve the press of Japan to the extent that press desires.
3. All communications facilities under government control shall be equally available to all national and international news agencies so that distribution of news within the Japanese home islands will not be the special privilege of one controlled organization.
4. The government will rescind its prohibition on reception of incoming wireless telegrams (foreign news) by any agency except the Ministry of Communications. Interception by any agency of radio news broadcast by the Allied Powers as a public service will be permitted. The property rights of news transmitted by recognized press services will be observed.
5. The present system of distribution of news within the home islands will be permitted under strict censorship until such time as private enterprise creates acceptable substitutes for the present monopoly.

For the Supreme Commander:
s/ Harold Fair
t/ Harold Fair
Lt Col, AGD
Asst Adjutant General[12]

Clearly, the directive intended to deal a fatal blow to the Dōmei News Agency, which had previously been banned from overseas activities. Three days later, Furuno Inosuke, Dōmei's president, announced his intention to dissolve the company.[13] On October 31, the board of directors approved the

12 *Operations of Military and Civil Censorship*, Documentary Appendices (I), Appendix 22.
13 Coughlin (1952), p. 24. *Nippon kin-gendaishi jiten* (1978), p. 461.

dissolution of the company, closing the books on Dōmei's 10-year history of wide-ranging activities.

A series of incidents took place immediately following the dissolution of Dōmei—events that tested the loyalty of Japanese newspapers.

On September 25, Frank Kluckhohn, a *New York Times* correspondent, and Hugh Baillie, head of the United Press (UP), became the first foreign journalists to receive an audience with Emperor Shōwa. Kluckhohn conducted his interview that morning; Baillie followed in the afternoon. Both interviews were released worldwide immediately. It was not until a few days later, however, that Japanese newspapers carried the interviews.[14]

On September 27, Emperor Shōwa visited General MacArthur at the American Embassy on his own volition. On this historical visit, the *Asahi Shimbun,* for instance, ran the following article and refrained from carrying the famous photo of the two at their meeting: the emperor in a swallow-tailed coat standing next to General MacArthur in an open-neck shirt at the American Embassy.

> His Imperial Majesty paid a visit to General Douglas MacArthur, Supreme Commander of the Allied Powers, on September 27 at the American Embassy in Enokizaka-chō, Akasaka-ku, Tokyo. This was an informal visit of His Majesty's own initiative. Dressed in a swallow-tailed coat and a silk hat, His Majesty rode a black official state limousine accompanied by Grand Chamberlain Fujita Hisanori and followed by an unceremonious procession of cars in which rode his entourage, including Ishiwata Sōtarō, minister of the Imperial Household; Tokudaiji Saneatsu, chamberlain; Court Physician Murayama; and Okumura, a general affairs official of the Imperial Household, instead of the customary Imperial cortège. The procession departed the Imperial Palace for the U.S. Embassy at 9:55 a.m. Received by Brigadier General Bonner F. Fellers and Major Faubion Bowers at the foyer, His Majesty met General MacArthur alone, with the aid of interpretation by Okumura. The entourage waited in the room next door. It was reported that His Majesty had a relaxed talk with General MacArthur for 35 minutes. His Majesty returned to the Imperial Palace at 10:45 a.m.[15]

---

14 Coughlin (1952), p. 24–25.

15 "Tennō Heika Makkāsā gensui o gohōmon/35-fun ni watari gokaidan" [His Majesty visited General MacArthur/25-minute long friendly talk], *The Asahi Shimbun*, September 28, 1945, p. 1.

When the formal photo and the interviews with Emperor Showa, which must have come via GHQ, appeared in Japanese newspapers on September 29, the Home Ministry immediately confiscated the papers and banned further distribution. Relevant here is Article 23 of the Press Law (promulgated in May 1909), which stipulated:

> Article 23: The Home Minister can ban the publication and distribution of newspaper articles that are found to be detrimental to public tranquility and order and liable of corrupting public morals. When necessary, he can confiscate these articles. When this occurs, the Home Minister can also forbid publication of articles with similar intentions.

The reason for banning the photo of Emperor Showa standing next to General MacArthur was self-evident. While Baillie's interview article was found to be free of potential complications, Kluckhohn's article was deemed problematic because it said, "He [Emperor Showa] had no intention of having his war rescript employed as former Premier Hideki Tojo had used it when Japan launched her attack on Pearl Harbor." It was judged that this exposé infringed on article 23 of the Press Law.[16]

In response to the inquiry from the UP, the secretary of the Board of Information explained:

> . . . It was traditional that the Emperor never accused any individual personally, that such accusations were left to the prime minister or some other public officials. . . . The Board believed that if the Japanese people thought the Emperor had made such an accusation, it "might have led to public disturbances." The ban was extended to the Baillie interview because the Board felt it would be unfair to permit the publication of one and ban the other . . .[17]

In short, the Home Ministry challenged SCAPIN-51 outright by using existing Japanese law to bluntly demand Japanese newspapers' loyalty to the state. This was tantamount to demanding that Japanese newspapers choose between allegiance to GHQ and loyalty to the state of Japan.

If there were two truths, the truth of the Allied Powers and the truth of Japan, which "truth" would Japanese newspapers opt for? If there were two

16 Coughlin (1952), p. 25–26.

17 Ibid.

censorships—that by the CCD and that by the Home Ministry of Japan—which one would Japanese newspapers choose to heed?

Thus, the reporting on the emperor unexpectedly raised the fundamental issue of where the Japanese news media's loyalty lay. And it appeared that the Japanese media, for the time being, chose to remain the Japanese media.

GHQ's response and retaliation to the Home Ministry was swift and relentless. The first blow came in the form of SCAPIN-66: Further Steps Toward Freedom of Press and Speech drafted by the CCD on September 27, 1945. It reads as follows:

> Office of the Supreme Commander for the Allied Powers
> AG 000.76 (27 Sep 45) CI   7 September 1945
> (SCAPIN - 66)
> Memorandum for: Imperial Japanese Government
> Through: Central Liaison Office, Tokyo
> Subject: Further Steps Toward Freedom of Press and Speech
>
> 1. The Japanese government forthwith will render inoperative the procedures for enforcement of peacetime and war-time restrictions on freedom of the press and freedom of communications.
> 2. Only such restrictions as are specifically approved by the Supreme Commander will be permitted in censorship of newspapers and other publications, wireless, and trans-oceanic telephone, cable, internal telephone and telegraph, mail, motion pictures or any other form of the written or spoken word.
> 3. Pending repeal of laws imposing restrictions which have given the government complete control of all channels of expression of public opinion their enforcement shall be suspended.
> 4. No punitive action shall be taken by the Japanese government against any newspaper or its publisher or employees for whatever policies or opinion it may express unless ordered by the Supreme Commander on the basis of publication of false news or reports disturbing public tranquility. The power of the government to revoke permission to publish, to arrest without prior approval of the Supreme Commander, to impose fines on publications and to curtail paper supplies as a punishment for editorial comment shall not be exercised.
> 5. Compulsory organizations of publishers and writers will be discontinued and voluntary organization will be encouraged.
> 6. No press bans will be issued by any government agency and no

pressure, direct or by inference, will be exerted on any medium to compel it to conform to any editorial policy not its own.

7. Steps shall be taken to repeal such parts of existing peacetime and war-time laws as are inconsistent with the Supreme Commander's directives of 10 September 1945 relating to dissemination of news, and of 24 September 1945 relating to disassociation of press from government; subject laws being:
    a. Shimbunshi-Ho
    b. Kokka Sodoin-Ho
    c. Shimbunshi-To-Keizai-Seigenrei
    d. Shimbun-Jigyo-Rei
    e. Genron, Shuppan, Shukai, Kessha Rinji Torishimari-Ho
    f. Genron, Shuppan, Shukai, Kessha To Rinji, Torishimari-Ho Shiko Kisoku
    g. Senji Keiji Tokubetsu-Ho
    h. Kokubo Hoan-Ho
    i. Ginki Hogo Ho
    j. Fuon Bunsho Torishimari-Ho
    k. Gunyo Shigen Himitsu Hogo Ho
    l. Juyo Sangyo Dantai Rei Oyobi Juyo Sangyo Dantai Rei Shiko Kisoku
8. A report will be submitted to the Supreme Commander on the first and the sixteenth day of each month describing in detail the progressive steps taken by the Japanese government to comply with this order and the orders of 10 September and 24 September.

FOR THE SUPREME COMMANDER:
s/ Harold Fair
t/ Harold Fair
Lt Col, AGD
Asst Adjutant General[18]

While this document was dated September 27, it was actually 11:30 in the morning of September 29 when the Japanese government received the directive.[19] The very day that the Home Ministry prohibited the publication

18 *Operations of Military and Civil Censorship*, Documentary Appendices (I), Appendix 22.

19 "Shimbun, genron no jiyū e/seigen hōrei o zenpai/rengōkoku shireikan, 'aratanaru sochi' tsūtatsu" [Toward Freer Press and Speech/All Restrictive Laws and Regulations to be Abolished/Supreme Commander for the Allied Forces Issues 'Further Steps Toward Freedom of Press and Speech'] in the *Asahi Shimbun*, September 30, 1945, p. 1.

of the emperor's photo and the articles by Baillie and Kluckhohn, the directive overruled the prohibition. The newspapers were distributed to readers after just a half-day delay.

Because of SCAPIN-66, the history-making photo of Emperor Shōwa with MacArthur as well as the interview by Clyde Kluckhohn were available to Japanese readers. The impact of SCAPIN-66 was much more profound than this one incident, however. SCAPIN-66 impacted subsequent journalism in Japan as a whole.

This was because the directive gave Japanese newspapers, their publishers, and their employees a privileged status in the sense that they would never be subject to sanctions by the Japanese government "for whatever policies or opinion [they] may express." (emphasis added). Because SCAPIN-66 assured Japanese newspapers they would be immune to government interventions no matter what policy or opinion they set out, even policies and opinions that could bring about dishonor or disadvantage to Japan were permissible—including those that, directly or by inference, aspired to the dissolution or annihilation of Japan as a state. In other words, the GHQ directive completely liberated Japanese newspapers from the duty to remain loyal to the state.

Newspapers in Japan were put fully under the supervision of the Supreme Commander for the Allied Forces (GHQ), a representative of the foreign authorities; as such, they were converted into mouthpieces for the supreme commander's views. In other words, newspapers in Japan came to speak for the values that GHQ represented. It goes without saying that censorship is a system that tests the loyalty of newspapers and other media organizations. Thus was the nature of the "freedom of speech" that Japanese media organizations obtained: for Japanese media organizations, that liberty was nothing but a coerced turnabout of allegiances. Japanese newspapers were unable to find any other way to survive and prosper commercially than to advocate the policies and opinions of the Allied forces.

An interesting document related to this development impacting Japanese newspapers sheds compelling light on the circumstances in play. Major Daniel C. Imboden, director of the Press and Publications Branch, Civil Information and Educational Section (CI&E), of the GHQ, gave a lecture on the freedom of the press to an audience of representatives of some eighty Japanese magazines on January 7, 1947; after the lecture came a question-and-answer session, which the document transcribes. The questions came from representatives of Japanese magazines, and Major Imboden himself answered all the questions. Below is a sampling of the discourse:

Q. About the publishing of salacious magazines, why hasn't Censorship taken action?
A. Have you read Gen. MacArthur's Press Code? (The answer was "yes.") Surely Japan has a Law against this type of magazine.
Q. The publishing law is out of existence. The only law of control is the Peace Preservation Law. That is also out of existence.
A. Then if that is true, what have the Japanese done about it?
Q. The Japanese people are leaving everything in the hands of CCD.
A. Japanese mothers bring to our office some of these magazines, saying that they are injuring their children's morals. I wonder if any of you have talked to the Governor here in Tokyo? He feels there is a law which can squelch these Japanese salacious magazines.
Q. I saw in the Japanese papers recently that there is no law in Japan which can control salacious magazines. The only thing the Japanese can do is suppress filthy pictures.
A. Do you have a magazine organization like the Japanese Editors' and Publishers' Association?
Q. Yes.
A. Do you have canons of journalism?
Q. We have our own society, but have no authority to control or do anything about the contents of magazines.
A. Do you have any canons or code like the Japanese Newspapers Publishers and Editors' Association in which you have agreed not to commit libel etc.?
Q. Japanese magazines have no press code, but should have one in the near future. If it is true that salacious magazines are being printed and circulated in Japan, I think it is because they have avoided censorship. The right of censorship has been transferred to CCD since the surrender. The Japanese can do nothing about it.
A. I think you are mistaken. The Japanese Government can do something about it if you people want it to. I can assure you that General MacArthur's Press Code does not encompass the printing of salacious literature. Have you ever considered where the newsprint comes from on which these magazines are printed?
Q. The black market.

. . .

Q. Are all Japanese publications subject to SCAP's direction?
A. No. We have attempted to assist the Japanese papers, and with some degree of success, in proper reporting of news items and in understanding the fundamental premise of freedom of the press.

We have attempted also to assist Japanese magazines publishers in publishing comprehensive articles when they so desired. We have attempted to give them a comprehensive insight into the operation of democratic papers and magazines. We have attempted to bring publishers up to date on how to educate themselves and their readers in democratic processes. I think you will find the magazine officer has many wonderful articles of value to your readers. We have not directed any Japanese publication. Of course we insist that the Press Code must be lived up to.

Q. So after all there is no such a thing as freedom of the press as far as the Japanese are concerned?

A. That is a trick question and will not be answered. No reference can be made to that insulting and impertinent question in any Japanese magazine.

Q. That was not intended as an insult. I thought we had a licensed press rather than a free press in Japan.

A. I will not discuss that. You are not in good faith. You are insincere.[20] (emphasis added)

This verbatim record of the questions and answers following Major Imboden's lecture is precious proof that Japanese publishers in those days had a fairly accurate grasp of the situation created by GHQ's SCAPIN-66 directive. Although they were well aware that there was no freedom of the press or freedom of speech in Japan, they were strictly banned from pointing that reality out or putting it in print.

In any event, the Japanese press was completely freed from a binding allegiance to its own country and instead coerced to obey a foreign authority completely. After 11:30 a.m. on September 29, 1945, Japanese media organizations in general—and newspapers, in particular—were converted into stateless organizations, an unprecedented situation in world history.

GHQ's retaliation went beyond SCAPIN-66. At 6:00 p.m. on October 4 came another directive, which imperiled the very existence of the Ministry of Home Affairs. The directive, SCAPIN-93, was titled "Removal of Restrictions on Political, Civil, and Religious Liberties."[21]

Drafted by the Government Section (GS) of the GHQ, the directive

---

20 *Magazine Conference 17 January 1947*. The National Records Center, Suitland, Maryland, RG 331, Box No. 8573.

21 *Political Reorientation of Japan, September 1945 to September 1948,* Westport, CT: Greenwood Press, Vol. II, Appendix B, 2nd, p. 463-465 (https://babel.hathitrust.org/cgi/pt?id=mdp.39015054029817&view=1up;seq=2 last visited on January 17, 2018)

essentially ordered (1) the immediate release of all political prisoners; (2) the abolishment of Special Higher Police to investigate and control political groups and ideologies deemed to be a threat to public order; (3) the removal from office and employment of the minister of home affairs, the chief of the Bureau of Police of the Ministry of Home Affairs, and other leaders of the national police organization; and (4) abrogation and immediate suspension of the operations of all provisions of all laws, decrees, orders, ordinances, and regulations that restricted freedom of thought, religion, assembly, or speech, including the Peace Preservation Law. The directive delivered a fatal blow to the Higashikuni cabinet, forcing its members to resign en masse.

At 11:00 a.m. on October 5, Major Peters, officer in charge of newspapers at the Civil Censorship Detachment, summoned the editors in chief of five national newspapers with headquarters in Tokyo to announce that the authorities would expand the pre-censorship, to which the Dōmei News Agency had been subject since September 14, to include their publications. Those five national dailies were the *Asahi Shimbun,* the *Mainichi Shimbun,* the *Yomiuri Shimbun,* the *Nippon Sangyo Keizai Shimbun,* and the *Tokyo Shimbun*.

Pre-censorship of these newspapers would begin on October 8, 1945, the announcement said.[22]

---

22 "Tokyo 5-shi ni jizen ken'etsu" [Pre-censorship on Five Tokyo Dailies], the *Asahi Shimbun,* October 6, 1945, p. 2.

CHAPTER 9

Shared Taboos

The second revision of the *AFPAC Basic Plan for Civil Censorship in Japan* was at last completed on September 30, 1945. Colonel Donald Hoover had to rush the revision of the Basic Plan, pushing his subordinates at the Civil Censorship Detachment (CCD) who had just arrived from Manila ten days earlier, while at the same time issuing a series of important directives.

The revision resulted in an official decision to establish a new Press, Pictorial, and Broadcast Division (PPB) within the CCD. Accordingly, the number of CCD personnel was also modified as follows:

Army Personnel: 234 commissioned officers (from the original 203 at the time of the first revision), and 546 noncommissioned officers and soldiers (from the original 420 at the time of the first revision)
Navy Personnel: 131 commissioned officers (from the original 288 at the time of the first revision), and 225 noncommissioned officers and marines (from the original 305 at the time of the first revision)[1]

Compared with the first revision of the Basic Plan, dated July 10, the second revision included a considerable reduction in naval manpower and, conversely, an expansion of army manpower. This indicates that the battle stage in the original plan was over and that the conditions of the occupation stage had also been totally transformed. The newly established PPB was manned entirely by U.S. Army personnel. In the second revision of the Basic Plan, the PPB's operations were stipulated as follows.

VIII. Operation of Press, Pictorial, and Broadcast Censorship
A. Basis of Operation
The Manual of Press, Pictorial, and Radio Broadcast Censorship in Japan is the basis of operating procedure. Directives of the Supreme Commander are incorporated immediately in the operations of this division.

1 *AFPAC Basic Plan for Civil Censorship in Japan*, revised September 30, 1945 by Chief of Counter-Intelligence, GHQ, AFPAC, p. 2, The National Records Center, Suitland, Maryland, RG 331, Box No. 8568.

B. Theory of Operation

The Press, Pictorial, and Broadcast Division is responsible for censorship of all material disseminated to the people of Japan through press, all forms of printed matter, news via agencies, radio, newsreels and motion pictures.

1. Press and Publications—Japanese newspapers in English are pre-censored. As far as personnel facilities permit, the major Japanese-language newspapers are pre-censored. All Japanese newspapers, other than the above, are post-censored.
2. News Agencies—All matter disseminated by any news agency inside Japan is pre-censored.
3. Radio broadcasts—News broadcasts are pre-censored. All other forms of voice broadcasts by Radio Tokyo, the only outlet as of the date of this plan, are submitted in script form for pre-censorship.
4. Pictorial—Rushes of Japanese newsreels are previewed and censored. The same system will apply to all motion pictures made by the Japanese. Additionally, other forms of entertainment which would fall under the form of propaganda media are censored.
5. Research Section—Makes checks on background of publishers and publications of Japan for use in special studies and analysis. Reactions of the Japanese people to various news items are surveyed by this group as the partial basis for reports prepared in the Information and Records Division.[2]

Based on the above, the authorities issued instructions concerning pre-censorship of magazines and other periodical publications to publishers in Japan. To paraphrase:

> Procedure for Pre-Publication Censorship of Magazines and Periodicals
>
> All publishers that intend to submit their magazines and other periodicals for pre-publication censorship should follow the following procedures:
>
> 1. Two identical galley proofs of the magazine to be censored should be submitted. Each galley proof must be a comprehensive copy complete with all the illustrations, the cover page, the colophon, the announcement of the next issue, the page num-

2 Ibid., p. 12.

bers, and the table of contents as well as all the print matter to be included in the finished magazine.

2. Galley proofs should be brought to the Newspaper and Magazine Censorship Division of the General Headquarters of the Supreme Commander for the Allied Powers located on the sixth floor of the Hōsō Kaikan, 2-2 Uchisaiwaichō, Kōjimachi-ku, Tokyo, by the magazine's editor-in-chief or equivalent.
3. Publishers outside the Tokyo metropolitan area, when given explicit permission to do so by the Newspaper and Magazine Censorship Division, can mail galley proofs of the magazine to be censored. After censorship is completed, however, someone in a responsible position with the magazine must report to the said Division to retrieve the galley proofs. The Division will not be responsible for the delayed arrival or loss of the mailed galley proofs.
4. a. A publisher submitting galley proofs for pre-publication censorship for the first time should also submit the following information, written both in Japanese and in roman letters:
   (1) Title of the magazine (and its English translation)
   (2) Name of the editor-in-chief
   (3) Name of the publisher
   (4) Location of the publisher
   (5) Frequency of publication (weekly, monthly, etc.)
   (6) Circulation
   (7) List price
   (8) Date of issue

   b. Changes to any of the above after submission should be conveyed to the said Division immediately.
5. The publisher should submit galley proofs for pre-publication censorship allowing plenty of time to revise the manuscript should revision be requested. It should be understood that the paper stencil should not be constructed until the publisher retrieves the approved galley and properly complies with all the revision instructions.
6. Censorship should be conducted on the basis of the articles of the Japan Publication Law issued by the Supreme Commander for the Allied Powers.
7. When the content of the submitted galley proofs of a magazine or other periodical is approved by the censors, a seal of approval will be stamped on the cover pages, after which one of the two submitted galley proofs will be returned to the publisher.

8. Portions to be deleted or eliminated are to be clearly marked on the submitted galley proofs with colored pencil. When the representative of the magazine comes to retrieve the galley proof, his attention will be called to these portions.
9. Corrections should always be made by resetting the type. Other methods, such as blacking out the portion to be corrected and leaving blank space, are unacceptable. After the revised galley proof is submitted, no addition or alteration is allowed without approval of the Newspaper and Magazine Censorship Division.
10. When magazines are published after required deletions are applied, two copies of the published magazine should be submitted to the said Division either directly or via mail. The submitted magazine will be compared with the previously submitted galley proofs to verify that all of the requested corrections have been properly made.
11. The publisher is not allowed to print, circulate, or market the magazine or other periodical until its representative retrieves one of the galley proofs submitted for pre-publication censorship and approved by the said Division.
12. Unless otherwise notified, pre-publication censorship on a magazine shall be continued for each issue through the above procedure.
13. The publisher should notify the said Division in writing that it has received these instructions.[3]

In addition, to supplement Article 9 of the aforementioned instructions, a note of caution (paraphrased below) was circulated among publishers. Obviously, the point was to drive home the need for censorship confidentiality.

Note of Caution to Publishers

1. When instructed to delete specific portions, reset the type. Do not resort to any of the following measures:
   (1) Blacking out the portion
   (2) Patching a white piece of paper over the portion
   (3) Filling up the portion with XXXX
   (4) Leaving the portion as blank space
   (5) Tearing off the page
2. Insertion, addition, deletion, or alteration of the cover, colophon, preface, table of contents, photos, advertisements, or any article is

3 The Prange Collection, East Asian Collection, University of Maryland.

not allowed without the Division's permission.

3. The galley proofs to be submitted should include all the articles to be bound as well as all the items listed in above 2. Two copies should be submitted.
4. All books must undergo pre-publication censorship without exception.
5. The censored galley proof should be retrieved on the designated date.
6. Use of such codes as =, ○, □, or × in the galley proofs should be avoided as much as possible and, when their use is unavoidable, make sure to add what they mean in kana or kanji.
7. Submission of the publication after printing should not be delayed for whatever reason.

Publication Section, Civil Censorship Detachment[4]

Related to item 7, the available primary documents include written apologies that publishers were obligated to present when they failed to submit a new publication to the CCD on time, even though the letters were written quite a few years later. Below are several examples:

(Paraphrase) Report of Delay in Submission
Submitted to:
Publication Section
Civil Censorship Detachment
~~Civil Information and Educational Section~~

Name of Author: Ishizaka Yōjirō
Name of Publication: *Basha Monogatari* (Tale of a Horse-Drawn Carriage)

We apologize for the delay in submission of the said book due to delay in the printing process.
July 20, 1948

Washio Yōzō (stamp)
Director of Publication
Bungei Shunjūsha[5]

---

4 Ibid.

5 Ibid.

Written in bold script with a calligraphy brush, the letter originally bore a target address reading "Civil Information and Educational Section," which was crossed out and amended to "Civil Censorship Detachment" by a different hand in pen. This and other similar cases seem to indicate that Japanese publishers often confused the CCD, a behind-the-scenes entity, with the Civil Information and Educational Section (CI&E), a visible organ. A considerable number of publication editors apparently submitted galley proofs and finished books to the CCD, believing that they were sending them to the CI&E.[6]

The CCD, which was mandated to conceal both its presence and its roles, did not bother to correct this confusion at every instance. Over time, the turf war between the CCD and the CI&E over jurisdiction of censorship became all the more internalized and, therefore, more combative. I will come back to this point later.

The second letter of apology was written on a Japanese typewriter. Given the frequent need to submit these apologies, publishers in Japan had apparently prepared boilerplate forms that they could fill out with the appropriate book titles, author names, and dates of submission.

> (Paraphrase) Letter of Apology
> Date: June 22, 1948
> To: Censorship Section, GHQ
> *Moto Zatsugeki Kenkyū* authored by Yoshikawa Kōjirō
>
> We accidentally put in the colophon of the said book a date of publication that was earlier than the actual date of publication. We hereto pledge that we shall avoid this kind of mistake as much as possible in the future.
>
> Iwanami Shoten (company seal)[7]

The letter of apology below was handwritten in pen.

> (Paraphrase) Reason for Delay in Registering a New Publication
> Date: June 17, 1948
> To: Books Section, Publication Censorship Division, Civil Censorship Detachment

6 The CCD partially occupied the sixth floor of the former Hōsō Kaikan building, where CI&E was also located on a different floor, contributing to the confusion among the Japanese publishers.

7 The Prange Collection, East Asian Collection, University of Maryland.

From: Mihashi Yoshitomo, Senior Managing Director
Meiji Shoin, Co. Ltd. (stamp)
Name of Book: *Chūko Bungakushiron*
Number of Volume: 1
Censorship Number: B1538

Although we were mandated to register publication of the said book no later than May 10, 1948, we failed to meet the deadline due to our hectic work schedule. We hope that this explanation is acceptable to you. We will try our best not to repeat this mistake and we ask for your forgiveness.[8]

A kind of complicity had naturally formed between the censors and their subjects through the concealment of the censorship and repeated apologies for delays in the requisite submissions of new publications.

For the Japanese newspapers and publishers subject to the censorship, the censor was a shadowy presence. They were uncertain whether the censor was the CCD or the CI&E. Nevertheless, they had to contact the censor, whether they liked it or not, as long as they continued to publish. And the moment they contacted the censor, they were mandated to keep the existence of censorship under wraps. In other words, they had no choice but to subscribe to the value system shaping the secrecy surrounding the censorship.

In effect, both sides were sharing a taboo. In every other aspect, the sides were in conflict with one another: the war victor and the loser, the conqueror and the conquered, the Americans and the Japanese, the censor and the journalists. Despite being in conflict in the "surface world," the two held hands tightly on one point in the shadowy, shady world. As far as the tacit agreement on the thorough concealment of the presence of censorship went, the censored were in no time drawn into intimate, collaborative relations with the censor.

Cultural anthropologists claim that a taboo is contagious. The *Encyclopedia of Religion and Ethics*, for example, observes, "Everything . . . which comes in contact with a tabooed person or thing becomes itself as dangerous as the original object, becomes a fresh center of infection, a fresh source of danger to the community."[9] In other words, the subject of censorship becomes a "thing that is as dangerous as the original object" by contacting

8 Ibid.

9 James Hastings, ed., *Encyclopedia of Religion and Ethics*, Edinburgh: T. & T. Clark, 1921, Vol. XII, p. 183, citing F.B. Jevons, *An Introduction to the History of Religion*, London, 1906, p. 61.

the "tabooed thing," upon which it becomes "a fresh center of infection" and, inevitably, "a fresh source of danger to the community."

What causes this infection of a taboo is fear—that is, the fear of "evil Japan" on the part of the censor and the fear of those who hide in the shadows, holding a life-or-death authority over them, on the part of the censored. The directive Further Steps Toward Freedom of Press and Speech (SCAPIN-66)—which liberated the Japanese press people and organizations from loyalty to the state—alone might not have been so effective in realizing GHQ's expectations without this fear factor. The surface "liberation" was able to affect the Japanese psychology and gain the leverage to transform that psyche only because of the accompanying fear element, on which the tacit agreement in the shadowy, shady world rested.

Important here is the notion that the most effective apparatus for infecting the censorship subjects with the taboo lay within the very structure of CCD's censorship, the top priority of which was to hide the existence of censorship at any cost. The censorship by the CCD in occupied Japan was also of a totally different nature relative to any type of censorship that the state authority had previously conducted in Japan.

Censorship by the Japanese government under the Publication Law, the Press Law, or the Press, Publication, Assembly, and Association Special Control Law was all announced publicly. As such, both the subjects of censorship and the Japanese people in general were fully aware of who the censors were. The expectation on those subject to censorship, then, was to avoid *violating* the taboo rather than *drawing attention* to it. This was because the Japanese censors demanded their censorship subjects share the same values, such as an intolerance toward blasphemy against the emperor.

In short, the domestic censorship by the Japanese state authority before and during World War II focused on prohibiting the mention of taboo topics. The emperor, the "national polity," or dangerous ideas were deemed taboos that could bring about "danger" and "infection" to the community when openly mentioned and, therefore, had to be strictly isolated. In other words, the censorship subjects and the Japanese people were basically "blindfolded," so to speak, by the state authority.

In contrast, the CCD's censorship made contact with taboos unavoidable. It aimed to have the censorship subjects deal with the taboos through the medium of concealed censorship. The censored, therefore, were lured into complicity. The censoring side intended to transform subjects into "a fresh center of infection" and "a fresh source of danger to the community" of "evil" Japan by making them party to taboos. In short, the ultimate goal of the GHQ was, in a way, to force the Japanese to hollow out their own eyes

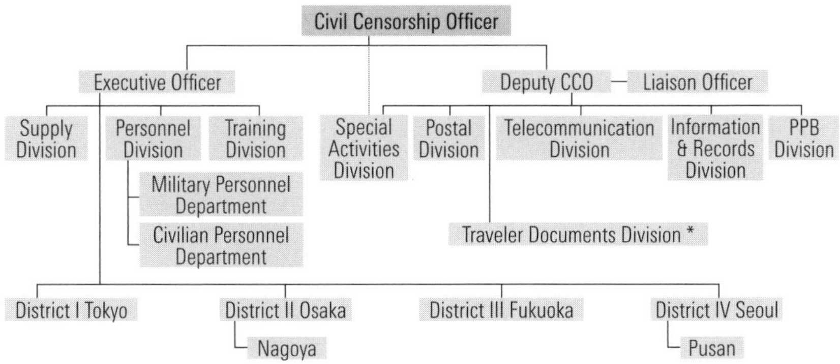

Figure 6. Organizational Chart of the Civil Censorship Detachment (CCD) (as of January 1946)
(Note: not actually established)

and implant artificial, U.S.-made eyes in their place.

The CCD organizational chart based on the second revision of the *AFPAC Basic Plan for Civil Censorship in Japan* (see Figure 6), sheds valuable light on the situation. The structure obviously took after the United States Office of Censorship (Part I, Chapter 4, Figure 1).[10]

Figure 7 shows the district-by-district deployment of CCD troops in Japan and southern Korea. According to this chart, the Japanese mainland was divided into three districts. The command center and headquarters of District 1 were located in Tokyo, the headquarters of District 2 in Osaka, and the headquarters of District 3 in Fukuoka. The District 4 headquarters were initially in Seoul, Korea, but operations later switched from the jurisdiction of the civil censorship officer (Civil Censorship Detachment) to the commander of the 24th Army as of July 15, 1947.[11] A new District 4 headquarters opened in Sapporo in October 1948.[12]

As noted earlier, the PPB commenced operations on September 10, 1945. PPB's censorship of newspapers and magazines began on September 26 in Fukuoka and October 23 in Osaka.[13] Figure 8 depicts the organizational structure of the PPB after its reorganization on December 21, 1948, one

10 Etō Jun, "Tozasareta gengo kūkan: Senryō gun no ken'etsu to sengo Nippon" [Closed Linguistic Space: Censhopship by the Occupation Forces and Postwar Japan], Monthly *Shokun*, February 1982, p. 69.

11 *Operations of Military and Civil Censorship*, p. 78.

12 Ibid., p. 79.

13 Ibid., p. 109.

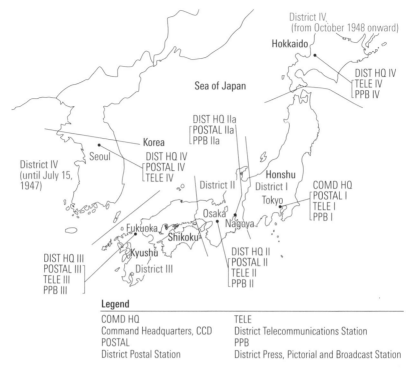

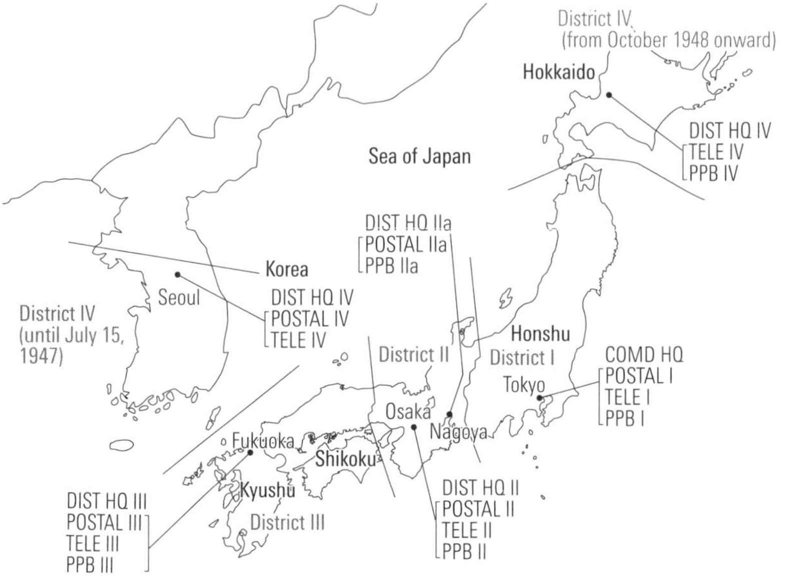

Legend

COMD HQ Command Headquarters, CCD	TELE District Telecommunications Station
POSTAL District Postal Station	PPB District Press, Pictorial and Broadcast Station

Figure 7. Deployment of CCD Troops in Japan and Southern Korea by District (as of December 1945)

that differed somewhat from the earlier, pre-reorganization structure that consisted of five divisions of personnel, newspapers, publications, motion pictures, and broadcasting and research.[14] Censorship of motion pictures began in October 1945.[15]

Branches of the PPB in each district operated in the following locations:

> (Paraphrase) District 1: Newspapers and publishers located in the prefectures of Tokyo, Hokkaidō, Akita, Aomori, Iwate, Fukushima, Miyagi, Yamagata, Gunma, Tochigi, Ibaraki, Chiba, Saitama, Kanagawa, Shizuoka, Nagano, and Yamanashi are to submit galley proofs and other specified products to the following address for censorship:
> For books and magazines

14 Ibid., p. 73.

15 Ibid., p. 109.

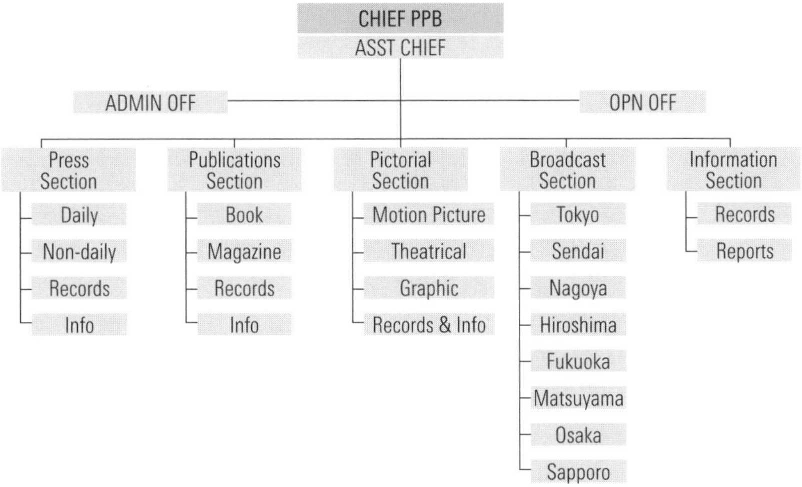

Figure 8. Organizational Structure of the Press, Pictorial, and Broadcast Division (PPB) (as of December 21, 1948)

Publication Department
PPB District 1
6th floor, Hōsō Kaikan
2-2, Uchisaiwai-chō
Kōjimachi-ku, Tokyo-to
(transferred later to 4th floor, Kantō Haiden Bldg., 1-1, Shiba-Tamura-chō, Minato-ku)

For newspapers

Newspaper Department
PPB District 1
Shisei Kaikan
Hibiya Kōen 2-gōchi
Kōjimachi-ku, Tokyo-to

District 2: Newspapers and publishers located in the prefectures of Ōsaka, Kyōto, Aichi, Gifu, Mie, Ishikawa, Toyama, Fukui, Hyōgo, Nara, Shiga, Wakayama, Okayama, Tottori, Ehime, Kōchi, Kagawa, and Tokushima are to submit galley proofs and other specified products to the following address for censorship:

Newspapers and Publications Department
PPB District 2
4th floor, Asahi Shimbunsha Bldg.

Nakanoshima, Kita-ku
Ōsaka-shi

District 3: Newspapers and publishers located in the prefectures of Fukuoka, Hiroshima, Shimane, Kagoshima, Kumamoto, Miyazaki, Ōita, Saga, Nagasaki, and Yamaguchi are to submit galley proofs and other specified products to the following address:
Publication Department
PPB District 3
Matsuya Bldg.
Hashiguchi-chō, Fukuoka-shi[16]

Figure 9 illustrates the workflow at the PPB's press section, which was similar to the process in the publication section. While the "Procedure of Pre-Publication Censorship on Magazines and Periodicals" only covered magazines and other periodicals, from the start of censorship, the PPB also demanded submission of two galley-proof copies of newspaper articles and books.[17] The Japanese personnel at the PPB were the first to peruse the submitted copies; they were looking for articles that ran counter to the censorship policy.

As I have noted several times, the CCD, from the beginning, suffered from a dearth of censors proficient in the Japanese language. Consequently, it was inevitable that the CCD had to employ Japanese nationals as censors under the supervision of personnel from the U.S. occupation forces. The Japanese censors translated newspaper headlines and tables of contents in magazines for review by U.S. military officers and civilian employees, who were their superiors.

When censors spotted articles and treatises subject to deletion or prohibition, they were instructed to test-translate them and report their findings to their superiors. Whenever a full, word-to-word translation was deemed necessary, however, the translation task was entrusted not to the Japanese censors, but to second-generation Japanese-American military personnel.[18] It goes without saying that the CCD did not trust the loyalty of the Japanese censors. More than that, the Japanese censors were given no power to make decisions, nor were they eligible for promotions to managerial posts. From a Japanese perspective, in a way, that might have been a blessing in disguise.

16 The Prange Collection, East Asian Collection, University of Maryland.

17 *Operations of Military and Civil Censorship*, p. 123–124.

18 Ibid., p. 118–120.

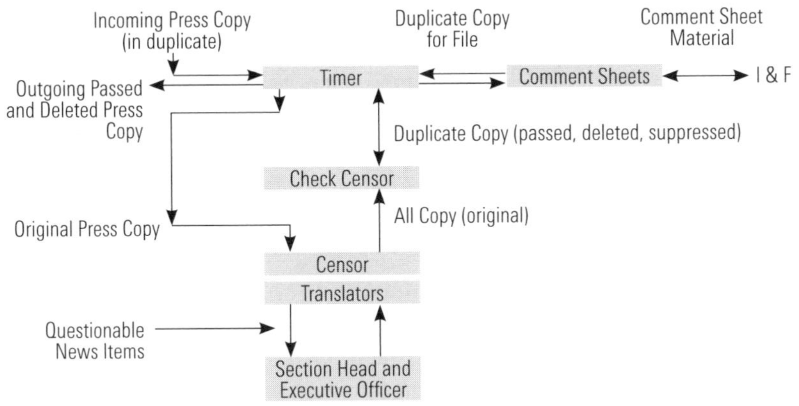

Figure 9. Flow Chart
Workflow at the Press Section of the PPB

The frequently quoted *Operations of Military and Civil Censorship* presents the following accurate observation on the working attitudes of the Japanese censors:

> Attitudes of recalcitrance, hostility, or fear of being labeled collaborationist, were conspicuously absent, or if extant, were well hidden.[19]

When the final decision was made on a selected article, instructions were scribbled on both galley-proof copies. One copy was sent back to the newspaper or publisher, and the other was kept at the CCD to be compared with what was actually published. The articles deemed permissible were marked with the censorship stamp; those articles that were earmarked for deletion or prohibition were marked with notifications in red ink. Newspapers and publishers were instructed to save the returned galley proofs for a certain period of time as evidence of permission for publication.[20]

As of March 1947, two years into the occupation, the CCD consisted of 88 commissioned military officers, 80 noncommissioned officers, 370 military civilians, 554 civilians from the Allied powers, and 5,076 Japanese citizens for a total complement of 6,168.[21] Of that total, records show, PPB personnel comprised 18 percent of the commissioned officers, 14 percent

---

19 Ibid., p. 119.

20 Ibid., p. 193–194.

21 *Civil Censorship Operations in Europe Compared with This Theater*, The National Records Center, RG 331, Box No. 8573.

of the noncommissioned officers, and 29 percent of the military civilians.[22] Although there are no records of the percentages of Japanese censors who worked for the PPB, one can conjecture that at least 30 percent of the PPB censors, or more than 1,500 of the total, were Japanese censors who engaged daily in the censorship of Japanese newspapers and magazines.

Ironically, it was the Japanese government that had to pay the Japanese censors' wages. This was because of the principle that called for the Japanese government to hire the Japanese citizens who worked for the Allied forces, set their wages, and pay accordingly. According to the Japanese government's "Table of Standard Wages for Full-Time Employees of the Allied Forces" effective as of January 16, 1946, Japanese censors were classified as professionals equivalent to "specialty interpreters/translators" and paid either ¥700 to ¥900 per month (in the case of "ordinary workers") or ¥900 to ¥1,200 per month (in the case of "expert workers"),[23] making them the highest-paid full-time Japanese employees of the Allied forces. Given the scarcity of Japanese censors, applicants who passed the examination then underwent further training for a certain period. Those who completed the training and were deemed employable were paid ¥350 per month to undergo further training, after which they entered formal employment.[24]

In light of this fact, the initial motivation of those who applied to work as CCD censors must have been, almost without exception, financial. The Japanese people in those days had to avoid starvation, first and foremost—and that meant taking full advantage of whatever abilities they had. In return for language ability, the CCD offered those who had lived in the United States, teachers of English, university professors, former diplomats, or students with confidence in their proficiency in English wages as high as ¥700 per month and sometimes even ¥1,200 per month. And the moment these applicants got hold of the compensation that the CCD offered, they automatically belonged to that shady, shadowy world.

Some of the Japanese CCD censors have already passed away, while some are still very much active today. If one adds the number of Japanese citizens who were employed by the Allied Translators and Interpreters Section (ATIS) to the some 5,000 Japanese CCD censors, the total would easily exceed 10,000. It is an open secret in some corners that this 10,000 includes people who later became heads of reformist local governments, executives of

---

22 Ibid.

23 Shūsen Renraku Chūō Jimukyoku Sōmubu Dai 1-ka, ed., *Shūsen jimu jōhō* [War termination operations information], No. 6, p. 19.

24 Interview with a person associated with the CCD.

major corporations, international lawyers, prominent journalists, editors of academic journals, and university professors. Needless to say, none of them included their CCD experience in their curricula vitae.

Whether those Japanese censors at the bottom of the censor hierarchy were required to maintain confidentiality about their duties—just like newspapers and magazines to be censored were instructed to keep silent about the censorship—or for other reasons, the Japanese censors, too, remained silent about the censorship. The people submerged in the first layer of postwar Japan's linguistic space were thus silent—and the depth of that silence perfectly corresponded to that of the shady, shadowy world.

Incidentally, the CCD opened a Censorship School for PPB personnel for six days (January 21–26, 1946). During those six days, four instructors (army first lieutenants Garner, Zahn, Bedigan, and Folkenstein [spellings unconfirmed]) gave one-hour classes from 9:15 to 10:15 every morning. Judging from the sixth rule in the guideline for the teachers at this school, which stressed that lectures must be slow-paced and easy to understand due to the students' limited English proficiency, the students must have been newly employed Japanese censors. The classroom was set up in a studio on the fourth floor of the former Hōsō Kaikan building in Uchisaiwai-chō.[25]

When all six classes were complete, fifty-one students took a Censorship School quiz consisting of the following questions on February 2.[26]

Censorship School QUIZ[27] 2 February 1946

1	Any article defending the Tenno System will always be considered a violation. FALSE
2	One of the principal aims of Censorship is to improve the morals of the Japanese people. FALSE
3	An article which stated that the occupation forces have issued ¥3,000,000 since occupying Japan would not be a violation of par 5 of the Press Code. TRUE
4	A news item simply stating that a Korean had been arrested for shooting 3 Japanese in Tokyo would not be a violation of the Press Code. TRUE

25 *Censorship School*, The National Records Center, RG 331, Box No. 8568.

26 *Censorship School-Quiz*, ibid.

27 Ibid.

5	An article which praised the American Occupation of Korea and criticized the Russian Occupation would not be a violation of the Press Code. FALSE
6	An article which states that State Shintoism should be encouraged would be a violation of the Press Code. TRUE
7	An article stating that an organized gang of 150 Chinese is terrorizing the people of Niigata prefecture would not be considered a violation. FALSE
8	An article stating that the Greater East Asia War was necessary to promote the peace of the world would be a violation. TRUE
9	An article implying that for the good of Japan no Allied troops except the American Forces should be allowed to occupy Japan would not be a violation. FALSE
10	If a newspaper reported in a straight news report which had been officially released that the Russian Forces were moving in to help occupy Japan and then added that in the opinion of the editor this was a good thing this would not be considered a violation. FALSE
11	A newspaper may take a news story and omit pertinent facts or details in order to have the news item conform to the policy of the paper. FALSE
12	In setting up its copy a newspaper printed a story about a Japanese being shot by a Chinaman and put it on the front page in a prominent place. This would not be considered a violation. FALSE
13	A magazine article reporting a formula for making a food substitute would be considered important enough to make an information item out of it. TRUE
14	It is permissible for a publisher to black out or paste strips over any items which are deleted by censorship so people can't read what was deleted. FALSE

15	A magazine article stating that America is trying to make Christians out of all the Japanese and that in the writer's opinion this is a good thing would be approved. FALSE
16	An article reporting that in Kanagawa Prefecture the thought police, in the opinion of the writer, are still operating would not be considered important enough to make an information item out of it, for the reason that GHQ could be expected to know about it anyway. FALSE
17	One of the principal aims of censorship is to keep foolish opinions from being printed. FALSE
18	The press code covers only news items and editorials, it does not cover advertisements. FALSE
19	There are 3 main types of censorship. FALSE
20	An article advocating total abolition of Buddhism would be passed as helpful to the occupation. FALSE

The breakdown of scores was:

100%	K. Arai, N. Kawamoto, J. Kawsjy, R. Kiriyama, Y. Kobayashi, J.A. Sargent, K. Suganuma, M. Yamamoto, Y. Yamamoto, M. Yukawa
95%	S. Furuya, M. Taniguchi, Saitō, M. Miyazaki, H. Pringsheim, H. Terada, N. Sakai, Gene Kiriyama
90%	T. Kanno, Klaus Pringsheim, K. Katsube, Miho, Y. Akiyoshi, T. Ōta
85%	T. Sasaki, T. Shimoyama, Y. Terasawa, M. Tateno, S. Ikehara
80%	S. Mitsuoka, R. Matsumoto, H. Itō, K. Ishii, M. Ōta, S. Nakamura
75%	J. Takeda, S. Arima, H. Nakamura, K. Saegusa, H. Yamauchi, T. Ōshima, N. Monma

70%	Ka Tai, I. Motohashi, S. Nakamura, S. Senda
65%	S. Ozeki
50%	A. Numano, R. Kimishima, T. Uchida, H. Tanaka

Note: Spellings of names could not be confirmed.[28]

Although it rarely happened, some of the Japanese censors were dismissed despite undergoing rigorous testing. Terasawa Yoshitaka, who scored 85% on the quiz and secured the post of senior censor/translator, was one such rare case. To paraphrase:

> Publication and Broadcast Section
> District I
> Civil Censorship Detachment
> General Headquarters, Supreme Commander for the Allied Powers
>
> September 9, 1946
>
> Richard H. Kunzman
> Censor
> Publication and Broadcast Section
> District I
> Civil Censorship Detachment
>
> Memorandum #19
>
> Re: Dismissal of Mr. Yoshitaka Terasawa
>
> Yoshitaka Terasawa
> Senior Censorship Translator
> Magazine Section, Publication Division
>
> 1. Civil Censorship Detachment has dismissed the above-cited person as of today for the following reasons: (1) Terasawa secretly conferred with a Japanese publisher on book censorship procedures; and (2) Terasawa showed defiance at the office of censors of the Civil Censorship Detachment, which could be interpreted as interference.

28 Ibid.

2. The above-cited was repeatedly warned that, unless specifically authorized by the Civil Censorship Detachment, personnel are not allowed to confer with publishers. When a publisher friend of the Civil Censorship Detachment personnel questions the censorship procedure, it is advised that this person should refrain from providing any authoritative information and, instead, refer his friend's questions to an appropriate section chief.[29]

The name of Sakagami Minoru, another Japanese censor who ended up being dismissed around the same time, does not appear in the student roster of the Censorship School. He was fired for mishandling a news photo. Again, to paraphrase:

September 18, 1946
Operational Management Memorandum #21

Dismissal of Personnel
1. Minoru Sakagami, Article Censor, News Agency Division, is dismissed as of today for negligence.
2. Any censor of the News Agency Division should be fully aware that handling of such a photo as the one of the U.S. M.P. lieutenant lighting a cigarette for former General Tōjō should be subject to consultation with his supervisor for the decision of the section in charge at the General Headquarters of the Supreme Commander for the Allied Powers.

Richard H. Kunzman
Censor[30]

These two dismissal letters suggest that the Japanese censors at the bottom of the censors' hierarchy were the first to be deeply indoctrinated in the CCD's censorship policy. The Japanese censors subsequently and unerringly passed that policy on to censorship subjects through comments and requests. It is apparent from documents at the National Records Center that, by the end of November 1946, two months after the dismissals of Terasawa and Sakagami, the following guideline on censorship had been compiled:

1. Criticism of SCAP:

29 The Prange Collection, East Asian Collection, University of Maryland
30 Ibid.

This is any general criticism of SCAP and criticism of any SCAP agency not specifically listed below.

2. Criticism of Military Tribunal:
   This is any general criticism of the Military Tribunal or specific criticism of anyone or thing connected with the Tribunal.
3. Criticism of SCAP Writing the Constitution:
   Any reference to the part played by SCAP in writing the new Japanese Constitution or any criticism of the part played by SCAP in the formation of the Constitution.
4. References to Censorship:
   Indirect or direct references to censorship of press, movies, newspapers, or magazines fall into this category.
5. Criticism of the United States:
   Any criticism, direct or indirect, of the United States, falls into this category.
6. Criticism of Russia:
   Any criticism of Russia, direct or indirect, falls into this category.
7. Criticism of Britain:
   Any criticism of Britain, direct or indirect, falls into this category.
8. Criticism of Koreans:
   Any criticism of Koreans, direct or indirect, falls into this category.
9. Criticism of China:
   Any criticism of China, direct or indirect, falls into this category.
10. Criticism of Other Allies:
    Any criticism of other Allies, direct or indirect, falls into this category.
11. General Criticism of Allies:
    General criticism of the Allies, not directed at any specific country falls into this category.
12. Criticism of Japanese Treatment in Manchuria:
    Criticisms referring specifically to treatment of Japanese in Manchuria falls into this category. These are not to be listed under criticism of Russia or China.
13. Criticism of Allies' Pre-War Policies:
    Any criticism of any policies of the Allies, singly or together, which existed prior to the war fall into this category. If criticism falls into this category, it will not be listed under criticism of any specific country.
14. Third World War Comment:
    Deletions made on the subject of the Third World War will be

included here, rather than under criticism of any particular country.

15. Russia vs. Western Powers Comments:
    Comments on the situation existing between the Western Powers and Russia fall into this category, and will not be listed under criticisms of Russia or any of the Western powers.
16. Defense of War Propaganda:
    Any propaganda which directly or indirectly defends Japan's conduct of and in the War will fall into this category.
17. Divine Descent Nation Propaganda:
    Propaganda which either directly or indirectly claims divine descent for either the Nation of Japan or the Emperor will fall into this category.
18. Militaristic Propaganda:
    This includes all propaganda strictly militaristic in nature, which is not included under Defense of War Propaganda.
19. Nationalistic Propaganda:
    This includes all propaganda strictly nationalistic in nature, but will not include militaristic, defense of war, or divine descent nation propaganda.
20. Greater East Asia Propaganda:
    This includes only propaganda relating to Great East Asia and will not include militaristic, nationalistic, defense of war, divine descent nation, or other propaganda.
21. Other Propaganda:
    This includes all other types of propaganda not specifically included above.
22. Justification or Defense of War Criminals:
    Any justification or defense of war criminals will fall under this category. It will not include criticisms of the Military Tribunal, however.
23. Fraternization:
    This will include stories dealing strictly with fraternization. These stories will not be included under criticism of the United States.
24. Black Market Activities:
    Reference to black market activities will fall into this category.
25. Criticism of Occupation Forces:
    Criticism of the Occupation Forces will fall into this category and will not therefore be included under criticism of any country.
26. Overplaying Starvation:
    Stories overplaying starvation in Japan will be under this category.

27. Incitement to Violence and Unrest:
    Stories of this nature will be included here.
28. Untrue Statements:
    Palpably untrue statements will fall into this category.
29. Inappropriate reference to SCAP or local military units.
30. Premature disclosure.[31]

Behind these thirty guidelines, as the document clearly suggests, was the intention to overhaul the traditional value system that the Japanese people had long cherished.

The only point at which the censored and the censor came into contact in the web of new taboos stretching around the Japanese people was the censorship and its concealment, as stipulated by the fourth prohibition in the censorship guideline. By repeating the process of being censored and keeping it secret, the subjects of censorship gradually became entangled in this web. By accepting new taboos themselves, the censored were transformed into "a fresh source of danger" to destroy the traditional value system that had supported the community of "evil" Japan.

In my view, this interactive process—the self-reproduction of new taboos through self-destruction—likely still persists in postwar Japan's linguistic space.

31 *A Brief Explanation of the Categories of Deletions and Suppressions*, dated November 25, 1946, The National Records Center, RG 331, Box No. 8568.

CHAPTER 10

Perspectives in a Closed Linguistic Space

A woman residing in Osaka wrote a letter and mailed it to a person incarcerated in the Sugamo Prison on suspicion of being a Class B war criminal. To paraphrase:

> Second Lieutenant Fujimori was kind enough to visit me and describe the detention center where you have been incarcerated. He warned me that it was nothing short of a regular prison.
>
> I have been lamenting over and over that, had you been a noncommissioned officer instead of a commissioned officer, you might never have been arrested.
>
> Knowing you well, I can swear that you can never have been abusive to prisoners of war. Whoever informed against you—I am shaking with outrage at the prisoner of war who repaid your kindness with ingratitude.
>
> But it is all because Japan lost a war that we have to put up with this kind of misery, isn't it?[1]

This letter was dated December 29, 1945, and the sender had apparently included her own photo in the envelope. She again wrote to the same person, who was presumed to be a young military officer, on February 3, 1946. In paraphrase, that letter read:

> I have been reliving the happy memories of working together with you in the office over and over. Although people say that working in the detention center is highly unpleasant, I consider myself lucky to have worked together with such a splendid gentleman like you. I have not worked anywhere else since then, because there can be no other working experience as enjoyable as the time I shared with you at the detention center. Alas, how short-lived that moment was! Every time I heard the air-raid warning siren, how I wished I could rush to the same bomb shelter with you! I would have been satisfied if I could

1 *Sympathetic Letter to War Criminal Suspect*, The National Records Center, Suitland, Maryland, RG 331, Box No. 8578, 86.

> have died with you. I don't think you were aware that I adored you so much. Since you are gone, my heart has been empty.
>
> But, in a sense, I also breathe easier now, since I no longer have to endure such heartache.[2]

I cannot forget, even today, the indescribable sensation that I experienced when I first read these letters in English translation in the reading room of the National Records Center in Suitland, Maryland. Even though it was typed on a standard comment form from the postal division of the Civil Censorship Detachment (CCD), I felt as if this sheet of paper vividly conveyed the writer's passionate adoration.

At the same time, I shuddered at the evidence in front of my eyes; a record of the fact that the CCD's censorship had reached even into the words emanating from someone's most intimate thoughts.

In a way, it might have been inevitable that a personal letter addressed to a war criminal suspect would be unsealed and exposed to the blunt scrutiny of a censor. To paraphrase linguist Ferdinand de Saussure, the CCD's censorship scrutinized even the deepest part of *parole* (language as manifested in the actual utterances produced by speakers of a language or, simply put, personal language as contrasted with *langue*, or social language)—equivalent to the censorship of a literary work. In other words, the CCD's censorship stretched beyond simply modifying the paradigm of *langue*, which formed the linguistic space of the Japanese language. What the CCD's censorship intended was to lower its sounding line into the very depths of *parole*. Given the nature of language, of course, there is no way to modify the paradigm of *langue* without attempting to transform *parole*.

The notion that the paradigm underlying *langue* (and, therefore, also *parole,* which is correlative with *langue*) is malleable to artificial, political modifications must have been alien to Saussure, who died on the eve of World War I.[3] But it was possible for the CCD. Coupled with the Japanese language-education policy promoted by the Civil Information and Education Section (CI&E)—the compulsory use of the *tōyō kanjihyō* (standard list of daily-use kanji) and adoption of *shin kanazukai* (new *kana* orthography)—the CCD at least contributed to making the impossible possible to no small extent.

This plaintive love letter that I dug out at Suitland was just a tiny drop in the sea of, on average, 19 to 20 million mail correspondences that the CCD's

---

2 Ibid., 234.

3 Ferdinand de Saussure (1857–1913).

postal division handled per month. Of these, the CCD unsealed some 4 million personal letters for closer scrutiny. In addition, the telephone and telegram division of the CCD censored some 3.5 million telegrams and tapped about 25,000 telephone conversations every month.[4] The CCD's bylaws included specific instructions on personal letters addressed to war criminal suspects:

> 2. Mail to war crimes prisoners who have been condemned to death and to or from all other classes of prisoners will be examined on its merits by the intercepting station and allowed to pass if unobjectionable.[5]

The handbook of the CCD's technical operations division (special activities division) gave the following strict directions on how to unseal personal letters:

> In dealing with individuals, it is dangerous to use secret censorship on all their communications. In dealing with organizations, at least 3% of the mail examined should be cut open and sealed. The message analyst in charge of the watch-list should attempt to ascertain from external appearances which letters contain innocuous messages. These should be cut open. If necessary, all communications can be steamed and the ones which proved to be innocuous can be cut open and sealed with tape after the secret sealing has been accomplished.[6]

In addition, the same handbook stressed that it was essential that the examination of watch-list mail not become a routine job and that no letters be examined purely on the basis of any established rules. Any contact may be important. Any letter may have a hidden message.[7]

Evidently, the CCD intended to concentrate on gathering information through censorship of postal mail, telephones, and telegrams in interlocking tandem with censorship of media like newspapers and magazines.

The function of civil censorship as the authority's restriction and regulation of speech and expression was only one side of a shield. Civil censorship also functioned as a source of information—and in enormous amounts.

4 *Operations of Military and Civilian Censorship*, Documentary Appendices (I), Vol. X, Intelligence Series, Appendix 3, Introduction.

5 Ibid., (II) Appendix 35, p. 62.

6 Ibid., (II) Appendix 38, p. 19.

7 Ibid., (II) Appendix 38, p. 18.

Information that was deleted or prohibited was not necessarily the only valuable intelligence, either. One cannot argue, then, that the information deemed harmless had no intelligence value. While information, of course, could also be collected from publications, it could be more efficiently tapped through censorship of personal letters. It was in these letters that the true, inner feelings of the Japanese people were revealed.

Taking these points into consideration, the CCD started a Public Opinion Tally in September 1946. Dividing all of Japan into nine districts, the CCD randomly drew 500 personal letters from each area (4,500 letters altogether) on a daily basis to unseal and read. The objective was to detect trends in Japanese public opinion on a few predetermined items. In December of the same year, the number of letters for sampling grew from 500 per day per district to 1,500 and, consequently, the CCD selected and studied as many as 337,500 letters a month. As a result, the CCD became capable of grasping trends in public sentiment more accurately than any public-opinion agency could even dream of.[8]

In the eyes of John LaCerda, an American journalist who visited Japan around the time, the effect of the CCD's censorship on newspapers and magazines in Japan appeared to be as follows.

> Within the limits of the liberal censorship which the occupation forces maintain, the press is permitted fairly free discussion. Editorial writers are aware of the social, political, and cultural differences between Russia and America. They are permitted to state their preferences and say why. But the comparisons are not generally invidious. Actually, comments on American beliefs and customs are generally so favorable as to be almost sycophantic.[9] (emphasis added)

This observation shows that, by that time, Japanese journalism had already been converted almost perfectly into the CCD's journalism. Nevertheless, contrary to the tone of newspapers, which were "generally so favorable as to be almost sycophantic," CCD people were accurately aware that the Japanese people still continued to maintain a certain sort of pride, at least inwardly. This should be obvious, for instance, from the following testimony:

> Letters intercepted from the Japanese mails, and to which I was given

8 *Operations of Military and Civil Censorship*, Chapter III. p. 89.

9 *American Opinion about Censorship in Japan*, The National Records Center, Suitland, Maryland, RG 331, Box No. 8575. John LaCerda, *The Conqueror Comes to Tea: Japan Under MacArthur*, New Brunswick: Rutgers University Press, 1946, p. 110.

access by American intelligence censors, indicated what the people are privately thinking. Look at these excerpts from letters which can be described as typifying the feelings of those who refuse to accept Japan's defeat as more than temporary and transitory.[10] (emphasis added)

Paul Vincent Miller, another American journalist, arrived in Japan in the spring of 1947, a few months later than LaCerda. Miller reported on the general condition of the CCD's censorship somewhat more critically. The following is a rather lengthy quote, but it provides a good clue to the overall picture of the contemporary situation.

> Quietly, unobtrusively, the Censor is at work in Japan. The quality of the censorship may be gauged by the following *haiku*, a Japanese poem of 17 syllables, which was submitted to the American authorities for pre-publication censorship and suppressed as containing material against American interests:
>
> "Small green vegetables
> are growing in the rain
> along the burned street."
>
> The reference is to a scene so familiar in present-day Japan, that of vegetable gardens planted by the Japanese wherever there is an available piece of ground whether it be along a busy thoroughfare or among ruins.
>
> And should you presume the above is simply an isolated case, consider the following:
>
> "It seems to be a dream far, far away
> that we wielded bamboo spears
> priced at only one yen and twenty sen
> against the big gun and giant ships."
>
> The reference here is to the fact that during the last days of the war the Japanese Government had instituted a kind of Home Guard equipped only with bamboo poles as weapons.
>
> It is rather difficult to determine why these poems were deemed dangerous. The *haiku*, as prescribed by long tradition, strives merely

10 Ibid., p. 22–23.

to evoke a mood by means of a paradox. The second poem probably is best interpreted as a wry comment by a Japanese on the astonishing lengths to which his war leaders could go in publicizing their asininity. Other interpretations of this second poem are possible, but they would not represent so well the current preference of the Japanese for sardonic comments on their political and military immaturity—an attitude that is commendable both for its common sense and its humility.

But the American authorities in Japan are very touchy about criticism. Indeed, when one Japanese writes a personal letter to another he has to be very careful not to express a derogatory opinion about censorship because censorship stations located in Tokyo, Osaka, Fukuoka, and Nagoya are very busy looking for just such things. The italicized portion of the following personal letter, sent by one Japanese civilian to another, was deleted by the censor:

> . . . As I have not received your answer to my letter which was probably mailed on the 10th and in which I enclosed my photograph taken in January, I am anxious to know what has become of it. *Because the Occupation Forces now censoring in Hakata are ill-reputed, I had some misgivings in sending a letter to you, and I was awaiting your answer still more eagerly.* I suppose it must have been lost on its way . . .

Not all letters received this kind of treatment. More frequently the offensive item is transcribed to what is known as a "comment sheet," which is forwarded to the main office in Tokyo. The original letter then is directed to the proper person without deletion. The following excerpt from another letter was not deleted, although the sentiments expressed probably are more bitter than those found in the first example:

> . . . Most of the letters are examined these days, you know. This is quite provoking. Although freedom of speech and freedom of thought are loudly proclaimed, at present day they are more limited than during the war...

On the basis of thousands of comment sheets pouring into Tokyo every week the Civil Censorship Detachment of GHQ has been able to state in its official publication:

> Broadly, the attitude toward SCAP and its policies is still favor-

able. However, strong exception is taken to certain directives and to the controls maintained on the press and, above all, to postal censorship, which Japanese in increasing numbers are criticizing.

From this and other statements issued by the Civil Censorship Detachment it is safe to say, first, that the American authorities are aware that our censorship policy is creating considerable bad feeling, and secondly, that they feel, despite the antagonism created, that the policy should be continued. But inasmuch as the reasons have been enshrouded in a mysterious secrecy the American observer cannot be blamed for viewing the whole situation with some suspicion, especially when he learns that deliberate efforts have been made to keep such information away from people in the United States.

Unfortunately I am not able to quote verbatim a memorandum sent by a high-ranking policy-making officer to the several District Censorship Stations throughout Japan and Korea but the substance of it was this: *that extreme secrecy must be maintained concerning all censorship operations inasmuch as there are groups in Congress and among the American people who would be adverse to the censorship policy. Those people must not be given access to the facts.*

While one naturally will make allowances for the fact that our military caste frequently prefers to impose a veil of secrecy over operations which, when disclosed, sometimes prove to have been quite offensive, one cannot avoid feeling uneasiness when a function so dangerous as censorship is wrapped in obscurity. Moreover, this uneasiness certainly is not allayed when the military authorities attempt to curtail the activities of American correspondents in Japan. One can find some justification in the exercise of censorship powers over a defeated nation which, at least theoretically, is still capable of disturbing the peace, but one finds it very hard to see how Americans, too, have deserved to be denied the opportunity to hear the truth.

Too much news is cut at the source so that the American public gets a bare trickle of information. There is hardly a day goes by in Japan when some important story does not come over the teletype machines with instructions from higher headquarters that it be canceled. Such was the story about the American general who stated that war with Russia could be expected not in a matter of years, months, or even weeks, but in a matter of days, and that the United States was making strong preparations in Japan for the event. Our militarists speak a strange language overseas which would quickly arouse the ire of the American people were if not for the activities of the Army's Public Relations Office which tactfully prevents disturbing stories from reaching the public.

Even a cursory glance at the censorship situation in Japan reveals the necessity for much of the secrecy with which its functions are conducted. The Japanese Theater, Dance, Radio, and the mails are all under close surveillance by our authorities. Nothing can be published or produced in Japan without first being submitted for our examination. This censorship is not mild and perfunctory; it is carried out with such methodical diligence that even a people as patient and subservient as the Japanese are obliged to wince at it.

We cannot demure, for instance, when a political candidate is made to submit his speech to the American government before he broadcasts it over the radio. But in many instances large portions of these speeches have been cut not because they contain anything seditious or disadvantageous to the United States but merely because the candidate had given too accurate a picture of Japan's present miserable condition.

The newspapers have been forced to become so circumspect that the Japanese people cannot help but feel that they merely are echoing SCAP policies. "Daily papers and the radio are doing their best to eulogize the Yankees," says one letter-writer. "The administration is entirely carried on under the direction of General MacArthur." Another letter-writer states, "I was told to be very careful in writing about the Allied nations' policies, tendencies, etc. Therefore, if my thesis is to be made public I should like to revise the proof again." A third letter-writer confides, "It makes me angry to think that this censorship is the work of an army which prides itself on its freedom." A fourth says, "If it (censorship) is for the purpose of investigating opinions there is no freedom of correspondence. . . I have often discovered that the Americans do not practice what they preach concerning freedom and equality, and they do not regard U.S. as human." Still another declares, "At present the radio, newspapers, and magazines are released only after being censored by MacArthur's headquarters. Is this the so-called "freedom of speech?" News or information cannot be released unless the crimes Japan committed in the past are compared to the perfect conduct of the Allied Forces, and are featured! Is this freedom of speech?"...

Anything sent through the mails is thoroughly investigated. Occasionally the mail of American soldiers is opened if it is suspected that they are assisting Japanese to send messages to friends or relations in

America. Business reports, descriptions of new inventions and appliances, new methods in the fields of mining, agriculture, and science—all these documents come under the scrutiny of American authorities. The information is transferred to comment sheets before the original communication is forwarded to its proper destination. A business man cannot expect to keep even his little trade secrets from U.S.; a struggling inventor his secretly developed gadget. He may try to circumvent our censorship by using the telephone rather than the mails but he soon discovers that part of the job of censorship is to record telephone conversations and telegrams.

Such is the quality of our censorship in Japan. I do not mean to imply that it is all bad or that it has not assisted U.S. in shaping our occupation policies. That would be far from correct. Thousands of comments sheets find their way to Tokyo every week. There they are classified, tabulated, and studied for possible trends. From them the authorities have been able to gather a wealth of information concerning every phase of life in Japan. The Japanese attitude is learned toward such subjects as Fraternization, Russia, SCAP, Reaction of Ex-Soldiers on the Return, Censorship, War Criminals, Rumors of Impending War, Education, the Black Market, Communism, etc. Not only is an accurate gauge of public opinion thus gained but a vast accumulation of data.

Many of the officers and War Department civilians working at censorship are liberal and broadminded men. Many more are worthless parasites who neither are fitted for their job nor have the slightest interest in anything but earning a salary with the least amount of effort possible. Generally speaking, however, censorship functions are carried out efficiently. Frequently the policies laid down in Tokyo are disregarded or misinterpreted by District Stations with the result that far too many individual instances of injustice and stupidity can be cited. But it would require a very painstaking study to determine accurately the operational efficiency of so complicated an agency.

It is probably true that censorship is necessary immediately after the defeat of an enemy nation, not so much to encourage in the defeated people a love of democracy—which it hardly can be expected to do—but simply to insure peace and to carry out a just Occupation Policy. In the first stages of occupation there is always the danger that anarchy and disorder will result. In Japan, however, that danger has passed and the people have proved themselves law-abiding and cooperative. It is also true that censorship does not coincide either with our professions or our ideals as a democratic nation. If we supplement this formal objection to censorship with the additional argument that its practical results in Japan have been only to antagonize the people who have come in contact with it, we present our military men with a case to which we have the right to expect them to make a reply.

But inasmuch as they continue to cloak their operations in secrecy and refuse to admit that the matter is one in which the American public has the right to ask questions, we can assume only that they are adopting the same fascistic methods and responding with the same lack of responsibility to the home government that has characterized so many military machines of the past and brought shame and reproach on the countries they represented.[11]

While the second reporter appeared to assume that there had been a discrepancy between the occupation forces and the U.S. government over civil censorship in Japan, it seems needless to point out that American journalists were liable to hold that kind of innocent misperception. As I have argued several times, censorship by the CCD took place on the basis of a Joint Chiefs of Staff directive (JCS873/3), and censorship could not be terminated in any district without prior permission from the Joint Chiefs of Staff.[12] Under the U.S. military system, the Joint Chiefs of Staff report directly to the president of the United States, who is concurrently commander in chief of the United States Armed Forces. Contrary to Miller's conjecture, therefore, the foundation for censorship in occupied Japan was the will of the U.S. commander-in-chief.

In any event, it appeared that journalists who had visited Japan from abroad, like Miller, were headaches for the CCD authorities. Japanese newspapers and magazines were seized media. Japanese reporters could not surpass the invisible wall around the closed linguistic space, even by an inch, no matter how hard they tried.

Overseas journalists, in contrast, be they from the United States or from other Allied powers or neutral countries, were able to traverse the closed linguistic space at will. They paid no heed to the taboos ruling the linguistic space, nor did they recognize the tacit agreement to conceal the censorship in the first place. Consequently, their criticisms of the civil censorship in Japan often became valuable testimonies to the true nature of the CCD censorship.

---

11 Paul Vincent Miller, "Censorship in Japan," *The Commonweal*, April 25, 1947, The National Records Center, Suitland, Maryland, RG 331, Box No. 8575.

12 The National Archives, RG No. 218, Copy No. 59, Records of the United States Joint Chiefs of Staff. Declassified 9-27-58.

CHAPTER 11

War Guilt

Not surprisingly, the extensive and rigorous information-gathering campaigns by the Civil Censorship Detachment (CCD) authorities paid particular attention to trends in people's sentiments toward war criminal suspects and the war-crimes tribunal.

Criticism of the Tokyo War Crimes Tribunal was the third of thirty items that merited "deletion or prohibition on publication" in the CCD's censorship policy. Of special note here is the fact that the Civil Information and Education Section (CI&E) conducted a vigorous, multi-phase War Guilt Information Program (WGIP) on the basis of highly accurate information from the CCD.

The CI&E issued a captivating document, titled "War Guilt Information Program," to the GHQ's Civil Intelligence Section (G-2) on February 6, 1948—only five days prior to the closing argument by Joseph Keenan, the chief prosecutor in the International Military Tribunal for the Far East, which had begun in Ichigaya on February 11.[1] The document opens as follows.

> (Paraphrase) Based on a recent consultation among the directors of the CIS and the CI&E and their deputies, the Civil Information and Education Section submits an outline of the civil censorship activities which it has launched and influenced with the purpose of implanting an awareness on their state's crimes and their origins in the minds of Japanese citizens. A recommendation is attached to the end of this document discussing the basic philosophy and general as well as specific methods that should be adopted when continuing the War Guilt Information Program and expanding it to include a series of countermeasures regarding the Japanese attitude toward the atomic bombings

1 Draft of c/n, Subject: War Guilt Information Program, From: CIE, To: G-2 (CIS), Date: 6 February 1948. This draft document was given to me by Dr. Ray A. Moore, professor of history at Amherst College while I was conducting research at the Woodrow Wilson Center for International Scholars. While the document did not carry a stamp to speak of, it could be conjectured that Dr. Moore had dug it out at the National Records Center in Suitland, Maryland, while he was browsing the GHQ-related documents. The author is immensely grateful for Dr. Moore's kindness and friendship.

on Hiroshima and Nagasaki and the ultra-nationalistic propaganda advocated during the International Military Tribunal for the Far East.

Subsequently, the document disclosed that the CI&E had launched a series of "war guilt" activities at the early stage of the occupation of Japan and that the activities were based on Section 2a (3) of the General Order No. 4 (Supreme Commander for the Allied Powers, October 2, 1945), which read as follows:

> "a. Make recommendations to:
> (3) Make clear to all levels of the Japanese public the true facts of their defeat, their war guilt, the responsibility of the militarists for present and future Japanese suffering and privation and the reasons for and objectives of the military occupation of the Allied Powers."

The document clarified that the first stage of the CI&E's WGIP, based on the above recommendation, was launched in the beginning of 1946 and continued through June of the same year. As far as newspapers were concerned, however, the program had already been activated in 1945.

> 1. A running story, entitled "Historical Articles on the War in the Pacific" (approximately 15,000 words) presenting the true history of the War, was prepared by CIE, approved by the Historian, C-3, and received almost complete coverage in the Japanese daily press from 8 December 1945 until the series ended. This history emphasized guilt for inception of the war, revelations of historical truth theretofore kept from the Japanese people, and facts about Japanese atrocities, particularly in Nanking and Manila.
> 2. Before the actual release of the above history, an information program emphasizing war atrocities was carried out in conjunction with the Yamashita trial in Manila, the issuance of lists of Japanese war criminals to be apprehended and tried in Yokohama and, after 8 December 1945 in conjunction with the "Historical Articles" series itself. . .

The program, timing-wise, synchronized impeccably with arrests of war criminal suspects and milestone developments at the Tokyo Trials—and that point is crucial. The program amounted to a tenacious challenge to the national sentiment of the majority of the Japanese people, who took the defeat as only a temporary and transitory occurrence. The date of the CI&E

document—February 6, 1948—is powerful evidence that, according to the information collected by the CCD, war guilt had not been embedded firmly in the Japanese people's minds in the way that the occupation authority wished it to be, even almost three years after the defeat.

The "Historical Articles on the War in the Pacific" that the CI&E document referred to was a propaganda newspaper serialization. The series had a grave influence on Japan, almost comparable to the CCD's censorship, in the sense that it not only defined the paradigm for historical descriptions of postwar Japan but also confined and closed the linguistic space where historical description took place. To ensure that the first installment in the series—courtesy of the General Headquarters of the Allied Powers, of course—would be carried on a two-page spread, the GHQ supplied extra reams of paper to all the newspapers in Japan. The series preamble stated:

> The crimes that the militarists in Japan committed to the Japanese people were too numerous to comprehensively list here. While some of them have already been publicized, the rest have not been exposed. But these, too, will be made public one by one by indisputable, unmistakable documentation in the course of time.
>
> While major war crimes include such conduct as abuse of authority by militarists, deprivation of people's freedom, and inhumane treatment by the Japanese government and the military which ignored the international customs on treatment of prisoners of war as well as noncombatants, what brought about the gravest consequences among their nefarious conduct was, by far, suppression of the truth. This "regulation" of truth was started immediately upon the passing of the Peace Preservation Law in the Imperial Diet in 1925. It is a well-known fact among the Japanese people that this law has been made fiercer each time it was amended for over 20 years to suppress people's freedom of speech and how barbarously political prisoners have been treated with their human rights violated.
>
> Developments in Japan in the beginning of the 1930s marked a major turning point in the country's political history with political conspiracies, purges of undesirable elements, and assassinations of high government officials who opposed the authoritarian policies of the military clique which was on the rise in those days.
>
> The number of those who were arrested on suspicion of being holders, advocates, and executioners of the so-called "dangerous ideas" exceeded 59,000 between 1933 and 1936. The organizational network of thought control centers was tightly organized under the strict lead-

ership of General Araki Sadao, teaching the Japanese people that they should blindly follow the instructions of their leaders and they should never criticize their leadership. It is highly significant that this period coincided with the rise of militarism. In February 1936, over 2,400 Imperial Japanese Army officers and soldiers rose in revolt, assassinating Saitō Makoto, Lord Keeper of the Privy Seal, Takahashi Korekiyo, Finance Minister, and Watanabe Jōtarō, Inspector General of Military Education, and severely injuring Grand Chamberlain Suzuki Kantarō. As the influence of the militarists increased, laws and rules on censorship were beefed up and a new law to deprive people of freedom of speech was instituted. And this system persisted in the Second Sino-Japanese War through the war with the Allied Powers.

It was possible to spread propaganda on Japan's victory with relatively few refutations from the Japanese people during the early stage of the war against the United States and Britain. As war continued and as it became increasingly difficult for the military to maintain its status, announcements by the government authorities became transformed into something that was farther from the truth. Even when the Japanese troops were defeated on numerous battlefields and the Imperial Japanese Navy de facto perished, the true state of war was never made public. As His Majesty announced lately, Japan's attack on Pearl Harbor without prior warning was never the wish of His Majesty. But the military police made the utmost efforts to keep this information from the Japanese people.

The Supreme Commander for the Allied Powers ordered the abolishment of the Peace Preservation Law on October 5, 1945, took a measure to demolish this system against newspapers, and declared that complete information on the war should be presented to the Japanese people. Today, it is absolutely imperative the Japanese people grasp the complete history of the war. It would allow the Japanese people to learn how Japan was defeated and understand why the Japanese people had to suffer from such miseries caused by the militarism. Only through this would the Japanese people obtain the knowledge and vigor to reconstruct their country to be a member of the peaceful international society, defying the pressure from the militaristic conducts. It is from the above viewpoint that the Headquarters of the U.S. Forces provide the Japanese people a special article on events which brought Japan and its people to the present outcome.[2]

---

2 *Asahi Shimbun*, December 8, 1945.

The above propaganda document played a historical role by introducing the name "Pacific War" into the Japanese linguistic space. The introduction of the new moniker, naturally, accompanied a ban on the older name. On December 15, 1945, exactly one week after the publication of the document, the following directive proscribed references to the "Greater East Asian War."

> The use in official writings of the terms "Greater East Asia War (*Dai Tōa Sensō*), "The Whole World under One Roof" (*Hakkō Ichi-u*), and all other terms whose connotation in Japanese is inextricably connected with State Shinto, militarism, and ultra-nationalism is prohibited and will cease immediately.
> (excerpted from the so-called "Shinto Directive," a memorandum issued on December 15, 1945, to the Japanese government via the Central Liaison Office as directive #3 from the General Headquarters, Supreme Commander for the Allied Powers) (Civil Information and Educational Section)

In the span of a mere week between December 8 and December 15, 1945, the "Greater East Asian War" that Japan had fought was deprived of its existence and significance and replaced by the "Pacific War" that the United States had fought. This was much more than just the replacement of a term, obviously. It was inevitable that, together with the replacement of the name of the war, the entire meaning and value surrounding the war also required a substitutive replacement. In other words, the modification of a term inevitably leads to a change in the paradigm of historical description. This paradigm shift, however, was by no means sprung from the spontaneous will of the Japanese people. It was, instead, forced through by the foreign occupation authority's coercions and prohibitions.

When the "Historical Articles on the War in the Pacific" newspaper series ended its run, the Takayama Shoin publishing house published the series in March and June of 1946. All 100,000 copies sold out. Although the translator contributed a carefully worded note reading, "In pursuit of being as faithful to the original English as possible when translating it, the translator requested rigorous revision of the draft Japanese translation by the GHQ's Civil Information and Education Section," CCD leaders rewrote the following portions in the translator's note.

> . . . It was through this document that we learned for the first time that the responsibilities for and the causes of the war which we had just

fought should not be attributed to the Greater East Asian War alone but that they dated back to the Manchurian Incident. It also taught U.S. how foolhardy the Greater East Asian War was for Japan. (emphasis added)[3]

Of course, these underlined portions were replaced by "the Pacific War." The translator of the book, published in book form as a compilation by the Civil Information and Education Section of General Headquarters, Supreme Commander for the Allied Powers, was Nakaya Ken'ichi. At that time, Nakaya was director of public relations at Kyodo News.

One of the reasons that the book sold as many as 100,000 copies was that the Japanese government instructed schools to use it as teaching material. On April 9, 1946, the directors-general of the School Education Bureau and the Textbook Bureau issued a notification on matters relating to classroom teaching for the new school year to prefectural governors and school principals. The notification contained the following instruction:

4. Textbook on Moral Training, National History, and Geography
   Classes on moral training, national history, and geography are currently suspended, and their textbooks are being recalled. The following preparations are being made to resume these classes:
   a. Prior to resumption of classes on moral training, national history, and geography, the curriculum guideline for teachers of the substitute educational plan (provisionally called "New Education Guidelines") is being compiled. It will be issued and circulated as soon as permission is granted by the General Headquarters, Supreme Commander for the Allied Powers.

      This guideline is divided into two sections. The first section introduces the general policy on education, while the second section discusses concrete teaching methods, such as how to organize a class around discussions among students, with the teaching materials as well as actual examples attached.

      The *Historical Articles on the War in the Pacific* provided by the Headquarters of the Supreme Commander for the Allied Powers will be shortly published by Takayama Shoin, and it will be distributed to each school through Nippon Shuppan Haikyū Tōsei Kabushiki Kaisha [a government-controlled publishing and distribution company]. Each school is instructed to purchase

3 The Prange Collection, McKeldin Library, University of Maryland.

the book and make appropriate use of it as a teaching material for temporarily suspended classes, including those on national history. (emphasis added)

As the above implies, the CI&E had instructed the immediate discontinuation of all courses in moral training, Japanese history, and geography on December 31, 1945. Upon the issue of that instruction, the vice-minister for education sent a notification titled "Matters Related to Discontinuation of Classes in Moral Training, National History, and Geography" to all the prefectural governors and school principals on January 11, 1946. The events go to show that, as the result of the amplification and effective, simultaneous use of the principle of prohibition on the one hand and the use of coercion on the other, the CI&E's propaganda document and publication of a book under the title *Historical Articles on the War in the Pacific* penetrated deep into the actual arena of Japan's school education.

To put it differently, this was nothing short of the penetration of the WGIP. After all, *Historical Articles on the War in the Pacific* had been compiled as the spearhead of the program from the beginning. Even though the book wore the dressings of a historical description, it was nothing but propaganda material. To begin with, the book had a motive to set "the Japanese militarists" against "the Japanese people." And the hidden agenda at the base of it all was the CI&E's intention to replace the Pacific War, which was a war between Japan and the Allied Powers, particularly the United States, with a fictional conflict between the militarists and the Japanese people. To accomplish that aim, it concocted a conflict between the two.

Needless to say, this was nothing but an attempt at either the internalization or the revolutionalization of war. By injecting the fictional scenario of "militarists" against "Japanese people," the GHQ could advocate a logic positioning the "militarists" as the ones that had committed a crime against the "Japanese people" and holding those militarists solely responsible for the "present as well as future sufferings and destitution of the Japanese people;" therefore, the logic had it, the United States was completely inculpable. The reasoning also led to the notion that the militarists were the only ones to blame for non-discriminatory air raids on major cities and even the atomic bombs dropped on Hiroshima and Nagasaki. There was nothing wrong, this argument concluded, with the Americans who actually dropped the bombs.

If there emerged some Japanese people who accepted this fictional picture of conflict as the reality or, for whatever reason, pretended to accept it, the CI&E's WGIP had more or less accomplished its intended purpose. And in that, the scheme for a perpetual revolution to destroy the traditional order in Japan took shape. Once that framework was in place, the tremendous amount of energy that the Japanese people had devoted to waging the war would never again target the United States. It would direct itself, instead, toward the destruction of the "militarists" and the old order in Japan.

The degree to which Marxist thinking influenced the CI&E when concocting this scheme is unclear. Again, the preamble of the *Historical Articles on the War in the Pacific* included the statement, "What brought about the gravest consequences among their nefarious conducts was, by far, suppression of the truth." One cannot help but detect something off-putting, something bizarrely incongruous about this statement for no other reason than its attempt to expose a so-called "truth" while completely concealing the self-evident truth that a war is a conflict between nations. By the time this propaganda document appeared in print, the CCD's censorship had already closed and begun monitoring Japan's linguistic space on a nearly total scale—an initiative whose existence itself was concealed and suppressed.

As the CI&E's *Historical Articles on the War in the Pacific* itself admitted, during the early stage of the occupation, from 1945 through 1948, the WGIP had not necessarily met the CI&E's expectations. Nevertheless, it seems that its impact is becoming increasingly remarkable recently, more than a generation after the end of the occupation.

I say this because subsequent developments in Japan, such as the so-called textbook controversy, the Suzuki Zenkō government's humiliating slavish diplomacy vis-à-vis China and Korea in the summer of 1982, the TV dramas *Oshin* and *Sanga Moyu*, and the *Asahi Shimbun* reporter Honda Katsuichi's excessive obsession with the Nanjing Massacre, were, in my judgment, all much ado about nothing—and they all had their roots in the CI&E's propaganda called the *Historical Articles on the War in the Pacific.* They all made a big fuss but left a strangely empty aftertaste. I strongly suspect that the vapid, lifeless upshot of it all lingered because the remote cause of these incidents was a mere propaganda document.

Some Japanese, it seems to me, continue to parrot the CI&E's propaganda lines even though more than a generation has passed since the end of the occupation. This phenomenon, an extremely strange view to some, is partly attributable to descriptions of postwar Japanese history that still tenaciously adhere to the old paradigm of the *Historical Articles on the War in the Pacific*. Moreover, the postwar generation, which has been inculcated on the basis of that historical account, has increasingly become the mainstream of Japanese society.

To put it more accurately, this is a generation of Japanese who were brainwashed—unknowingly and indirectly—by WGIP propaganda instead of learning historical descriptions based on legitimate assessments of historical documents. As long as an occupation authority takes firm control of education and speech, it can continue to exercise an effective influence on the occupied country for generations, in some cases, after the termination of the occupation. This is what the CCD's censorship and the CI&E's WGIP have illustrated.

The first stage of the WGIP was not limited to publication of the "Historical Articles on the War in the Pacific" series in Japanese newspapers and the instruction to make schools adopt the book version as teaching material. Along with conducting these activities, the CI&E also carried out a vigorous radio campaign. The radio program was called *Shinsō wa Kōda* (Now It Can Be Told), and Japanese people in their late forties or older today likely remember it, if only remotely. The CI&E document titled "Implementation of First War Guilt Information Program" reads:

> 1. "Now It Can Be Told," a dramatization of the Historical Articles was broadcast in a series of ten weekly program, from 9 December to 10 February 1946.
> 2. Concurrently, CIE initiated a nationwide radio program, known as the "Now It Can Be Told 'Question Box,'" to allow for audiences participation in asking questions prompted by the original program. When the original program ended, the "Question Box" became the "Truth Box." This new program ran for 41 consecutive weeks, ending on 4 December 1946. It had a listener reaction which averaged 900 to 1,200 letters weekly, a very high response for Japan at that time.

In other words, along with an attempt to instill the WGIP in school education, the CI&E also tried to make maximum use of radio for social education. This was only natural. Even today, I cannot shake the memory of the bizarre opening of the radio program *Shinsō wa Kōda* accompanied by the fate motif of Beethoven's 5th Symphony. It was odd, come to think of it, that our radio, which had broadcast the Eastern District Army information and, only half a year earlier, Emperor Showa's Jewel Voice Broadcast in which Emperor Showa read out the Imperial Rescript on the Termination of the War, blared out the gaudy opening of *Shinsō wa Kōda.*

The same "War Guilt Information Program" document explained the program's second stage as follows.

> 4. Early in 1946. . . a second information program was initiated and

has continued to the present. This program carried a more positive tone of democratization and hope for the future of Japan as an orderly, peaceful member of the family of nations. Recurring references have been made, however, to the causes of the war, Japan's war guilt and war crimes. Some of these references have been continuous and pointed. This program has been implemented through the press (Tab G), the radio (Tab H), motion pictures (Tab I), and books (Tab J).

a. Press

1. Most press activity, including thrice-weekly press conferences, daily press releases, and indoctrination of newspaper executives and writers, has been devoted to a positive program of democratization. Thus, the entire press of Japan, through CI&E at the national level and through Military Government at the prefectural level, has been kept aware of daily developments in SCAP's accomplishment of the primary missions of the Occupation. Detailed statements and answers to questions on all phases of the Occupation have been handled through this medium, specifically in the fields of politics and government, social trends, economics, public health and welfare and foreign trade. SCAP, through this medium, has shown the Japanese what steps it has taken to advise and assist them. It has also detailed philosophies and methods whereby the nation not only could achieve democracy but could help itself economically and socially.

2. While this process of democratization was in progress, direct reminders of Japan's war guilt and ultra-nationalism, which led to disaster, have not been neglected. Before the War Crimes Trials opened in June 1946, CIE held two press conferences for the Chief of the International Prosecution Section and one for the Defense Section, attended by representatives of Kyodo News Service and all leading newspapers in the nation. The purposes and methods of the International Tribunal were discussed thoroughly and were covered thoroughly by the press. Conferences were held at Yokohama to launch the information program for the Class B war criminal trials there. Since the opening of both series of trials, CIE has distributed daily the PIO releases on the Class B trials and has conducted a full-time information program on the major trials by assigning a liaison officer to daily duty with Japanese

correspondents at the Tribunal.

3. Particular attention has been paid, through the War Guilt Information Program, to obtaining for Japanese press all possible information on the trials, particularly on details of the prosecution's case and the testimony of prosecution witnesses. (emphasis added)
4. Through the activities of the CIC, the Press and Publication Unit, press and magazine executives have been made aware of the fact that the economic, social, and human waste of war is such that no civilized person can countenance it as a method of resolving conflicts between nations; that a free press manned by journalists of integrity is feared by all tyrants, bosses, and dictators who would impose one will upon the many. Such a press is the voice of the people.

At the annual convention of the Japan Newspaper Publishers & Editors Association in July 1947, Major Daniel C. Imboden, director of the Press and Publications Branch (Civil Information and Education Section) and the guest of honor at the convention, said basically:

A few Japanese newspaper editors that I spoke with told me that they do not believe it the newspaper's responsibility to meddle in political discussions. To this, I must express my disagreement. I have been convinced that, had the Japanese newspapers exerted influence on political discussions in prewar Japan, Tojo and his fellow conspirators would not have and could not have thrown Japan into the present misery . . .

He also said:

Our mission is to assist Japan to create accountable newspapers that will someday grow into free newspapers. General MacArthur permitted Japanese newspapers to continue to publish after Japan's surrender, which is an unprecedented treatment. Past history shows that it is customary for the commander of the occupation forces to ban publication of newspapers in the enemy country.

The document continued on to discuss the second-stage programs in the fields of radio and films. The proposal for the third-stage program in the document, which operated on the basis of experiences from the first and second stages, will be a topic of discussion in subsequent chapters.

CHAPTER 12
The Tokyo Trials

The document by the Civil Information and Education Section (CI&E) on the War Guilt Information Program enumerated several issues to note when launching the third stage of the program.

It goes without saying that this third stage reflected, as of February 6, 1948, the tense atmosphere on the eve of the prosecutor's concluding speech and summation at the International Military Tribunal for the Far East (Tokyo Trials) in Ichigaya.

> 5. Information recently received from G-2 (CIS) and other sources indicates that:
>   a. Some individuals and groups in Japan, inspired by the writings and public remarks of certain scientists, clergymen, authors, journalists and professional do-gooders in the United States, are branding the atom bombing of Hiroshima and Nagasaki as "atrocities." There is also a growing feeling among some of these Americans, reflected in corresponding sentiments of certain Japanese, that whatever educational or philosophical movements are undertaken in Hiroshima with American funds should be done in a spirit of "atonement" for the alleged atrocity.
>   b. There is a growing feeling among certain Japanese, particularly among those seeking to justify to the world and the Japanese the nation's aggression and ultra-nationalism, that Tojo has stated the case convincingly and should be admired by the Japanese people for his courage. This could even extend to martyrdom of Tojo, in the event of his execution.
>   c. Both of these points constitute a foundation upon which the now quiescent ultra-nationalists conceivable [sic] might seek to rebuild their structure after the Occupation has been terminated.
>
> (Item 6 paraphrased) 6. It has been informally proposed to the CI&E that the Japanese should once again be made aware of the history of Japan's ruffian invasions, particularly regarding the atrocities that the Japanese military committed in the Far East, in order to counteract these emerging attitudes. In particular, it has been suggested that the

history of atrocities committed by the Japanese troops, most notably the Manila massacre, be published and widely distributed and that a highly intensive campaign be launched to counter the growing criticism of the atomic bombing of Hiroshima and Nagasaki.

(Item 7 paraphrased until a.) 7. Based on previous studies on this issue and consultations with the G-2 (CIS) officers in charge of media as well as the inhouse media officers, the CI&E believes that the third phase of the current campaign should be conducted in line with the following basic policies and methods.

a. Considerations Basic to Planning
(1) Extreme caution is indicated on the grounds that a direct, frontal attack information program might act as a boomerang and be the means of inciting and solidifying the majority of public opinion whereas present available documentation points to "ultra-nationalist" and "atrocity" thinking being confined to a minority.
(2) The question of whether there is a conflict in policy also must be considered in relation to an all-out information program. Present policy indicates that Japan is to be re-built economically, and that a quick peace treaty is desirable. In instituting a "frontal-attack" program on these subjects, the Occupation tacitly admits to the American people that the Japanese are not to be trusted and that, therefore, economic assistance is debatable, and a peace treaty is undesirable.
(3) It is the consensus that the Tojo trials and the Hiroshima-Nagasaki "atrocities" properly should be considered as coming under the heading of a "war guilt" program. Treatment, however, may vary in specific methods as outlined in the following plan.

b. General Methods to Be Employed
(1) Strong emphasis on political information and education as an antidote for ultra-nationalism. (This has and is being covered to a large extent, but an even more concentrated program has been evolved and is now awaiting approval).
(2) Full coverage to be given in the expose of any concrete movements which show resurgence of ultra-nationalistic movements, the fallacious thinking in the back of such movements,

and the inevitable consequences of such movements.
(3) Constant liaison with influential editors and leaders in the fields of labor, agriculture, education, government, etc., emphasizing the virtue of a free society versus a totalitarian state.
(4) Encouragement of the development of progressive, liberal groups.

c. Specific Methods and Media to Be Utilized
(1) The Press:
(a) The Press and Publications Unit, CIE, has appointed a special press officer whose sole duty is to maintain liaison with Japanese editors and endeavor to impress upon them not only the ideologies expressed in Tab b-(3), but also to attempt to encourage <u>objective editorial comment</u> and news coverage on the summation and verdict of the Tojo and other war criminal trials, as well as news items on Hiroshima projects.
(b) The Press and Publications liaison officer at the IMTFE (Tab G),[1] will continue informational activities on the objectives and duties of a free press, with special emphasis during the Tojo summation and verdict phases.
(c) Press and Publications Unit will send a press representative to the dedication ceremonies scheduled for April, 1948 at Hiroshima to encourage <u>correct interpretation</u> by the Japanese press.
(d) Appropriate material for news releases will be requested from interested SCAP sections on both the Tojo and Hiroshima phases, which will help to counteract impressions mentioned previously. (A statement from General MacArthur would be of great assistance.)

(2) Radio:
(a) CIE Radio Unit will continue to stress the "war guilt" theme in regularly scheduled programs as outlined in Tab 4b (1) and (2) for the duration of the war crime trials, and will continue constantly to refer to this subject in other programs as outlined in Tab 4b (4).
(b) Major coverage will be given the summation and verdict of the Toho phase of the trials.

---

1 It appears that this female officer was a U.S. Army first lieutenant. See Asahi Shimbun Hōtei Kishadan, *Tōkyō Saiban, jō* [Tokyo Trials, Part I], Tokyo Saiban Kankōkai, 1977, p. 59.

(c) A special CIE representative, who will counsel and guide Japanese radio people in correct interpretation, will be sent to Hiroshima for the April dedication ceremonies.

(3) Exhibits:
(a) CIE Exhibits Unit has already prepared in rough outline form a series (13) of posters on War Crimes Trials, subject to the approval of interested SCAP sections, with themes based on why war trials are held. . . how a minority group threw the nation and the world into chaos. . . the average citizen did not have a true voice in management of his own life. . . consequences of accepting false information. . . moneys spent on warships, planes, ammunition in relation to what could have been spent in peaceful pursuits, vis., new housing, power, modernization, etc. . . lessons to be learned from war trials. (emphasis added)[2]

The name of former Prime Minister Tōjō Hideki, the central figure among the accused, appeared quite often in the CI&E's document. The aftereffects of various Tōjō-related developments still lingered. the submission of the Tōjō affidavit to the court on December 19, 1947, Tōjō's own testimony on December 26, and the cross-examination by chief prosecutor Joseph Keenan and completion of the examination by William Webb, president of the Tribunal, on January 7, 1948, for example, all had a palpable influence.[3]

Toward the end of the affidavit—a 245-page document whose English translation took attorney George F. Blewett three days to recite—former Prime Minister Tōjō declared:

> In concluding my evidence at this and perhaps the only time permitted to me under the rules of this Court, may I reiterate that the policy of Japan, and certainly choice of her duly constituted officials of state, involved neither aggression nor exploitation. Step by step, through numberous [sic] legally selected Cabinets, and without a variance in regularly constituted governmental procedure, our country finally was brought face to face with stark reality, and to U.S. who at that period

2 Draft of c/n, Subject: War Guilt Information Program, From: CIE, To: G-2 (CIS), Date: 6 February 1948.

3 Asahi Shimbun Hōtei Kishadan. *Tōkyō Saiban, chū, dai 5-hen Tōjō jinmonroku* [Tokyo Trials, Part II Vol. 5: Record of Tojo Examination], Tokyo Saiban Kankōkai, 1977, p. 813–963. Def. Doc. #3000—Affidavit of Tojo, Hideki, Individual Defense (available at https://dspace2.creighton.edu/xmlui/handle/10504/74577, last visited on February 17, 2018).

were weighted with the duty of deciding the fate of our nation, a war of self-existence was our only alternative. We staked the fate of our country on that decision and lost, bringing about the present plight as we see it before our eyes.

The query as to whether or not the war was a just one considered from the viewpoint of international law and the responsibility for defeat are two different matters clearly distinguishable. The former is a problem between foreign countries and a legal one, but I believe firmly and will contend to the last that it was a war of self-defense and in no manner a violation of presently acknowledged international law. Never at any time did I ever conceive that the waging of this war would or could be challenged by the victors as an international crime or that regularly constituted public officials of the vanquished nation would be charged individually as criminals under any recognized international law or under alleged violations of treaties between nations.

As to the other question, the responsibility for defeat, I feel that it devolves upon myself as Premier. The responsibility in that sense I am not only willing but sincerely desire to accept fully.[4]

Chief Prosecutor Keenan, obviously conscious of Blewett, who addressed former Prime Minister Tōjō as "General Tōjō" and showed him considerable respect when examining the accused, addressed Tōjō as "Defendant Tōjō." When starting his cross-examination, Keenan defiantly said, "Defendant Tōjō, I shall not address you General Tōjō, because, as you are well aware, Japan no longer has an army."[5] During the subsequent four-day exchange with Keenan, Tōjō never reversed his position.

For instance, when Keenan questioned Tōjō about Proposal B (Otsu-an; the final offer from Japan for a diplomatic settlement with the United States, which was adopted by the Imperial Conference on November 5, 1941), saying, "Had the United States accepted the conditions of Proposal B, would there not be the attack on Pearl Harbor and, therefore, eruption of the war?" Tōjō instantly replied as follows: "Had Proposal B been accepted, there would have been no war. Even if half of the conditions of the Proposal had been accepted, there would have been no war. . . . if the United States had truly hoped for peace in the Pacific, if I may add."

"Just a minute," Keenan cross-questioned Tōjō, saying, "Pray point out

4 Ibid., p. 904–905.

5 Ibid., p. 906, 916.

which were the conditions of Proposal B that Japan would not have started the war if the United States had accepted."

"I would say any of the conditions," Tōjō replied, "if only your country truly wished for peace in the Pacific and showed the willingness to make concessions . . ."

When Keenan said, "How interesting! Are you saying that, if the United States had accepted any one of the conditions of Proposal B, there would have been no war?" Tōjō replied, saying, "Yes, that is what I mean. I thought we could mitigate our conditions if the United States showed the willingness for mutual concession."

When Keenan asked if Tōjō was present when Proposals A and B were decided by the Imperial Conference, Tōjō triumphantly said, "Of course. Not only was I present, I was the person with ultimate responsibility." Furthermore, when Keenan asked if Proposal B had not been Japan's last word to the United States about the bilateral negotiation, Tōjō refuted the notion, saying, "Our last word to the United States was handed to Washington on December 7. Between this date and presentation of Proposal B, your country slammed down a Hull Note on U.S. on November 26."

Keenan retorted, "The question is whether Japan used Proposal B as the final conditions that it could offer in the bilateral negotiation." When Tōjō said, "Diplomatically, the answer is yes," Keenan followed up, saying, "I am not asking for a diplomatic nicety. What I like to know is the truth. Wasn't Proposal B the final and ultimate condition from your side in the negotiation?" To this, Tōjō said, "And I am giving you the truth," without missing a beat.

Shifting his target, Keenan demanded, "Then, let me ask you. When the Japanese government adopted Proposals A and B, was it its intention to enter war against the Allied Powers when the United States rejected these conditions? Yes or no?"

When Tōjō shrugged off Keenan, saying, "It is not that simple. It takes two to negotiate," Keenan repeated the question. Tōjō replied, raising his voice:

"Let me explain. When a nation had to stake its existence on whether to enter a war, you cannot make a decision in such a simple language. The foreign minister would take a due measure of his own as the foreign minister. When it comes to a life or death problem for the country, however, I had my own thinking as prime minister of the country. If your country had presented the modus vivendi proposal, which we understand had been prepared according to President Roosevelt's will, the situation would have been altered significantly. Although the modus vivendi proposal was quite different from our Proposal B in key points, it might have been overcome with a heart-to-heart talk. It is utterly unthinkable for a prime minister of a country to tenaciously persist in what has already been decided and forcibly lead the country to a war."

In response to this statement, Keenan said, "I have tried to be as patient as possible to hear your view . . . But my question is a simple one. When Foreign Minister Togo presented both proposals as the maximum concessions Japan could make, was that based on your own intention?" Tōjō responded, saying, "I endorse the conduct as a diplomatic measure taken by my own intention," to which Keenan followed up with, "So, you will take responsibility?" Tōjō concurred, declaring, "But of course."[6]

At the end of Chief Prosecutor Keenan's cross-examination around 3:00 p.m. on January 6, 1948, he sat up straight and squarely faced the accused before saying, "At this point, I wish to hear the defendant's state of mind concerning whether he feels guilty, both morally and legally, for starting a war." Former Prime Minister Tōjō, too, held up his head and squarely faced Keenan, resting his left hand on the witness stand and declaring triumphantly, "I never did err. I believe I did the right thing."

Next, Keenan tried to corner Tōjō, saying, "Are you then prepared to repeat the same thing with your colleagues when and if you are acquitted?" Attorney Blewett rushed to the podium to raise an objection to Keenan's cross-examination, questioning its validity. Blewett's objection was sustained.[7]

The examination of former Prime Minister Tōjō on the witness stand by Webb and the re-examination by the defense attorney concluded at 11:15 on the morning of January 7. The "Tensei Jingo" (Vox Populi, Vox Dei) daily column in the *Asahi Shimbun* newspaper on January 8 wrote about Tōjō's testimony:

> To chief prosecutor Keenan's examination, defendant Tōjō replied that it was just, both morally and legally, to start a war as prime minister.
>
> It does not matter what Tōjō says in the courtroom. He is entitled to say whatever comes to his mind. It simply would do no good if Tōjō alone repents his past sin and turns submissive at this stage. We do not wish to start a debate on Tōjō's remarks, either.

---

6 Ibid., p. 941–943.

7 Ibid., p. 957–958.

> The question is how the Japanese people react to Tōjō's testimonies. Overseas attention, too, is focused on this question.
>
> Foreign correspondents say, "People all over the world are not watching Tōjō's lips. They are watching the Japanese people's reactions to what he says."
>
> Recently, I sometimes hear people on trains saying, "Tōjō seems to have regained his popularity." Letters that we have received from readers also include, occasionally, those that praise Tōjō. Although it is hard to imagine that the silent majority of the Japanese people, after all that has happened, will become intoxicated with Tōjō's cultish, scandalous, magazine-like nonsense, we must not overlook a mood among a few to sympathize with his testimonies that we glimpse every once in a while today.
>
> It is like fast-forwarding a film of history. It can be likened to a competitive swimmer, who must have jumped into a pool of democracy, being rewound to a prewar jumping stand, ready to invade neighboring countries. This trend also reminds us of the German people, who had created the beautiful Weimar Constitution, being corroded by a venomous insect called the Nazi.[8] (emphasis added)

The author of the "Tensei Jingo" column must have been subject to pre-censoring by the Civil Censorship Detachment (CCD). As an "influential journalist," the author must have also been in daily contact with liaison officers of the CI&E and, therefore, contributed to the CI&E's propaganda plans. I would say it was not surprising at all for this writer to use an apparent "language of the enslaved" to narrate his story.

More noteworthy here, however, was that this column—despite being in the "language of the enslaved"—noted train-commute gossip on Tōjō's recovering popularity and Tōjō's testimonies finding sympathetic ears.

Needless to say, the sentiment speaks to the following perception evident in the CI&E's document: "There is a growing feeling among certain Japanese. . . that Tōjō has stated the case convincingly and should be admired by the Japanese people for his courage. This could even extend to martyrdom of Tōjō, in the event of his execution." The third stage of the War Guilt Information Program was to proceed with that exact sense of crisis serving as leverage.

When it comes to propaganda plans, the International Military Tribunal for the Far East itself stands as a much larger-scale form of propaganda for

8 Ibid., p. 964.

the War Guilt Information Program (WGIP). The CI&E planned the third stage of WGIP to further perfect the initiative's propaganda effect. Together with the CCD's censorship, the third stage continued to hurl abuse at defendants' statements—on which they put their lives on the line—sometimes through concealment of the true nature of the Tokyo Trials in the name of "objective reporting" and, other times, by "giving guidance" to Japanese news media.

CHAPTER 13

Dissenting Voices

The censorship of books written about the International Military Tribunal for the Far East by the Civil Censorship Detachment (CCD) was not always as thoroughly effective as the War Guilt Information Program of the Civil Information and Education Section (CI&E) was. One reason appears to be the shift from pre-censorship to ex post facto censorship that had taken place by that time.

The shift from pre-censorship to post-publication censorship for books came into effect on October 15, 1947, with the exception of fourteen publishers specializing in ultra-right or ultra-left books. The mode of censorship for magazines followed suit on December 15 of the same year, excluding twenty-eight blacklisted titles.[1] A document issued by the Press, Pictorial, and Broadcast Division (PPB) of the CCD on June 29, 1948, betrayed the irritation of an officer in charge regarding the change:

> (Paraphrase) 2. . . . Our basic stance toward scheduling of operational progress is that this kind of publication should be directly commissioned to competent military civilians of the Publication Section or Re-censorship Section or, at least, the first-class Japanese censors for examination rather than having it go haltingly through the ladder of censors from the bottom. Miyoko has produced such an excellent summary of Kiyose's book in a matter of a day, when the only thing the Publication Section accomplished in fifty-six days was translation of the book's thirteen-page preface into English. Of course, we cannot expect a similar capability from our publication censors. Nevertheless, it is my conviction that censorship on this kind of publication should reach the final conclusion within a week of its arrival. Witnessing this kind of tardiness again even after the two scandalous disasters over the IMTFE-related books, makes it obvious that a fundamental reform of publication censorship is urgently needed.

1 *Operations of Military and Civil Censorship*, Vol. X, p. 120-128.

> 3. Decision concerning *Bengo Nijūnen*: Immediately prepare comment sheet on malignant censorship violations. RMS[2]

"Kiyose's book" was *25 hikoku no hyōjō* (Views of the 25 Defendants),[3] compiled by the Yomiuri Shimbun Kishadan (*Yomiuri Shimbun* newspaper reporters), to which Kiyose Ichirō—Tōjō Hideki's defense counsel—contributed a lengthy preface and afterword. *Bengo nijūnen* (Twenty Years a Lawyer),[4] meanwhile, was by Ōta Kinjirō, the defense counsel for General Doihara Kenji.

The first of these two Tokyo Trials–related publications, *25 hikoku no hyōjō,* was published by Rōdō Bunkasha on April 5, 1948. Copies of the work were immediately submitted to the CCD for post-publication censorship. The book had a first-run printing of 3,000 copies and sold for 100 yen.[5]

Bengo nijūnen was published by Chūbunkan Shoten on May 15, 1948, and submitted to the CCD for post-publication censorship. With an initial run of 5,000 copies, the book sold for 80 yen.[6]

Both books failed to clear post-publication censorship. The decision regarding *25 hikoku no hyōjō* came on June 24.[7] with the rejection of *Bengo nijūnen* on July 1.[8] It took the CCD eighty days and forty-seven days, respectively, to reach its decisions on the two books.

Given the slowness of the censorship process, it is not surprising that CCD personnel felt frustrated with the situation. Even more agitating to the GHQ's censorship authority than that sluggish pace, however, appeared to be the fact that both of the books—but particularly *25 hikoku no hyōjō*—repeated the arguments of Defense Counsel Kiyose at the International Military Tribunal for the Far East almost word for word.

---

2 *RMS Note to Press and Publication Section*, The National Records Center, RG 331, Box No. 8574.

3 *25 hikoku no hyōjō* [Views of the 25 Defendants], The National Records Center, RG 331, Box No. 8574.

4 *Bengo nijūnen* [Twenty Years a Lawyer], The National Records Center, RG 331, Box No. 8574.

5 *25 hikoku no hyōjō*, p. 21.

6 *Bengo nijūnen,* p. 17.

7 *25 hikoku no hyōjō*, p. 1.

8 *Bengo nijūnen*, p. 1. A memorandum dated 8:50, June 28, 1948, and initialed RMS urges, in summary, that, while the comment sheet on malicious censorship violation concerning *Bengo nijūnen* was being prepared, the Press and Publication Section should contact the publisher to acquire and submit whatever information considered important. The memorandum also encouraged the Press and Publication Section to determine the range of information to be acquired based on its own experiences during the "Tōjō testimony" and "*25 hikoku no hyōjō*" incidents. The memorandum particularly stressed the importance of the information on how many copies were printed and who obtained the copies. It is stated that the time and date on which publication was banned should be 16:00 on Thursday, July 1.

Obviously, the longer post-publication censorship took, the more widely the books would circulate. As the process plodded slowly on, the CCD might have even suspected an unspoken agreement among the Japanese censors to sabotage the process.

At the outset of the International Military Tribunal for the Far East, Defense Counsel Kiyose made a motion challenging the legality of the court head-on during the third court hearing on May 13, 1946.[9]

Entering the court room in soldier boots and worn-out clothes, Kiyose looked like an old student with no care at all about his appearance. "I should now like to be permitted to explain the motion with respect to the jurisdiction of this Tribunal," he said, and started giving a statement that affected the very basis of the tribunal itself:[10]

> The first point is that this Tribunal does not have the authority to try "Crimes Against Peace" and "Crimes Against Humanity." Needless to say, the Potsdam Declaration, advising surrender to Japan, issued on the 26th of July, 1945, states that "stern justice shall be meted out to all war criminals, including those who have visited cruelties upon our prisoners." This Declaration was acknowledged and signed when the Instrument of Surrender was signed in Tokyo Bay on the 2d of September, the same year.
>
> The Potsdam Declaration not only binds our country but also binds the Allies. In other words, this Tribunal is empowered to make charges and try what are called "war criminals" in accordance with the tenth article of the Potsdam Declaration, but not so empowered to try those who cannot be considered as war criminals.
>
> The Charter of this Tribunal stipulates "Crimes Against Peace" and "Crimes Against Humanity." However, if the Allies do not have the authority to try these cases, neither does the Supreme Commander appointed by the Allied Powers to represent the Allied Powers have the power to consider such charges.
>
> To grant authority or powers to others which one does not possess himself is, in the light of international law, unfounded. Hence, it is necessary, rationally and strictly, to circumscribe the limit of what are considered war criminals as stated in the Declaration of Potsdam.

9 Asahi Shimbun Hōtei Kishadan. *Tōkyō Saiban, jō* [Tokyo Trials, vol 1], Tokyo Saiban Kankōkai, 1977, p.175

10 Ibid., p. 179.

In other words, we must limit the interpretation of what is meant by "war criminals" to that existing up to the 26th of July, 1945—in other words, at the time when this Declaration of Potsdam was issued by the Allied Powers and at the time accepted by Japan. In other words, up to that time the meaning of "war crimes," as generally accepted by the nations of the world, was those crimes relative to the violation of the laws and rules of war—rules and conventions of war.

To give some concrete examples, there are four typical crimes: One, the violations by belligerents; two, violations by non-belligerents; three, plunder, espionage; and another, war treason.

A Judge representing Britain is sitting in this Tribunal. According to the British Manual of the Laws of War, Article 441, a definition of "war crimes" is set forth. In the next Article, namely, Article 442 the various types of war crimes are given. These, in other words, are the four that I have just mentioned.

This meaning of "war crimes" is not confined only to the Manual on the Laws of War of Great Britain which I have just mentioned, but it is also likewise understood in other countries.

"Crimes Against Peace." And, speaking of this, whatever the nature of the war or character of the war, the planning, the preparing, the initiating and the waging of war cannot be considered as "Crimes Against Peace" in accordance with the conception of war held by the civilized nations of the world up to July, 1945.

I need not say that the Honorable Judges here, the learned Judges here, are learned on the books on international law and such well known books on international law as that of Oppenheim or Hall. There is no mention of planning a war as a war crime. Works on international law widely known and well read in Japan, namely, that by Dr. Sakutaro TACHI and by Dr. Jumpei SHINOBU, mention war crimes but confine them to violations of the laws and customs of war.

Some of the books give five classifications; but, substantially, they are the same as that listed in the Manual on the Laws of War published in Britain.

On the occasion of the promulgation of the Charter of this Tribunal on the 19th of January, this year, a special order was issued by His Excellency, General of the Army, MacArthur, Supreme Commander of the Allied Powers, stating that the Supreme Commander from time to time declared that war criminals will be punished from time to time. That is mentioned in this special order, to the effect that it will be declared from time to time in our interpretation, means that they apply to Japan.

Declarations made against Germany or other European Axis nations cannot be applied to Japan. Whatever declarations are made, whether at the Moscow or Yalta Conferences, against Germany cannot under any circumstances be made applicable to Japan.

Mr. President, this is a very important point. There is a very great difference between the way in which Germany surrendered and Japan surrendered. Germany, as you well know, Mr. President, resisted to the very last, Hitler died or was killed, Goering departed from the ranks, and Germany ultimately collapsed. In the case of Germany, it was literally an unconditional surrender. In other words, as regards German war criminals, the Allies, if I may be permitted to say so, could just as well have punished war criminals without trial.

The forces of the Allied Powers had not yet landed in Japan when the Potsdam Declaration was proclaimed. In that Declaration, Article 5, it is mentioned that the "Following are our terms. We will not deviate from them."

It is an absolute mistake to bring charges against Japanese war criminals—that is, charges for "Crimes Against Peace" and "Crimes Against Humanity"—because the same charges happen to be made at the trials at Nuerenberg [sic].

The Potsdam Declaration proposed to Japan contained conditions; to borrow the words from civil law, it presented Japan an offer. In other words, there was a condition. It was this that was accepted, and it is this that the Allies must observe.

One of the war aims of the Allies in this war was respect for international law. If that is the case, it has been our strong belief that interpretation of the question of war crimes would under no circumstances go beyond the interpretations made by existing international law. The Japanese people have also so believed.

The Potsdam Declaration was accepted by the Cabinet at that time headed by Premier Kantaro SUZUKI. The question of punishing war criminals, or punishment of war criminals—the Potsdam Declaration was accepted on the understanding that the punishment of war criminals will take place in accordance with the commonly accepted understanding of that term throughout the world. To go beyond that is overstepping the bounds of international law. We would like to know, therefore, why new crimes should be charged after the acceptance of that Declaration.[11]

11 Ibid., p. 180–182.

Defense Counsel Kiyose continued on to point out a second objection. The war referred to in the Potsdam Declaration was the war "then existing between Japan and the Allies" as of July 26, 1945—in Japan, the Greater East Asian War. Kiyose therefore insisted that other incidents like the Manchurian Incident, the Battle of Lake Khasan, and the Nomonhan Incident should not fall under the definition of war. Third, Kiyose tried to invite the court's attention to the fact that "at that time there was no state of war existing between our country [Japan] and Thailand."[12]

Throughout, Kiyose maintained an impassioned tone, raising his voice, sometimes swinging his right arm, and sometimes banging the manuscript on the speaker's stand, which, according to the *Asahi Shimbun* reporters, impressed those in the court with the presence of a genuine jurist. According to the *Tōkyō Saiban, jō* (The Tokyo Trials, vol. 1) which the Asahi Shimbun Hōtei Kishadan (court reporters) wrote and compiled, "It appears that everyone in the court was deeply impressed with Kiyose's oratory preparation, logical way of speaking, and courage to refute the prosecution whoever the opponent might be—and all in the midst of that confusion."[13]

Kiyose's motion was countered by prosecutors Joseph Keenan and Arthur Strettell Comyns Carr and then defended by Ben Bruce Blakeney. William Webb, president of the International Military Tribunal for the Far East, rejected the motion at the seventh court gathering on May 17. The reason for rejection was not cited at that time; instead, it was announced that the reason would be disclosed in the future.[14] Nevertheless, together with the dissenting judgment of Judge Radhabinod Pal from India, which was banned during the occupation period, the Kiyose motion came to be long remembered as a historical document that questioned the fundamental legality of the Tokyo Trials head-on.

In Kiyose's long preface to *25 hikoku no hyōjō*, he states:

> . . . Indeed, a trial of the defeated by the war winner is historically and globally unprecedented. No such trial took place after, for instance, the Punic Wars, the Thirty Years' War, or the Napoleonic Wars. After World War I, the German emperor was not prosecuted. This court, therefore, marks the beginning of a new era from the viewpoint of international public law and common law. This court derives its ratio-

12 Ibid., p. 184–186.

13 Ibid., p. 179.

14 Ibid., p. 201.

nale from Japan's acceptance of the Potsdam Declaration. Article 10 of the said declaration stipulates as follows.

> "We do not intend that the Japanese shall be enslaved as a race or destroyed as a nation, but stern justice shall be meted out to all war criminals, including those who have visited cruelties upon our prisoners. The Japanese Government shall remove all obstacles to the revival and strengthening of democratic tendencies among the Japanese people. Freedom of speech, of religion, and of thought, as well as respect for the fundamental human rights shall be established."

> This stipulation is the basis for this court. Therefore, all the war criminals, including those who brutalized prisoners of war, are to be tried in this court. On this particular point, I made an objection immediately after the opening of this court last year. My personal view on a war criminal is that such designation should be limited to those who actually brutalized prisoners of war or those who violated existing international laws, including:
>
> 1. the violation of international law of war by military personnel and military civilians;
> 2. acts of war by non-belligerents;
> 3. espionage and wartime mutiny; and
> 4. plunder.
>
> Whether a war is a justifiable one or not, any country has the right of belligerency. Thus, the exercise of this right cannot be regarded as criminal. But my motion was denied for a reason to be announced at a future time.[15]

Having thus touched briefly on his motion, Kiyose discussed the composition of the court of the International Military Tribunal for the Far East and the charges facing the defendants by quoting part of his own opening statement that he recited on February 24, 1947:

> During my opening statement, representing the defendants, I announced that evidence would be produced on each of the following categories.

15 *25 hikoku no hyōjō*, p. 4-5.

1. General questions.
2. Matters concerning Manchuria and Manchoukuo.
3. Matters concerning China.
4. Matters concerning the Soviet Union.
5. Matters concerning the Pacific War.
6. Matters concerning individual defendants.

In order to introduce the defense's arguments, I believe it most appropriate to quote the main points of my opening statement. First, on the general issue, I argued as follows.

> "There are three vital considerations which should be outlined in this opening statement in order properly to comprehend the exact nature of the internal and external policies of Japan during the period covered by the indictment. These are independence, abolition of racial discrimination and diplomacy.
>
> The first of these national characteristics is the fervent desire of the Japanese people to preserve the nation as a completely independent and sovereign state. The sincere desire of foremost leaders throughout Japan in the Meiji period was to elevate and enhance the standing of the nation to a position of complete independence and sovereignty. Since that purpose was a worthy one, consistent with the principles advocated by President Wilson after World War I, its attainment should be recognized by this Tribunal.
>
> The second point is the demand for the abolition of racial discrimination. Racial discrimination affects those who are discriminated against much more keenly than those who discriminate. However, in order to eliminate racial discrimination the standards of culture and education for this nation needed to be raised. The government and the people of Japan were not blind to these necessary requisites. Where morality and custom called for certain modifications and improvements they willingly admitted their necessity and adopted them, but the culture of the world is not singular but plural according to the number of nations and races concerned. Each nation has its own history and tradition, and culture is created and developed accordingly. The aspiration for racial equality cannot be realized simply by raising the position of the Japanese to the standard of Europeans and Americans. It was the unanimously held hope of the Japanese people, together with all other peoples of East Asia, to reach that standard attained by

Europeans and Americans. We shall further develop that Dr. Sun Yat-Sen, the father of the Chinese revolution, and other leaders in India and throughout East Asia expressed sympathy with this idea.

The third fact to be referred to is what has been termed "the fundamental principles and doctrines of diplomacy" of Japan. Since the Meiji Period the prevailing ideal held by the government and the people of Japan in respect to foreign relations was to maintain peace in East Asia and thereby contribute to the welfare of the whole world. This was called the "cardinal principle of diplomacy" in official documents and Imperial Rescripts, that is to say, the fundamental ideal of Japan which guided its foreign policy. The war with China 1894 to 1895 and the war with Russia 1904 and 1905 were fought with that aim and consideration in view. This principle has been recognized by the great powers, and we expect to prove that the Anglo-Japanese Alliance was concluded and renewed as a result of its recognition. The Japanese people cannot forget the sympathy of the government and people of the United States shown toward Japan at the time of the Russo-Japanese war, which was fought for the maintenance of the cardinal principle. That principle of stabilization was never an aggressive nature. On the one hand, it prevented East Asia from falling into political and economic confusion, and on the other hand it promoted the common development of all Asiatic races and thus their contribution to the progress of mankind. Only in the light of the foregoing ideals can the true relations between Japan and her neighbors be fully understood."

We shall also try to prove the following facts with a view to providing this Honorable Tribunal with materials which we hope will be useful for its decision whether the attack on Pearl Harbor was a surprise attack or not.

The State Department authorities considered Japan's note to the United States dated November 20, 1941, as the last one and after November 26, the whole matter was thrown into the lap of the fighting services. On the morning of November 27, 1941, the highest official of the State Department stated that the matter of relations with Japan was in the hands of the Army and Navy. On the same day the Chief of Naval Operations and the Chief of Staff sent war warnings to the forces in Hawaii…

On the evening of December 6, 1941, even upon reading thirteen parts of the Japanese notes, the President said: 'This means war.'"

> On December 6, 1941, Washington time, the Japanese Foreign Ministry sent a dispatch to the Japanese Ambassador at Washington intimating that a note in English to be addressed to the State Department was ready. . . The United States intercepted that part of the dispatch by 9:30 p.m. December 6, and the President gave them personal perusal. Had the note been delivered as was intended at one o'clock p.m. December 7, 1941, the delivery would have preceded the attack at Pearl Harbor, which took place at 25 minutes past 1:00 p.m., Washington time. But the Embassy's deciphering and typing took so much time that, as the prosecution pointed out, Ambassador Nomura was unable to arrive at the State Department until 2:00 p.m.[16]

To conclude, Kiyose added the following three points.

1. This was a court for an international trial. Therefore, it differs in its implications as well as the impression it projects to the world, from the Pétain trial in France by the French people and the Chinese trials of *hanjian* [national traitors to the Han Chinese state] in China. In this international court, former enemies denounced the war that Japan fought as a violation of laws. The accused who had started and led the war in full conviction of its legitimacy were the representative people of Japan, which was a fully independent nation at the time. The accused must therefore not only plead and prove their innocence, but also plead and prove their state's innocence. Defeated in the war, the accused were keenly aware of their responsibility for the defeat. If this trial were, like those in France and China, about the responsibility of the accused to the nation, some of them may not have pleaded innocent. We should strictly refrain from misinterpreting the defendants' plea of innocence at the outset of this court as their attempt to evade their responsibility to the nation for the defeat.
2. In this court, only the conduct of twenty-five defendants, including the defendant Tōjō, were to be tried. In other words, only incidents related to the defendants' conduct were subject to testimonies. It takes two, however, to fight a war. From our viewpoint, therefore, it is only natural for U.S. to question the responsibility for the war of aggression, cases of violations of treaties, and legitimacy of the use of atomic bombs on the part of our enemy in the world war. In

16 Ibid., p. 9–11.

fact, there are tremendous amounts of points that we, the Japanese, wish to argue. But President Webb repeatedly claimed that an act of stealing committed by B cannot be used for the defense of thief A. And this set a limit to our efforts as defense counsel.

3. To our delight, people's understanding of the mission of jurists has deepened in recent years. Protection of basic human rights and exercise of the right to self-defense are inseparable, and they are closely interrelated. The purpose of basic human rights should not be limited to the protection of one's life, freedom, and fortune. Honor is also an important element to be protected. We must fight against distortion of truth and malicious criticism. Tried in this court were legitimate government officials who were authorized to exercise the right of self-defense for the country. Also on trial was the individual right of self-defense of the accused. Facing the gravity of this mission, I am deeply ashamed of my powerlessness.[17]

The preface was dated October 19, 1947. While the book's afterword, also written by Kiyose, was not dated, the wording of the text suggests that he had penned it toward the end of February or in early March of 1948. Concerning this book, *25 hikoku no hyōjō*, the Examiner's Note attached toward the end of the comment sheet reads:

> (Paraphrase) The volume includes portions implying that the writers were sympathetic with, if not committed to, the defendants and contains very little genuine criticism of the defendants or their testimonies in the court. In addition, newspaper reporters included in their articles a number of *tanka* poems recited by defendants and others during the trial, which are obviously a violation of censorship. A letter from a defendant to his family criticizes that the prosecution used the tactics of obstructing defendants' 'rightful arguments' and 'depriving the defendant side of everything.'[18]

The June 29 document of the Pictorial and Broadcast Division (PPB) of the CCD (mentioned above) quite belatedly criticized the *25 hikoku no hyōjō*, to which Kiyose had contributed the preface and afterword, as "flagrantly bad."[19] It must have been significantly damaging not only for the CCD

17 Ibid., p. 11–12.

18 Ibid., p. 20–21.

19 *RMS Note to Press and Publication Section*, Part 1.

authority but, more broadly, for the United States' whole Japan occupation policy that it took the PPB eighty long days to come up with a judgment on the book due to its clumsy post-publication censorship process. This was because it all depended on whether the authorities could dispossess not only the defendants, but also the Japanese people as a whole of whatever trust they had in their own country's history.

As I mentioned earlier, the War Guilt Information Program began with the simultaneous posting of the "Historical Articles on the War in the Pacific" series in all the daily newspapers in Japan on December 8, 1945. It seems redundant to point out that the historical view that permeated Chief Justice Keenan's opening statement in the Ichigaya Court on June 24, 1946, a half year later, aligned with this "Historical Articles on the War in the Pacific" and was cut from the same cloth.[20]

It goes to show that the International Military Tribunal for the Far East itself was a gigantic-scale War Guilt Information Program. More than that, it harbored a systematic and tenacious intention to completely deprive the Japanese people of their history and their trust in their own history—and even in their future, too.

The documents in this Chapter reveal that the do-or-die battle between those scheming to deprive the Japanese people, on the one hand, and those determined to defend "honor" and "resist distortion of the truth and malicious criticism," on the other, was fought not only in the Ichigaya Court, but also throughout the linguistic space of occupied Japan.

One might go as far as to say that a similar battle is still being waged today. This is because the mechanisms of the propaganda plan during the occupation, after all, allowed governments and countries that had not sent delegates to the Ichigaya Court to eternally play the same role as "those scheming to deprive the Japanese people."

---

20 *Tōkyō Saiban, jō*, p. 202–253.

CHAPTER 14

Germany and Japan

The post-publication censorship of *25 hikoku no hyōjō* and *Bengo nijūnen* accidentally exposed the existence of a tear in GHQ censorship. This makes it clear that the shift from pre-publication censorship to post-publication censorship by the Civil Censorship Detachment (CCD) was by no means a measure taken in conjunction with the International Military Tribunal for the Far East.

On the contrary, facing a variety of new circumstances, the GHQ authority had to make the shift against its wishes. The following document (in paraphrase) clearly shows that the GHQ's General Staff Section 2 (G-2) itself, not to mention the CCD's Press, Pictorial, and Broadcast Division (PPB), was reluctant to make the shift:

> Draft Directive from CS to AC of S, G-2
> Concerning Censorship in Japan and Korea
> G-2 Deputy Chief of Staff 5 June 1947
> FEC
>
> 1. The attached draft of Directive from Chief of Staff to Assistant Chief of Staff, G2, is to be enclosed as Tab C to Gen. Almond's staff study on future censorship requirements in Japan and Korea.
> 2. Previously G-2 has recommended to Gen. Almond that PPB Censorship remain as previously established, as a protection against objectionable material (See 4-b).
> 3. Gen. Almond did not concur in this recommendation, but recommends that those PPB media which have not consistently violated the press or radio code for Japan be transferred to a post-censorship basis, (except that foreign motion pictures imported under SCAP Circular 12, dated 5 December 1946, continue to be pre-censored) except that all PPB media, currently pre-censored, be required to continue to submit for pre-censorship material concerning the Allied Powers, the Occupation, or its objectives.
> 4. G-2 concurred in the essential principle per C/N No. 2 from G-2 to DCS FEC dated 31 May 47 subj: "Draft of Study 'Civil Censorship in Occupied Areas,'" only if the disadvantages and reservations are recognized:

a. The essential principles of relaxation of censorship over Press, Pictorial and Broadcast media is understood by G-2 to transfer to a post-censorship basis all the Japanese press, (including book and magazine publishers, newspapers and news agencies, except the ultra-rightist and ultra-leftist press); all Japanese radio stations, current production Japanese motion pictures, and all theatrical productions (except the ultra-rightist and ultra-leftist producers), except that currently pre-censored press, pictorial and broadcast media shall be required to continue to submit for pre-censorship material concerning the Allied Powers, the Occupation, or its objectives.
b. It should be noted that I have on repeated occasions (C-in-C) exercised stoppage of both "Stars and Stripes" and "Nippon Times," during printing and before distribution. This was possible because we caught the offending material in process. If and when post-censorship is in effect, the offending material in many cases will already have been circulating. Hence, we should not assume responsibility for adverse items not submitted to pre-censorship. The C-in-C should be made cognizant of this circumstance.
c. Compliance with directives for post-censored material is successful only when violations are corrected by punitive action. It is the belief of G-2 that, at this stage of the Occupation, punitive measures adequate to correct post-censorship violations would be impossible to effect without public protest both in Japan and abroad. Therefore, CCD, CIS, G-2 points out that no staff section should be held responsible for dissemination of specific material inimical to the Occupation and its objectives that was not pre-censored.
d. The requirement that the Japanese PPB media, currently precensored, submit for pre-censorship, material concerning the Allied Powers, Occupation or its objectives, places upon the Japanese the responsibility for selecting material within this category. This will in many cases be a responsibility which they will not be capable of performing, due to the wide range of subjects that concern the Allied Powers, the Occupation or its objectives, without direct reference thereto. It is the belief of CCD, CIS, G-2 that placing this responsibility upon the Japanese will be a source of criticism and resentment.

C. A. W.[1]

---

1 *Draft Directive from CS to AC of S, G-2, Concerning Censorship in Japan and Korea*, The National Records Center, Suitland, Maryland, RG 331, Box No. 8573.

Some of the GHQ authority's reasoning for suggesting the policy to relax censorship at that particular juncture seems to lie in the contradiction and inconsistency between the CCD's censorship and clauses in the Constitution of Japan enacted on May 3, 1947.

Article 21 of the Constitution of Japan, which was promulgated on the basis of the draft prepared by the G-2, stipulates:

> Article 21. Freedom of assembly and association as well as speech, press and all other forms of expression are guaranteed. No censorship shall be maintained, nor shall the secrecy of any means of communication be violated.

By having Japan adopt a constitution including the above stipulation, the United States, at least officially, appeared to have attempted to make Japan's linguistic space almost homogenous with that of the United States under the First Amendment of the U.S. Constitution.[2] It would thus have seemed utterly unjustifiable for the U.S. occupation authority itself to conduct censorship on a massive scale and, moreover, keep it secret to the end. As I wrote earlier, American journalists visiting occupied Japan had already called attention to that inconsistency from an early stage.[3]

The second reason behind the relaxation of censorship by the GHQ was a chain of criticism from within the United States. *The Commonweal*, the magazine that ran "Censorship in Japan" by Paul Vincent Miller, carried a note from the editor to the effect that "It is an indication of the Army's awareness of the problem that Mr. Roger Baldwin of the American Civil Liberties Union has been invited to survey the situation in Japan and Korea, acting as a private citizen" (April 25, 1947).[4] The American Civil Liberties Union was a nationwide human rights organization then located at 170 Fifth Avenue, New York City, and Roger Baldwin was its executive director.[5]

It is not certain exactly when Baldwin visited Japan and Korea, but he sent a personal letter to Lieutenant General Robert Eichelberger, commander of the Eighth United States Army, on July 9, 1947. In his letter,

---

2 See Part I, Chapter 6.

3 See Part II, Chapter 10.

4 Paul Vincent Miller, "Censorship in Japan," *The Commonweal*, April 25, 1947, The National Records Center, Suitland, Maryland, RG 331, Box No. 8575.

5 *Roger Baldwin's Letter to Lt. Gen. Eichelberger, July 9, 1947*, Regarded Unclassified, Order Sec Army by Tag per 50753, given to the author by Mr. Richard Finn, formerly of the Department of State.

Baldwin enclosed a memorandum titled *Civil Liberties in Japan*.[6] Given the letter's date of June 9, 1947, he most likely made his way to Japan in May or June of that year. At the outset of the memorandum, Baldwin writes:

> 1. The new constitution and the laws to implement it, not yet complete, afford a solid basis for civil rights. The occupation has gone as far as practicable in assisting the Japanese to set up the forms and institutions essential to democratic liberties. The constitution and laws are not however, the supreme law of the land under an occupation which has final powers. The supreme law is in theory the Far Eastern Commission, whose decisions are "implemented" by SCP directives. Few are issued now because the structure of the new democracy is pretty well completed.
> 2. The occupation necessarily restricts civil liberties by repressing anti-democratic forces and directing the course of democratic development. It does this (1) by censorship of all forms of communications, domestic and international, inspection of the mails, and controlling all meetings and organizations; (2) by trial in provost courts of Japanese offenders against directives and; (3) by ordering the purge of militarists and their supporters. It also raises issues [(4)] by putting on trial war-time offenders against the "laws of war" in the treatment of prisoners, and the leaders who waged aggressive war; (5) by restrictions on the relations of occupation personnel with the Japanese, and; (6) by opposing Communism in principle, while according Communists the rights exercised by others, [though] with far greater supervision.[7]

Subsequently, after offering his detailed views on each of the above points, Baldwin made the following ten recommendations.

> a. Remove all forms of SCAP censorship, domestic and international.
> b. Adopt a code of directives to press, radio etc., concerning criticism of U.S. and Allies.
> c. Reform the provost courts, limit jurisdiction to acts. Abolish deportation of aliens. Review the purges, and reform procedure,
> d. Release or try the war offenders.

---

6 *Civil Liberties in Japan* by Roger Baldwin, Memorandum attached to his letter to Lt. Gen. Eichelberger.

7 Ibid.

e. Liberalize the fraternization rules; abolish the curfew, free relief workers from restraints, restrain MP searches.
f. Remove the ban on marriages to Japanese.
g. Make clear distinction between Communism and labor and liberal movements.
h. Reorganize the M1 teams and provide direct access of civilians to SCAP agencies.
i. Permit affiliation of Japanese agencies with international, travel of representatives, air mail, printed matter.[8]
j Approve Japanese institutions' participation in international organizations, allow their representatives to travel abroad by sea or by air, and approve foreign publications.

In response, Major General Charles Willoughby, General Douglas MacArthur's chief of intelligence or G-2, who had received Baldwin's memorandum from Eichelberger, wrote a rebuttal on July 22. Willoughby argued that, at least as far as censorship was concerned, Baldwin's conclusions were based on "inaccurate data and statistics."[9]

Major General Edward M. Almond, GHQ's chief of staff, verbally asked Willoughby on April 28 whether civil censorship was still taking place on the European front. Willoughby immediately instructed Colonel William Putnam, his subordinate and commander of the CCD, to produce a document comparing civil censorships in the occupied European regions (Germany and Austria) with that in Japan and Korea under the occupation.[10]

The appendix to Putnam's document disclosed that, in several aspects, the mode of civil censorship in occupied Germany was remarkably different from the CCD's censorship in Japan—something that appeared to be somewhat related to the issue raised during the International Military Tribunal for the Far East.

This difference between occupied Europe and occupied Japan tied into the motion that defense counsel Kiyose Ichirō made at the outset of the Tokyo Trials:

Mr. President, this is a very important point. There is a very great

8 Ibid.

9 *Brig. Gen. Willoughby's letter to Roger Baldwin*, attached to the aforementioned memorandum.

10 *Civil Censorship Operations in Europe Compared with This Theater*, The National Records Center, Suitland, Maryland, RG 331, Box 8573.

difference between the way in which Germany surrendered and Japan surrendered. Germany, as you well know, Mr. President, resisted to the very last, Hitler died or was killed, Goering departed from the ranks, and Germany ultimately collapsed. In the case of Germany, it was literally an unconditional surrender. In other words, as regards German war criminals, the Allies, if I may be permitted to say so, could just as well have punished war criminals without trial.

> The forces of the Allied Powers had not yet landed in Japan when the Potsdam Declaration was proclaimed. In that Declaration, Article 5, it is mentioned that the "Following are our terms. We will not deviate from them."[11]

From the standpoint of international law theory, then, Kiyose posited that the state of Germany had temporarily perished through its collapse, and its former territory was reduced to a domain jointly shared by the United States, Britain, France, and the Soviet Union.[12] It follows that, legally, German war criminals could be treated as offenders of the domestic criminal laws of the Allied powers. Therefore, there could be no room in their trials for interference related to international problems, excepting problems that could arise among the four Allied powers countries.

Equally, the civil censorship that the occupation authorities conducted in Germany was, legally speaking, a purely domestic censorship. By no means was it an international censorship like the CCD's activities in Japan. Substantially speaking, the censorship in Germany was literally based on the crumbling of the state. Thus, the aforementioned appendix attached to the CCD document (*Civil Censorship Operations in Europe Compared with This Theater*) reads:

> Information Control (Censorship) in U.S. Zone of Germany, in press, pictorial and Broadcast fields.
>
> A. History:
>
> 1. At the outset of the occupation all printing plants, radio stations and motion picture theatres were closed. All German produced motion pictures were impounded. Military Government published 7 semi-

11 Asahi Shimbun Hōtei Kishadan, *Tōkyō Saiban, jō* [Tokyo Trials, Part I], Tokyo Saiban Kankōkai, 1977, p. 181–182.

12 Taoka Ryōichi, *Shūsengo no Nippon no hōteki chii* [Legal Position of Japan After the End of WWII], an annex to *Shūsen shiroku* [History of the end of war], Hokuyōsha, 1980, p. 159–162.

weekly newspapers to combat rumors, communicate news and instructions to the German people, and operated 3 radio stations.

2. "Politically reliable" and professionally qualified Germans to be permitted to engage in press, pictorial and broadcast field were sought out. "Because of necessity for finding men who were completely reliable and also were qualified to play a positive part in the democratic reorientation of Germany . . . political qualifications demanded in the informational services were necessarily more rigorous than in other fields of public life, and investigations were exhaustive."
3. On 31 July 46, first license to enter information field was given to publisher of *Frankfurter Rundschau*, who had passed the strict selection tests, and as U.S. licensed organs increased in press, publication and broadcast field, U.S. Military Government organs were gradually discontinued.

B. Present Status:

1. Press—As of 30 November 1946, only 44 German newspapers have been licensed to publish in U.S. Zone; only one news agency, DANA, has been licensed to operate. As of 31 July 46, 71 publishers had been licensed to operate.
2. Radio—No German radio stations have been licensed to operate. There are 6 radio stations in U.S. Zone, all run by Military Government.
3. Pictorial—10 licenses have been issued to German film producers, but no films, as of 29 November 46, had been allowed to be produced by Germans in Germany. Licenses have been issued to 269 musical and theatrical producers, and to 867 motion picture theatres. . .[13]

The arrangement was thus a system of information control under direct military administration, a framework of control (or censorship) operating on four core components:

1. Licensing
2. Monitoring
3. Limitation of themes
4. Management of news sources[14]

---

13 Information Control (Censorship) in U.S. Zone of Germany, in Press, Pictorial, and Broadcast Fields. The National Records Center. Suitland, Maryland, RG 331, Box No. 8573.

14 Ibid.

Of the four pillars of the censorship system, license to operate was withheld from organs of political parties, labor unions, or churches from the outset. Violators had their licenses suspended and publications confiscated, while their editors were reprimanded.

As for the monitoring of media, in the case of the DANA News Agency, several representatives of the U.S. military administration went straight to top management for constant monitoring of compliance with the directives and policies of the military administration. Even at the six radio stations under direct control of the U.S. military administration, all the scripts—without exception—underwent pre-broadcast censorship by censors of the military administration. All of their programs were monitored by censors of the U.S. forces, as well.

The third component, "limitation of themes," entailed the prohibition of criticism of the military administration and the occupation forces via adherence to a code of conduct. Offenders were deprived of their licenses to operate and ordered to suspend operations. Section 2 of Allied Control Authority Directive No. 40, equivalent to the Press Code for Japan, enumerated the following four areas subject to prohibition:

> 2. Members of German political parties and the German press must refrain from all statements and from the publication or reproduction of articles which:
>   (a) contribute towards the spreading of nationalistic, pan-Germanic militarist, fascist, or anti-democratic ideas;
>   (b) spread rumors aimed at disrupting unity amongst the Allies, or which cause distrust and a hostile attitude on the part of the German people towards any of the Occupying Powers;
>   (c) embody criticism directed against the decisions of the Conferences of the Allied Powers on Germany, or against the decisions of the Control Council;
>   (d) appeal to Germans to take action against democratic measures undertaken by the Commanders-in-Chief in their zones;[15]

The ensuing third section of the directive clearly stated that offenders would be punished.

The "management of news sources," the last of the four pillars, concerned the limitation of sources of foreign news and censorship thereof—on top of the monitoring of the media. As for foreign books, theatrical plays,

15 Ibid.

and music, only those permitted by the military administration were allowed to be imported to the U.S. occupied area.

What the directive shows is that the most salient feature of the military administration's information control (censorship) in Germany was its openness, the complete lack of a need to conceal anything at all.

Seeing as occupied Germany was nothing other than the former territory of a now-defunct state jointly owned by four alien countries (the United States, Britain, France, and the Soviet Union), there could be no international agreement to constrain the four nor any domestic law that contradicted the censorship. On this particular point, civil censorship in occupied Germany was markedly different in nature from the CCD's censorship in occupied Japan.

Moreover, in U.S. occupied Germany, operations of PPB media were completely banned at the outset of the occupation and then gradually resumed through qualification screening and the provision of licenses. The methodology stood in stark contrast to the CCD's censorship in Japan, which secretly applied pre-publication censorship to operating newspapers, publishers, and broadcasting stations.

From the viewpoint of the U.S. occupation authorities, civil censorship in U.S. occupied Germany was, both in terms of legal theory as well as actual practice, much more straightforward. The CCD's censorship in Japan was altogether different—it was rife with complicated, knotty factors from the very beginning. Defense counsel Kiyose's observation—"Germany and Japan differed in the way we surrendered"—encapsulated that reality.

As of late April 1947, when Almond verbally posed his question to Willoughby, civil censorship was still in place in U.S. occupied Germany. Moreover, Putnam's comparison of censorship in occupied Germany and that in occupied Japan revealed that the manpower mobilized in occupied Germany exceeded the personnel for CCD censorship in Japan and Korea—both quantitatively and qualitatively. The table below points to those differences.[16]

	Germany	Japan/Korea
Commissioned officers	1	83
Noncommissioned officers	8	80
Military dependents	946	370
Civilians from Allied Powers	2,937	554
Local civilians	4,436	5,076
Total	8,328	6,163

16 Ibid.

The same document also explained why more manpower went into Germany than Japan and Korea:

> a. More extensive time for planning civil censorship program. (Civil Censorship for the ETO was planned in England 18 months prior to the invasion of France; censorship for Japan was planned merely three months prior to the landing of U.S. forces in Japan.)
> b. Greater allotment of personnel.
> c. When the U.S. forces arrived in Japan, the Japanese communications system was still operating, although damaged from the war. External communications were permitted and it was necessary to quickly organize an effective system of internal censorship control. In Germany no Government existed, all communications were greatly curtailed, and were gradually opened step by step, commencing with intra-city, intra-district, and finally intra-zone communications.
> d. The recruiting team from Europe assigned the mission of screening potential WDC employees for censorship positions in Europe arrived in the United States during the Spring of 1945 (six months prior to the invasion of Japan). The European recruiting team fortunately arrived in the States just prior to the liquidation of the Office of Censorship, Washington, D.C. Approximately 12,000 Civil Services personnel engaged in the wartime function of civil censorship in the U.S. were gradually released from their positions. Accordingly, the European recruiting team had first priority on interviewing such trained censorship personnel for the purpose of determining whether or not they were interested in going to Europe for the purpose of accepting positions with civil censorship (the first recruiting team from Japan was sent to Hawaii and the U.S. in March 1946).
> e. Greater attractions in Europe for civilian personnel than Japan or Korea.
> f. There are available in the United States a large number of personnel that fit into the European language requirements; personnel in the U.S. qualified for handling the difficulties of oriental languages are few and far between.[17] (emphasis added)

In addition, Putnam's dossier also disclosed another major difference between the censorship in the two occupied zones: while there was no across-

17 Ibid.

the-board censorship of such PPB media as newspapers, publications, films, and broadcasts in Europe, as many as 18 percent of commissioned officers, 14 percent of noncommissioned officers, and 29 percent of military civilians of the total of 6,163 persons were assigned to PPB censorship in Japan.[18]

In other words, Willoughby, who submitted the document comparing Germany with Japan and Korea to Almond, used Almond's question to demonstrate the disadvantageous position of CCD censorship in Japan and justify the continuation of pre-publication censorship.

As a matter of fact, this attempt by the GHQ's G-2 to resist the shift to post-publication censorship proved effective to a certain extent. Notwithstanding criticism from the U.S. homeland—of which Baldwin's memorandum was a typical example—the only medium for which pre-publication censorship ended immediately on August 2, 1947, was broadcasting.[19]

As I noted previously, pre-publication censorship of books was suspended on October 15 and of magazines on December 15 of the same year. Pre-publication censorship of major national dailies in Japan was not terminated until July 25, 1948.[20]

It seems redundant to point out that these measures were taken in consideration of the progress at the International Military Tribunal for the Far East. The prosecutors' final statement was made on April 16, 1948, and the verdict was expected to be delivered in the fall. Considering the sensitive situation, with so much hanging in the balance, it was utterly impermissible for the censorship authorities to repeat their *25 hikoku no hyōjō* and *Bengo nijūnen* blunders in influential media like newspapers.

The G-2's tense apprehension about the censorship of newspapers is conspicuous in the document that forms the basis for the next Chapter: one pertaining to a lengthy commentary that the *Nippon Times* had submitted for pre-publication censorship on May 26, 1947.

---

18 Ibid.

19 *Operations of Military and Civil Censorship USAFFE/SWPA/AFPAC/FEC*, Vol. X, Intelligence Series, p. 135.

20 Ibid., p. 120–128.

CHAPTER 15

Internalization

The *Nippon Times* commentary discussed in this Chapter was labeled a "magazine commentary," implying that the piece may have been intended for publication in the *Nippon Times Magazine*, a weekly or monthly supplement to the daily *Nippon Times*.[1]

What follows is a paraphrase of the U.S. occupation authorities' first reaction to the piece.

> From: Press Section
> To: District I Headquarters
> May 28, 1948
>
> I had a meeting with Lieutenant Colonel D.S. Tate from G-2 at 13:30 concerning the attached *Nipp Times* [sic] editorial. His view was as follows: "I am against the publication of this editorial at this particular time. This is exactly the same argument that Tōjō defenders are going to make when he is sentenced to death. The analogy with General MacArthur is too direct; it will only be interpreted that the great patriot Tōjō must be acquitted by the SCAP and that any other verdict is tantamount to what Tokutomi calls 'a mistake committed by Emperor Meiji.'"
>
> Donald R[2]

In the margin next to the above passage was the comment:

> (Paraphrase) This document was presented to Lieutenant Colonel Nugent [author's note: Chief of the Civilian Information and Education] at 14:00 on May 28, 1954, by an orderly. What follows is Lieutenant Colonel Nugent's view: "While it will cause no problem if this editorial is printed six months from now, it will be extremely inconvenient if this is published <u>now, when the War Guilt Information</u>

1 *Magazines: Tokutomi's Speech* by Asahara Jōhei, The National Records Center, RG 331, Box No. 8574.

2 *From News Agency to Dist. 1*, The National Records Center, RG 331, Box No. 8574.

Program is being launched in earnest. Although I tend to be quite tolerant regarding this sort of thing, the editorial is too timely and could conceivably do tremendous damage to what we are trying to accomplish through the War Guilt Information Program. It is my impression that this editorial does more harm than good, particularly at this point. While I do not intend to fight to block publication of this, I do not believe its publication at this stage furthers the goal of the occupation."[3] (emphasis added)

Following this exchange of views, Lieutenant Colonel J. A. Thompson, acting commander of the Civil Censorship Detachment (CCD), drew up the following memorandum paraphrased here that very day and submitted it to the Civil Intelligence Section (CIS):

> 1. The attached editorial was submitted by the *Nippon Times* for pre-censorship.
> 2. The editorial is about a historical incident in the Meiji era in which twenty-four anarchists attempted to assassinate the emperor. The "secret court" sentenced twelve gang members to life in prison and the remaining twelve gang members to death by hanging. The majority of the text of the editorial is the protest of Tokutomi Kenjirō, who asks why the execution of the twelve anarchists should not have been carried out.
> 3. It appears that the aim of the *Nippon Times* in choosing to publish this editorial at this particular time is to stir up public opinion sympathetic to war criminals who are waiting for the final verdict and against their execution. Taken one step further, it could be conceived as a scheme to place General MacArthur in a position where he might grant a pardon to war criminals found guilty by the court.
> 4. It is appropriate to prohibit publication of this editorial.[4]

The lengthy commentary in question, simply titled "Tokutomi's Speech," was the work of one Asahara Jōhei. While I have no knowledge of this author, he might have been one of the reporters at the *Nippon Times* (now the *Japan Times*). Even a basic profile on who he was would be illuminating, but his identity remains unknown.

---

3 Ibid.

4 *G-2, GHQ, Inter-Office Memorandum, 28 May 48*, The National Records Center, RG 331, Box No. 8574.

Asahara opened the piece as follows.

> This incident took place in June of the 43rd Year of Meiji [1910]. The news about a gang of anarchists led by Kōtoku Shūsui attempting to assassinate the emperor and the crown prince stirred up the entire nation. Rumor had it that the entire gang was immediately arrested and tried by a special court.
>
> Six months later, on January 18 in the 44th Year of Meiji [1911], the silence was broken when it was revealed that the special court had sentenced all twenty-four implicated individuals to death.
>
> Because the truth of the incident remained hidden, the people showed symptoms of considerable anxiety and a hint of unrest. The tension eased somewhat, however, when reports on the ensuing day said that twelve of the twenty-four defendants would serve out life imprisonments. Rumor had it that the lives of the remaining twelve defendants would also be spared.
>
> But this wishful thinking was all for naught. Five days after the verdict, the twelve were hanged all at once. This gave cold shivers to people in Japan.
>
> Tokutomi Kenjirō, a writer using the pen name Roka, was a well-known humanist in those days. Particularly after the spiritual awakening that he had experienced a few years prior, Tokutomi had devoted himself to the salvation of man's soul based on his belief in world peace and the Christian faith.
>
> When Roka learned of the death sentence for the anarchists, he wrote a letter to Prime Minister Katsura [Tarō] requesting that the executions be called off. Roka was outraged by the execution of the twelve and furious about the government's handling of the incident.
>
> It was around that time that students of the First Higher School [in Tokyo] visited Roka, asking him to deliver a speech at their school. Although he rarely agreed to give lectures, he readily accepted the invitation.
>
> Roka spent three days and nights preparing the lecture, and yet he still continued to polish his manuscript. How earnestly and painstakingly he went about this task is evident in the two speech drafts in the collection at the Roka Park Library in Tokyo. Each is so full of deletions, corrections, additions, and rewordings that even Aiko, Mrs. Tokutomi, had difficulty reconstructing his speech from the drafts after his death. I imagine Roka perhaps had written a draft first and completed it after editing the manuscript to his satisfaction. And yet,

finding it still unsatisfactory, he must have continued to add corrections.

Roka's lecture was given on February 1 at the auditorium of the First Higher School. The auditorium, which had a capacity of 1,000, overflowed with attendees. A large signboard with the title of Roka's lecture, *Muhonron*, hung on the wall, and the venue teemed with the babble of excited voices.

Roka walked to the podium in black-crested garment and Kokura hakama [formal men's divided skirt]. He wore a pair of colored glasses on his thickly bearded face. And Roka started his speech composed, calm.[5]

The rest of Asahara's piece was devoted almost entirely to a verbatim introduction of Tokutomi Roka's *Muhonron* (On Rebellion). Comparing Asahara's commentary with the text of the *Muhonron* (draft) in *Tokutomi Roka-shū* (Collection of Tokutomi Roka's works),[6] I found the former a to-the-point summary translation of Tokutomi's treatise; the translation attains the level of fluency.

Asahara wrote:

I reside in a corner of the Musashino region near Tokyo. Every time I come to the Aoyama area of Tokyo, I must go through Setagaya. About 1-*ri* (roughly four kilometers) away from home, there is a scanty clump of Japanese red pines on the southern side of the road. Beyond the clump is Gōtoku-ji temple, which is well known for the tomb of Ii Kamonnokami Naosuke. A little way ahead of this temple, over a valley, one sees a mound covered with Japanese cedar and pine trees. The tomb of Yoshida Shōin and Shōin Shrine sit atop this mound. Ii and Yoshida were archrivals fifty years earlier. While Ii beheaded Yoshida during the Ansei Purge, Ii was subsequently assassinated by discontented *rōnin* samurai outside the Sakurada Gate of Edo Castle [the Sakuradamon Incident]. Fifty years after the bloody feud, the two found their resting places across a valley, all vengeances forgotten. From the sentimental viewpoint of today's Japanese, Shōin was, needless to say, the typical, purest of pure revolutionaries, and Ii was also a fine fellow who singlehandedly shouldered the heavy burden of man-

5 *Tokutomi's Speech*, p.1 of galley proof.

6 *Tokutomi Roka-shū* (Collection of Tokutomi Roka's works), Vol. 42 of *Meiji Bungaku Zenshū* [Collection of the Meiji Literature], Tokyo: Chikuma Shobō, 1966, p. 369–374.

aging Japan toward the end of the Tokugawa shogunate. Departing home in the morning, they took different paths in the field, jumping into the fervor of the killing games. Looking back at them from the vantage point of fifty years later, they simply exchanged blows from opposite directions toward the same goal of creating today's Japan. [Author's note: Three lines skipped.]

Ladies and gentlemen, we were all born in the Meiji era and, therefore, have not experienced the extremely restrictive, inflexible society of Japan fifty to sixty years ago. In those days, this tiny island country was divided into some sixty feudal domains like a *go* board, where one had to go through a checkpoint and pay taxes to move from one domain to another. Between men, there were castes, formalities, and social standings. Imagine an era when people were constrained by prohibitions and customs, when anything new was prohibited, and anyone who tried anything new was labeled a rebel. Is it not truly unbearable? Fortunately, the aftereffect of the major global tidal current also flooded into Japan over the dikes, which had been closed against the outside world for quite some time, triggering the revolution known as the Meiji Restoration, a transformation swept through sixty some feudal domains all at once and integrated Japan into a unified nation. [Three lines skipped.] The morale of Japan in the first year of Meiji was so high, as people shed layers of old clothes one by one, so to speak, leading to the emperor's promulgation of the Charter Oath, feudal lords' abandoning their domains, and samurai putting down their swords. . . . Japan grew rapidly like a bamboo shoot steamed by the air of liberty, equality, and reformation. [Two lines skipped.] Who was responsible for creating such momentum? It was the major tidal current of human emotions that ran around the globe. Who, then, invited such a tide to Japan? It was none other than our pioneer Meiji Restoration revolutionaries. Those revolutionaries had to suffer tremendously. Whether they were *rangakusha* [a person who studied Western sciences by means of the Dutch language] who pioneered new thought or advocates of *kinnōjōi* [supporters of the doctrine of restoring the emperor and expelling the foreign barbarians] who devoted themselves to an attempt to break the deadlock, they were all rebels from the viewpoint of the authority of the time. It would be impossible to narrate in a short space of time all the sufferings, all the twists and turns, that they had to undergo. All of U.S. who enjoy life today in the Meiji era must give grateful thought to their pains.

This is the direction my thoughts turn whenever I pass through

Setagaya. It has already been fifty years since both Yoshida and Ii were diminished to bones. It was with the power given to U.S. on the sacrifice of these revolutionaries and countless others that Japan was able to attain today's position. Japan is no longer a child. It has become quite the adult. While Japan had madly galloped through time in the first years of Meiji, it has now become composed enough to watch its steps as it walks, looks inward, and reflects on where it has been. Now that rules for internal affairs have somehow been established, and with the expansion of the territories through two external wars, it appears that unification of the new Japan has reached the end of its first chapter. The painful efforts of the revolutionaries before and after the Meiji Restoration have been rewarded, to some extent. Has, then, the history of the new Japan reached completion? Will the history of Japan now shift into the maintenance phase? Is there no more need to open new avenues? Do we no longer need revolutionaries? Absolutely not! The global current, which swept away the 300-year-old feudal state under the Tokugawa shogunate at a single stroke and unified Japan some fifty years ago, is still surging. This current represents the human tendency to become one—the heart of humankind to aspire for realization of universal brotherhood. Today's world, in a sense, can be likened to the Tokugawa Japan of fifty to sixty years earlier, where each and every country builds up its own army and navy, raising the walls of customs duties high, so that every other nation is either friend or foe, so that one has to hold on to a pistol in the pocket with his left hand while shaking hands with his right. When you realize that today's world is stuffy and absurd, it becomes unbearable, even for a minute, does it not? Nevertheless, the pursuit of the grand ideal of humankind will not stop until all the barriers between peoples are knocked down, until all can be unified. The human race continues to struggle toward unification, to be one. And the same can be said about the countries of the world, the races of the world, the social strata among people, genders, religions, and so on. Parts aspire to join with other parts so as to unify, while the wholes wish to be integrated with other wholes.

Thus, we in Japan stand in the dead center of this great turmoil of big whirlpools and countless smaller whirlpools, like the Naruto Whirlpools. Is the friction caused by this great turmoil endless and limitless? Like the Japanese people in the first years of Meiji who, at the apex of elation, madly abandoned themselves in order to attain emancipation from worldly attachments, will the time not come to this world of ours when all the kings throw away their crowns, billionaires abandon their fortunes, warriors give up their swords, and wise men, fools, the strong, and the weak disregard all the differences among them to embrace, shake hands, and dance with joy with each other under a white sun in a blue sky? It may be just a dream, but, even so, that is just fine. No one can live without a dream. [Three and a half lines skipped.] The time will come. It is steadily coming. Our innermost heart is whispering so to U.S.. Nevertheless, the happy fulfillment of this dream must be redeemed with our own blood, sweat, and tears. It calls for a number of people willing to sacrifice themselves for this realization without our knowing it. [Two and a half lines skipped.] "A newer version of Yoshida Shōin must appear in today's world. . . ." That is what I always murmur to myself whenever I pass through Setagaya. Then, without the slightest warning, at the outset of the 44th Year of Meiji, Japan ended up killing twelve rebels. This happened only one week ago.

Ladies and gentlemen, I must inform you that I somewhat differ with Kōtoku Shūsui and his comrades. I am a coward and I hate bloodshed. I do not know whether Kōtoku and his comrades seriously intended to commit high treason. I do not know if it was more of a case of "truth comes out of falsehood"—if they were actually driven by momentum and dragged into a pitfall before they realized where they were going, as one of the gang members, Ōishi Seinosuke, allegedly said. I do not know if they schemed to commit a forced double suicide with the emperor out of desperation, having realized that they were hopelessly deprived of the right to speak or write. And I do not know, from a strictly legal viewpoint, whether the execution of the twelve was appropriate and justifiable.

Did they just kill one innocent person and fail to accomplish their goal? Whatever the causes and circumstances of the incident, I lament deeply if there indeed was a scheme of high treason as the judgment of the Supreme Court of Judicature seemed to endorse. I do not approve of violence. I do not wish to sacrifice others even if I must sacrifice myself instead. Still, as much as I absolutely disapprove of a high-treason scheme and rejoice at the failure of such attempts, I did not like to see those twelve executed. I wanted them to be alive. Even though they were labeled "mutinous subjects and unfilial children," they were not simple villains. They were revolutionaries. I do not approve of the execution of a simple villain, to say nothing of revolutionaries who were youths with promising futures. They attempted to devote themselves to humankind, dreaming of a new heaven and earth of freedom and equality. Even though their conduct might have been akin to madness, shouldn't their aspirations deserve our sympathy?

They were socialists, originally, who found society's unequal distribution of wealth defective and advocated public ownership of means of production, instead. What is so fearful about socialism? It is found everywhere in the world. Nevertheless, the narrow-minded and uptight government suddenly became oversensitive to the presence of socialism and suppressive of it, particularly when socialists vocally opposed the Russo-Japanese War. [Four and half lines skipped.] Undergoing governmental suppression and oppression, those socialists in Japan finally became anarchistic. What is so fearful about anarchism? If the government is really so fearful of them, the prime minister or the home minister, someone high in the government, should have had a heart-to-heart talk with Kōtoku before the matter became serious. Low-level bureaucrats will never do. But government authorities are too authoritarian and pompous to take such an unconventional measure. They are more inclined to tenaciously impose severe restrictions on the likes of Kōtoku, using their long arms. Kōtoku and his comrades found these restrictions unbearable; eventually they were transformed from something like a rat to a tiger. And some of them came to the resolution that they no longer had any option other than the last resort, leading to the emergence of a ghost-like scheme. They should not have been so short-tempered, and they should not have become so desperate. They should have been just a little more patient. But, who, then, made them so self-destructive? Whatever the judicial judgment was, Kōtoku and his comrades were not mutinous subjects or unfilial children in heaven's judgment. They were revolutionaries. They were martyrs.[7] (emphasis added)

The final "They were martyrs" was not in Tokutomi's original text. Whether the CCD censors were aware of it or not, Asahara had obviously added that tailpiece.

Asahara's summary translation of *Muhonron* continued:

. . . Providence took pity on their good intentions, and their scheme failed before its time arrived. The successful accomplishment of their scheme would have meant a setback of their good intentions. Prov-

7 *Tokutomi's Speech*, p. 1–2 of galley proof.

idence took pity on the imperial family, as well as Kōtoku's group, and the scheme failed, leading to the arrest of the conspirators, the lives of twelve of whom were spared out of political considerations. The remaining twelve were executed, which was a god-sent grace. Actually, twelve plus one lives were lost. We should not forget about Kōtoku's mother, who died in Tosa of a suspected suicide.

Thus the twelve died. Death, however, was a victory for them. Paradoxical as it may sound, in the rule of human affairs, the loser is the winner. To die is to live. They were without a doubt confident about that. That one of the accused hailed, "*Banzai, banzai*" ["Long live!"] when he walked out of the court room after being sentenced to death is proof of that conviction. They all died with smiles on their faces. Uchiyama Gudō, one of the executed who was reputed to be a dissolute priest, looked very peaceful. With the death of those twelve anarchists, countless seeds of anarchists were sown. Those twelve successfully died sacrificial deaths.

Still, I find fault with those who created these victims.

Ladies and gentlemen, in our veins runs the blood of loyalists to the emperor. I, for one, treasure His Majesty. . . . The present emperor is the embodiment of simplicity and fortitude, a model of a genuine Japanese man. . . . As can be depicted in His Majesty's *waka* poems, such as "Like the clear blue heaven in the morning, how I wish I can be as magnanimous as that," the emperor is an aspirational monarch. This is highly commendable. Ladies and gentlemen, as subjects to such a monarch, why did we have to kill those twelve—even though they might have been devils to plot the assassination of the emperor—while sparing the lives of the other twelve? Was the emperor devoid of clemency? Or was he ambivalent toward the gang members? The answer to these questions is definitely no. The outcome was solely the fault of the advisors to the emperor. Had there been a loyal man of principle close to the emperor who directly pleaded for equal royal pardons for all the twenty-four accused, regardless of the seriousness of their offenses, and for a chance for the twenty-four to reflect on and repent of their sins, His Majesty must have concurred. This would have spared U.S. of the task of burying twelve revolutionaries. . . If only Yamaoka Tesshū had been alive at a time such as this to advise the emperor! Yamaoka was the bravest and most loyal of all. Once, when the emperor was still young, Yamaoka became concerned about the emperor's vulgar conduct of wrestling with vassals and throwing them to the ground for fun. Yamaoka took it upon himself to throw the young emperor until he had had more than enough and then reprimanded the emperor. Or if only Kido Shōgiku had been there. In the first year of Meiji, in the presence of the emperor, flanked by Princesses Sanjō Sanetomi and Iwakura Tomomi and other princes and lords, Kido faced the emperor squarely and commandingly preached that the emperor must heed trends overseas where some countries had already abolished their monarchs and adopted republican political systems. The emperor listened to Kido with respectful attention, while the attending princes and lords went pale. Or if only Baron Motoda Nagazane had been alive at that time. Motoda had genuinely revered the emperor from the bottom of his heart and had made it his lifelong goal to guide the emperor to be morally perfect and intelligent in the mold of such sage-kings as Emperor Yao and Emperor Shun, two legendary leaders of ancient China. Or if only Ito [Hirobumi] had been alive. . . . Nay, had the crown prince been a child by birth of the empress, His Majesty might have thought differently. . . (<u>Here, the speaker's voice choked, and attendants' eyes warmed.</u>)[8] (emphasis added)

The sentence, "Here, the speaker's voice choked and attendants' eyes warmed" was not included in Tokutomi's original text. There is no knowing what prompted Asahara to add this line.

The middle portion of Asahara's lengthy summary translation points clearly to his intentions.

> [G]overnment officials should look back at their original ideals and become humble learners. They may defend themselves, claiming that they had confidently carried out their duty as far as the crime committed by Kōtoku and his comrades was concerned. From the detached viewpoint of history, those officials may even appear to represent a kind of savior who killed anarchists and provided a breakthrough. . . .However, the Meiji government cannot evade the responsibility of having tortured and enraged twelve of His Majesty's children—and those with good works to do, at that—framing them as rebels and shamelessly hanging them in the well-governed 44th Year of Meiji. Those officials must apologize to His Majesty, to the Japanese people, and to those twelve victims. You should not kill even if you are to be killed. Sacrifice is service to the emperor and the Japanese people. Human dignity deserves respect. It does not matter what bad name those offi-

8 Ibid., p. 3 of galley proof.

cials might incur as a consequence. Whether theirs was a successful endeavor or not is not necessarily the question at hand. The final judgment rests on something that resides in our deepest corners.

[Subsequent eighteen lines skipped.]

Ladies and gentlemen, Kōtoku and his comrades have perished at the gallows as mutinous subjects and unfilial children. Even though their actions may have been objectionable, who could question these revolutionaries' motives? Ladies and gentlemen, let us remember that Saigō Takamori, too, was once labeled a rebel. Today, however, can anyone think of someone who is not as un-rebellious as Saigō? Kōtoku and his comrades, too, accidentally became "mutinous subjects and unfilial children." Public opinion 100 years from now will resent this incident and grieve over forsaken ideals. It is a matter of character, something that we must not fail to refine.[9]

The summary translation of Tokutomi's speech ended here, but the *Nippon Times* commentary continued:

When Roka finished his speech, a momentary silence lingered until the entire house suddenly exploded in thunderous applause. Every last member of the audience felt that whatever indescribable emotion they had had toward the incident had found a conduit in the speaker's words. It was a moment when their deep resentment toward death by hanging and their deep emotions toward the emperor, both harbored deep in their hearts, found the perfect expression.

Among the audience was Tanaka Kōtarō, a student at the First Higher School who later became professor at Tokyo Imperial University and, eventually, minister of education. He wrote in his journal, "It was the most memorable speech I have ever heard. Had it been delivered eight days earlier, the lives of all of the executed anarchists would have been spared."

This lecture was banned from publication, and Nitobe Inazō, schoolmaster at the First Higher School, was reprimanded by the Ministry of Education. The manuscript of this lecture, included in Vol. 18 of *Roka Zenshū* [Complete Works of Tokutomi Roka], published in 1929, is full of omissions due to censorship. Since then, there has been a remarkable change of the times. Some may question if the people feel deep-seated

9 Ibid., p. 4 of galley proof.

emotions toward the emperor, but judging from the cheers welcoming the emperor wherever His Majesty visits and the overwhelming votes that candidates advocating continuation of the emperor system have obtained in the past two general elections, this is impossible to refute.[10] (emphasis added)

The "remarkable change of the times" might have occurred—or might not have occurred. To be sure, censorship by the Japanese authorities and official reprimands were abolished.[11] Nevertheless, Asahara's draft did not make it to publication, with "Suppress" written in blue pencil with a stamp on the first page of the four-page galley proof. This was no different from the situation in, say, 1911.

Attached to the galley proof was a memo by a U.S. military censor, who found the article inappropriate for publication as it was. He backed up his judgment by saying that the defense argument for Tōjō after his guilty verdict was likely to resemble Tokutomi's argument. In spite of the apparent similarity, however, the censorship in 1911 by Japan's Home Ministry authorities and the international censorship by the CCD could by no means be of the same nature. The control of press and speech regarding a high-treason trial on the one hand and censorship and propaganda related to the International Military Tribunal for the Far East on the other cannot be discussed in the same breath. While the former was a defensive measure intended to protect the existing order and incumbent regime, the latter was an offensive measure obviously fueled by an aggressive and destructive purpose. Needless to say, the latter was driven by the tenacious and chronic intent to mobilize whatever means necessary to destroy the identity of the Japanese people and their confidence in their own history—whatever may come—as the War Guilt Information Program exemplified.

It goes further. Once this structure of censorship and propaganda was firmly embedded and sustained in Japan's media organizations and the educational system, the identity of the Japanese people and their confidence in their own history would continue to be destroyed from within, ad infinitum, even after the abolishment of the CCD and termination of the occupation. The Japanese people, too, would continue to obsess constantly over the threat of international censorship. It was exactly this nightmare—the resurgence of international censorship—that emerged during the so-called "textbook issue" in the summer of 1982.

---

10 Ibid., p. 4 of galley proof.

11 See Chapter 8.

CHAPTER 16

The Politicization of Language

Thus far, I have discussed how the censorship of speech and expression by the Civil Censorship Detachment (CCD) has continued to constrain the linguistic space of postwar Japan.

I have also said, in the previous Chapter:

Once this structure of censorship and propaganda was firmly embedded and sustained in Japan's media organizations and the educational system, the identity of the Japanese people and their confidence in their own history would continue to be destroyed from within, ad infinitum, even after the abolishment of the CCD and termination of the occupation. The Japanese people, too, would continue to obsess constantly over the threat of international censorship. It was exactly this nightmare—the resurgence of international censorship—that emerged during the so-called "textbook issue" in the summer of 1982.

This threat, however, is not necessarily confined to that of international censorship. In fact, I have had firsthand experience witnessing unmistakable censorship in Japan by none other than Japanese media organizations themselves. I have documents that could prove the existence of censorship in today's Japan, too. The incident in question had close connections to the Imperial Household and the roots of Japanese culture, and the following is an outline of the case for the record.

I have no detailed knowledge on when the Nippon o Mamoru Kokumin Kaigi (People's Council for the Protection of Japan, chaired by Kase Toshikazu) decided to produce a documentary film as part of the celebration of the sixtieth anniversary of the present emperor's [Shōwa's] reign. If I recall correctly, though, it was around the spring of 1985 that I received a phone call from Mayuzumi Toshirō, chairman of the celebration event, who asked me to supervise the production of the film.

According to Mayuzumi, my task as supervising consultant would be to ensure that the film's scenario reflected the People's Council's intentions for the celebration as much as possible. Remembering that I had contributed to the production of NHK's television program "Meiji no Gunzō: Umi ni Karin o" (A Lively Crowd of the Meiji Era: Ring of Fire to the Sea) some ten years earlier, I decided that I could handle the mission and accepted Mayuzumi's invitation.

On the evening of June 12 that same year, I met with Mayuzumi, Soejima

Hiroyuki (secretary-general of the People's Council), and representatives from Mainichi Eigasha, the filmmaker commissioned to produce the film. During the meeting, I was puzzled by the group's reluctance regarding the revised version of the first draft of the scenario that the People's Council had presented.

Of course, their concern was that the full depiction of the revised scenario would make the film excessively long—so long as to make showing the film practically impossible. The more you trim down manuscripts, including scenarios, the more powerful and sharp-focused they become—that truth always holds. So convinced, I was motivated as the film's supervisor to cut the scenario down to size.

A few episodes seemed to be of some significance, but the filmmaker explained that they could not find the corresponding takes in their documentary film library. I told them that we did not always have to have perfectly matching pictures to explain all the episodes, like a picture-story show; they could, instead, evoke the images in the audience's minds through music and narration, a much more sophisticated method. After hearing my suggestion, the filmmaker agreed and decided to go ahead with that approach.

Thus, we saw some progress during the meeting as far as technical issues were concerned. What puzzled me, though, was the apparent shift of mood on the part of the filmmaker whenever it came to the question of the wording in reference to the emperor and the imperial family: as soon as the issue came up, they immediately got nervous and defensive. And it was not about us being insufficiently deferential. On the contrary, they insisted, we should constantly remain vigilant so as not to be *excessively* deferential.

For instance, since accepting my supervisory role on the documentary, I realized that I wanted the film to quote as many poems by the emperor as possible. Needless to say, poems by the emperor are an expression of His Majesty's mind in his own words. One way or another, people can quibble over the present emperor's personal weakness in the sixty-some years since his appointment as regent. Nobody, however, can cast doubt on the candid manifestations of His Majesty's heart in his poems. Let His Majesty's own words tell his accomplishments, I believed. There can be no truer record of His Majesty's sixty-year reign than his verse.

The reaction from the filmmaker, however, went against my expectation to no small degree. First, they reacted negatively to the term "poems by His Majesty." When I asked what was wrong with it, they said that we should not use that term. To my question on an alternative term, they replied that, nowadays, we were supposed to refer, simply, to "his poems."

At this point, I had to say, "Wait a minute." We are not talking about a poem by someone off the street. How could we possibly call a poem composed by His Majesty simply "his poem?" This goes against the original linguistic sensitivities of the Japanese people. And what on earth would anyone gain by replacing "His Majesty's poem" with "his poem?" It would just go against the Japanese sensitivity to words, making the meaning obscure, diminishing the due awe, and violating the emperor's sanctity. To begin with, where in the world did that prohibition come from? Who banned it? More than that, who would claim the authority to do so?

In response to my outburst, the filmmaker tried to explain roughly as follows. My phrasing, a "poem by His Majesty," was anachronistic. They claimed that the Imperial Household Agency was so particular about terminology that each broadcasting company and filmmaker had compiled its own in-house manual so that it would never make such a crucial mistake as calling "his poem" a "poem by His Majesty."

Hence started my rebuttal. If that was indeed the case, then the practice was tantamount to self-censorship by each broadcasting company and filmmaker, stemming from suggestions or interference by the Imperial Household Agency. While the current Constitution of Japan was based on a draft that the GHQ's General Staff Section 2 (G-2) had submitted to the Japanese government, even the GHQ-initiated constitution explicitly stipulates in Article 21 that "No censorship shall be maintained, nor shall the secrecy of any means of communication be violated."

For broadcasting companies and filmmakers themselves to employ self-imposed restrictions on wording under the guidance of the Imperial Household Agency would violate Article 21 of the constitution. Even more, the idea of it all seemed like a perpetuation of decades-old constraints: it was as if a linguistic space similar to that in place during the occupation period, when CCD censors discreetly monitored the media, was still limiting the free expression of the Japanese people even under the current constitution—at least when it came to the emperor and the imperial family.

Now that I have been commissioned to supervise the production, I continued, I will not tolerate such inscrutable nonsense. A "poem by His Majesty" is nothing other than a poem by His Majesty and it simply cannot be "his poem." I will take full responsibility for whatever comes of that choice. When the Imperial Household Agency complains, let me handle that immediately. If necessary, I am prepared to argue that the Imperial Household Agency's requests are tantamount to censorship prohibited by the Constitution of Japan, and I will not hesitate to take legal action against the agency. Needless to say, I have no intention of burdening the filmmaker or the People's Council with any legal expenses, either.

When I had said that much, I could sense the Mainichi Eigasha softening a bit. Its executives, who had shown apparent bewilderment in the beginning, started saying that they would try to satisfy my wish as much as they could. Thus, with this agreement, the meeting was adjourned.

About two months after the meeting, when I was recuperating at my mountain villa after two months of intensive deliberations at a council on the visit to Yasukuni Shrine by cabinet members in June and July, the People's Council secretariat contacted me with a request to take a look at the revised scenario and film in early August. Hearing my explanation on why I could not come to Tokyo, the secretariat personnel offered to mail the scenario to my villa and then come to nearby Karuizawa with a projector so that I could see an unedited cut of the film. We arranged for a viewing at 3:00 p.m. on Wednesday, August 14, 1985, at the Hotel New Hoshino in Sengataki, Karuizawa.

Reading the scenario, which was just a simple copy of the script, I found the overall structure quite satisfactory. However, it did have intolerable problems with the use of honorifics, including the non-use of terms reserved for the emperor and the imperial family for sickness, death, accession to the throne, and so on. I was particularly annoyed by the improper use of honorific titles, including that for the emperor, who had to be called Imperial Prince Hirohito in his youth instead of merely Prince Hirohito. And Empress Kōjun had to be referred to as Princess Nagako before her marriage to the emperor. A special term reserved for an emperor's death should have been used for the passing of Emperor Taishō, but if that was against their policy, at least a special term commonly used for the death of a person in a high position until recently should have been employed.

When I met the film director and People's Council secretariat people, who visited me in the afternoon of August 14 as agreed, I candidly shared my concerns with them. I showed them the scenario on which I had scribbled my proposals in red.

The film director was an up-front, open type, one who gave me the impression of being a proficient editor. He was refreshingly civil; he calmly listened to my thoughts on the scenario with a wry grin. Then, nonchalantly, I floated an idea to the staff from the People's Council secretariat, "Now that you've produced such an excellent film, why don't you consider shortening it for TV broadcast?"

Hearing this casual comment of mine, the film director appeared a little tense, even if only momentarily. Subsequently, he demurred. "No, not TV," he said. "We wouldn't be allowed to run it on TV."

"Oh, you couldn't run this on TV?" I replied. "Are the TV standards that high?" I deliberately did not pursue the issue any further.

Somehow, the director's comment weighed on my mind. It bothered me that he had said that the film would not run on TV. When I later took a look at a handbook on terminology that Mainichi Eigasha had given to the People's Council, I understood instantly why our film would never hit the small screen. I knew that the handbook was a de facto censorship guideline.

The handbook was compiled by Mainichi Broadcasting System, Inc., and its formal title was *Kōshitsu kankei yōgoshū: Kaitei-ban* (Imperial Household–Related Glossary: Revised Edition). It had been compiled in September 1975, which made it already some ten years old when I took a look at it. An executive director on the broadcasting program examination board and chairman of the broadcast terminology liaison committee at Mainichi Broadcasting System, Inc., contributed a section titled "In Place of a Preface," which reads:

> The unexpectedly strong feedback from many corners on *Kōshitsu kankei yōgoshū* that we had published earlier have brought home the keen interest [among Japanese media] in terminology related to the imperial household.
>
> In light of all the comments on errors, complaints, and requests, we resigned ourselves to compiling the revised edition.
>
> Given the image of prewar imperial household–related terminology—that it is arcane, banal, antiquated, and so on—it was quite a time-consuming and arduous task to reconstruct it in simple, contemporary Japanese. In any event, we have managed to revise the original glossary in a year, and it is our hope that it will be widely used.
>
> Last but not least, we wish to express our deepest gratitude to all who rendered their assistance in compiling the manuscript. (emphasis added)

The introduction, which follows the "In Place of a Preface," includes the following points.

(1) All the terms were reviewed carefully in light of contemporary sensibilities. Extra care was taken to avoid being anachronistic. To avoid rendering the glossary dry and bland, we tried to add easy-to-understand explanations to the entries wherever possible. We hope that the compilation might serve as a mini–imperial household dictionary.

(2) Facing pages are given to *Sokuishiki* (coronation ceremony), *Sokui no rei* (ceremony of accession), and *Taisō no rei* (rites of imperial

funeral). Right-hand pages provide detailed descriptions of ceremonial procedures in chronological sequence.

(3) The "Examples" in the explanations are mainly quoted from newspaper articles on Emperor Taishō and the incumbent emperor. Note that it remains unknown how ceremonies such as *Sokuishiki*, *Sokui no Rei*, and *Taisō no Rei* will actually be conducted in the future and, therefore, the handling of terms related to these ceremonies calls for extra care. (emphasis added)

The guideline's explanatory note included the astonishing passage:

(1) Words no longer in use today are marked with an *X* for the benefit of users. In cases where words no longer in contemporary use are parts of the names of traditional ceremonies, however, they are presented without *X*. An example is *Senso-go Chōken no Gi,* in which the word *senso* is one that is no longer used.)

(2) The △ symbol indicates a word that is still used today but should be accompanied by a simple, straightforward explanation wherever possible.

(3) An underline marking Chinese characters in words that are no longer in use today, words that are still in use, names of ceremonies, and names of events signifies that the characters are not *tōyō kanji* (Chinese characters designated for daily use in Japan). Underlines do not appear under *jinmeiyō kanji* (Chinese characters officially for use in names) not listed as *tōyō kanji.* (emphasis added)

Below is the table of contents for *Kōshitsu kankei yōgoshū: Kaitei-ban.*

I. Coronation/Accession to the Throne/Enthronement of the Emperor of Japan
II. Illness/Demise/Rites of Imperial Funeral
III. Emperor/Imperial Family
IV. Birth/Marriage
V. Events/Ceremonies
VI. Terminology on Deeds/Outings/State Acts/Decorations/Imperial Family
VII. Attire
VIII. Buildings, etc.
IX. Appendix: Laws Related to the Imperial Family, Index

The list of principle references included, among others, *Kōshitsu kankei hōsō yōgoshū: Kettei-ban* (Imperial household–related broadcast terminology: Final edition) compiled by Nippon Hōsō Kyōkai (NHK); *Kōshitsu kankei yōgoshū: Sono 1* (Imperial Household–related glossary: Vol. 1) by Tokyo Hōsō (Tokyo Broadcasting); *Kōshitsu kankei yōgoshū* (Imperial Household–related glossary) by Nippon Shimbun Kyōkai (Japan Newspaper Publishers & Editors Association); and *Kōshitsu yōgo* (Imperial Household–related terminology) by Kyōdō Tsūshinsha (Kyodo News). Judging from this list, it would appear that a standard for self-censorship had been established not only at the Mainichi Broadcasting System, but also across Japan's broadcasting and newspaper industries in general.

Seeing that such basic terms as *gofurei* (illness of a great personage) and *okakure ni naru* (to pass away) were among the words "no longer in contemporary usage," I had to concur that our documentary celebrating the sixtieth anniversary of the emperor's reign could not possibly air on TV. The glossaries frequently marked such terms with an *X*, signifying obsolescence—and, because of that, our documentary film would not pass the self-censorship of broadcasters and newspaper companies in Japan.

In any event, I wonder how the broadcasters and newspaper companies had interfered so rudely in the Japanese language—how in the world could they justify that authority? What legal grounds did they have? As I have already pointed out, this conduct violates the prohibition of censorship stipulated by the Constitution of Japan. Of the constitutional articles concerning the emperor, Article 1 says, "The Emperor shall be the symbol of the state and of the unity of the people, <u>deriving his position from the will of the people</u> with whom resides sovereign power" (emphasis added). Article 2, meanwhile, states, "The imperial throne shall be <u>dynastic</u> and succeeded to in accordance with the imperial house law passed by the Diet" (emphasis added). These two articles harbor a fundamental contradiction—the emperor deriving his position from the will of the people even as the imperial throne is a dynastic one. I wonder if the censors in the broadcasting and newspaper industries have ever pondered why the constitution had to uphold such a fundamental contradiction.

And if the Imperial Household Agency's wishes had indeed been behind the self-censorship by the broadcasting and newspaper industries, as the executives of Mainichi Eigasha had implied, I just wonder, to begin with, what kind of role this public office is playing in today's Japan.

Come to think of it, even if the imperial throne is dynastic, can the will of the people ever be dynastic? If this "will of the people" does actually exist, it should be something transitory and ever-changing—and, by extension, cannot automatically and logically guarantee the unbroken succession of the imperial throne.

Dynastic succession is an institution only sustainable where the succession of the imperial throne is guaranteed regardless of the people's will. Stepping further into the hidden logic pervading the constitution, one finds that "the will of the people" in Article 1 on the one hand and the dynastic succession of the imperial throne in Article 2 on the other seem mutually contradictory. Not even the present constitution permits upholding one and discarding the other.

Examining these two constitutional articles on the emperor from the succession angle, one naturally concludes that "the will of the people" in Article 1 is an obvious fiction—a make-believe, if you will. When interpreting the institutional fact that the emperor is actually on the throne and that the throne is a dynastic succession, we deliberately, consciously choose to believe that the emperor's position derives from the will of the people; otherwise, the significance of the dynastic succession in Article 2 would be hard to comprehend.

Censors at broadcasters and newspaper companies, however, seem to have failed to pay due attention to the subtle interaction between Article 1 and Article 2. Instead, they only pursue the substantialization of "the will of the people." "In Place of a Preface" in *Kōshitsu kankei yōgoshū: Kaitei-ban* says, after all, "Given the image of prewar imperial household–related terminology—that it is arcane, banal, antiquated, and so on— it was quite a time-consuming and arduous task to reconstruct it in simple, contemporary Japanese." And the book's introduction states, "All the terms were reviewed carefully in light of contemporary sensibilities. Extra care was taken to avoid being anachronistic. To avoid rendering the glossary dry and bland, we tried to add easy-to-understand explanations to the entries wherever possible. We hope that the compilation might serve as a mini–imperial household dictionary." The implicit assumption in these statements is the undisputed primacy of "contemporary sensibility" over "prewar imperial household–related terminology," the clearest evidence of how the broadcasters and newspaper industries perceived the apparent contradiction in the constitution.

Let me pose some questions here. Is today's Japanese language truly easier to understand, and is the contemporary sensibility really superior to prewar imperial household–related terminology? And how did these people acquire the arrogance to unilaterally label some words "anachronistic?" Who granted broadcasters and newspaper companies the authority and power to reconstruct the imperial household–related terminology into easy-to-understand contemporary Japanese language?

For argument's sake, assume that broadcasters and newspapers have that authority. Even on that assumption, using the obscure gauge of "contemporary sensibility" as the only criterion for eliminating anachronism would be arbitrary, to say the least. Is it really justifiable to demarcate "words no longer in use" and "words that are still in use" according to such an arbitrary criterion?

Would replacing *gyōkō* (or *miyuki*, words reserved for an outing by the emperor) with *odekake* (a word for an "outing" that can be used for anyone) and *gofurei* (an illness of a great personage) with *gobyōki* (an illness of anyone) really accomplish the reconstruction of older terms into simple Japanese? To eliminate a term that was reserved for the emperor's outings by designating it as a "word no longer in use today" would only make contemporary Japanese more inaccurate and impoverish the vocabulary. Are broadcasters and newspapers in Japan today prepared to commit an act of such stupidity as calling the road Gyōkō Dōro in Hayama an Odekake Dōro and the street Miyuki Dōri in Ginza an Odekake Dōri instead? Was that not exactly what the media companies were doing in their foolish word-hunting?

A passage from Natsume Sōseki's *Kokoro* illustrates my point, I believe:

> And then, at the height of the summer, Emperor Meiji passed away. I felt then that as the spirit of the Meiji era had begun with him, so it had ended with his death. I was struck with an overwhelming sense that my generation, we who had felt Meiji's influence most deeply, were doomed to linger on simply as anachronisms as long as we remained alive. When I said this in so many words to my wife, she laughed it off. But then for some reason she added teasingly, "Well, then, you could follow the old style and die with your lord, couldn't you." (translation by Meredith McKinney, Penguin Books, New York, 2010) (emphasis added)

The word *hōgyo* was used to describe the demise of Emperor Meiji, the underlined part of the above passage. Is the term "arcane," "banal," and "anachronistic?" It cannot be because it is, indeed, contemporary Japanese. According to a survey of favorite books among junior and senior high school students, *Kokoro* by Natsume Sōseki has almost always been in the top five over the past twenty years. Today's teens, who figure to be at the cutting edge of contemporary sensibilities, continue to read Natsume Sōseki's *Kokoro* as an essential linguistic experience of their own; to contemporary Japanese readers, then, *Kokoro* resides in the vernacular. If *Kokoro* and its linguistic conventions are not "contemporary Japanese," then what is?

Culturally speaking, even the Japanese language in the Meiji and Taishō eras are both integral parts of contemporary Japanese usage. More than that—even the language of *Genji Monogatari* (The Tale of Genji) is also an indispensable component of contemporary Japanese usage. A language as a form of culture is always synchronic—and sustainable only through being synchronic.

Genji Monogatari is a tale of honorifics, so to speak. It would be no overstatement to say that the essence of the honorifics of classical Japanese grammar that high school students in Japan learn today inhabits this tale. *Genji Monogatari* is narrated with virtually no personal pronouns; the tale is woven with a tremendous number of honorifics, used accurately and rigorously. It goes without saying that at the apex of the *Genji* world are the honorifics reserved for the emperor.

From that standpoint, honorifics not only point to the apex of the world of a tale but, more importantly, also function as the nucleus and root of the Japanese language that forms the text of the *Genji* tale. This characteristic of the Japanese language is firmly present in contemporary Japanese, synchronically, as well. After all, the Japanese language remains a language of honorifics.

To discard honorifics as anachronistic and demarcate words no longer in use from words still in use is an artificial attempt to divide the Japanese language diachronically based on political value judgments. It represents the destruction of the language itself and, by extension, the destruction of the roots of the Japanese culture. I wonder if those who drew the line between obsolete and current ever gave even a minute's thought to the horrors of bringing political and diachronic arbitrariness to a language.

Let a national language remain natural. That is how language should exist. It has been some six years since I started studying primary sources to examine the Civil Censorship Detachment's censorship in occupied Japan, and the process has stirred quite a few thoughts in me. There may be peace, democracy, and people's sovereignty in today's Japan, but freedom is still missing. Let the language—the Japanese language—go au naturel. Let the language live. There can be no freedom in a linguistic space that cannot promise a natural existence to its own language.

Afterword

This book represents the culmination of my research on censorship in occupied Japan, which I conducted at the Woodrow Wilson International Center for Scholars in Washington, DC, from October 1979 through June 1980.

As a Japan Foundation visiting fellow, I devoted myself day and night during those nine months at the Wilson Center to searching for and reading through documents related to the U.S. occupation forces' censorship activities in Japan. Even though my stay was short, the experience was illuminating. Much of what I learned informed two books of mine: *1946-nen kenpō: Sono kōsoku* (1946 Constitution: Its Constraints) and *Ochiba no hakiyose* (Sweeping up Fallen Leaves) from Tokyo's Bungei Shunjūsha. Nevertheless, I still felt that I had to get the truth out about the censorship in occupied Japan, which, after all, had been the focus of my study. I started compiling what I had found in Washington soon after I returned home, and I began writing this book in the summer of 1981.

In February 1982, the manuscript, which now constitutes the first part of the present volume, appeared in the monthly *Shokun!*. I continued to write the subsequent sections, which ran in the same monthly magazine in five installments from December 1982 through February 1986.

Out of my desire as an author to create the best opportunity for getting my work out into the world, I decided to compile the manuscripts and publish them as a book more than three and a half years after their first appearance in *Shokun!*. I, for one, am confident that this book is unrivaled in its field. As far as I know, there has been no other comprehensive study on the hidden censorship by the U.S. occupation forces in Japan with grounding in primary sources not only in Japan but also in the United States.

There is, of course, *Press Control around the World* (New York: Praeger, 1982), co-edited by Jane Leftwich Curry and Joan R. Dassin, to which I contributed a chapter titled "The Censorship Operation in Occupied Japan."

In the preface to *Press Control around the World*, Joan Dassin praised my chapter as an empirical study on a censorship system that had been completely unknown in the United States. While that individual chapter may be the only exception to my earlier claim that no other such work in this field exists, it is no match for the present volume in terms of comprehensiveness. I hope that this book will resonate not only with Japanese readers but, more importantly, from my viewpoint, also with intellectuals in the United States. Disclosing the relentlessness of the occupation forces' hidden censorship in postwar Japan will undoubtedly provide American intellectuals with considerable food for thought about the ideal of freedom of speech.

Regarding Japanese readers, there is only one thing I expect. I hope the book convinces them of the extremely succinct principle that, as long as a person has no other recourse than thinking in language, he or she can never think freely without knowing the true nature of the linguistic space that constrains and conditions his or her thinking.

I would like to take this opportunity to express my deepest gratitude to the Japan Foundation and the Woodrow Wilson International Center for Scholars for making it possible for me to conduct my research. I also wish to express my heartfelt appreciation to Tsutsumi Takashi, then editor in chief at *Shokun!*, Saitō Tadashi, who was in charge of the monthly, and Mr. Takahashi Kazukiyo, whose meticulous efforts greatly facilitated the publication of the book.

Etō Jun
Nishimikado, Kamakura
July 4, 1989

Afterword to the Paperback Edition

In the early spring of this year, I unexpectedly received a lengthy letter from Mr. Okai Takashi, a *waka* poet.

In his letter, he confessed that he had long wondered about the silence and change of style that Saitō Mokichi, a *waka* luminary of the Taishō era, showed after Japan's defeat in the war. During his pursuit of an answer to his question, Mr. Okai came across this book, *Tozasareta gengo kūkan: Senryōgun no ken'etsu to sengo Nippon*. Finding the work thought-provoking, he wrote me a cordial letter:

> Seeing as your book is not readily available today, I had to borrow it from a library. I wish that the publisher would publish a paperback edition of your book and make it more accessible; after all, the work is a valuable document—required reading, I think. I very much hope that the book can reach as many readers as possible.

I was immensely moved by the undeserved honor that Mr. Okai had lavished on the book—but at the same time, the letter made me realize that my book had become "not readily available." I needed to do something about the problem. That realization found its end in the publication of the paperback edition of *Tozasareta gengo kūkan: Senryōgun no ken'etsu to sengo Nip-*

pon from Bungeishunjūsha as a volume in its Bunshun Bunko collection. I would like to take this opportunity to express my deepest gratitude to Mr. Okai for offering that unprompted cue and to the publication department of Bungeishunjūsha for its kind response to my request.

I made no changes to the text for the paperback edition. Oddly enough, the system of hidden self-censorship in Japanese journalism, which had its origin in the censorship conducted by U.S. occupation forces, appears to have regained momentum since the end of the Shōwa era and beginning of the Heisei era. In my judgment, hidden self-censorship has gradually become a menace once again. As long as a "closed linguistic space" persists in Japan, I am convinced that my humble study will continue to maintain its raison d'être.

I also wish to express my gratitude to Terada Hidemi in Bungeishunjūsha's publication department for assisting with the editing and publication of the paperback edition.

Etō Jun
September 25, 1993
Nishimikado, Kamakura

About the author

Etō Jun was one of Japan's foremost literary and cultural commentators. Born in Tokyo in 1933, he published his first literary commentary (on Natsume Sōseki) while still a student at Keio University. Much of his literary criticism seeks to tie literary works to their authors' lives, and much of that is critical of lives that he sees as insufficiently rooted in Japanese tradition. He was also an acclaimed cultural commentator. Among his best-known works are *Kotoba to chinmoku* (Words and Silence), *Amerika to watakushi* (America and I), *Seijuku to sōshitsu: Haha no hōkai* (Maturity and Loss: Collapse of mothers' role), and *Jiyū to kinki* (Freedom and Taboos). His epic *Sōseki to sono jidai* (Sōseki [Natsume] and His Times) won the Noma Literary Prize in 1970. He was elected a member of the Japan Arts Academy in 1991.

Much of his writing was caught up in questions of identity as he spent much of his intellectual energy seeking to identify Japan's real identity and to promote its revival. Arguing for a return to what he thought were traditional values, Etō was a conservative icon. He committed suicide at his home in Kamakura in 1999, apparently distraught over his wife's death and his own debilitating illness.

（英文版）閉された言語空間—占領軍の検閲と戦後日本
Closed Linguistic Space: Censorship by the Occupation Forces and Postwar Japan

2020年3月24日　第1刷発行

著　者　江藤 淳
英　訳　公益財団法人日本国際問題研究所
発行所　一般財団法人出版文化産業振興財団
〒101-0051 東京都千代田区神田神保町2-2-30
電話　03-5211-7283
ホームページ　https://www.jpic.or.jp/

印刷・製本所　大日本印刷株式会社

ISBN 978-4-86658-114-9